Milestones in Developmental Physiology of Insects

papers in development and heredity

Milestones in Developmental Physiology of Insects

edited by
DIETRICH BODENSTEIN
University of Virginia

Appleton-Century-Crofts

Educational Division

Meredith Corporation

New York

PRINTED IN THE UNITED STATES OF AMERICA
390-10493-0

Contents

Milestones in Developmental Physiology of Insects

Introduction

When I set out four years ago to put together a number of papers on the developmental physiology of insects, I wanted to focus on those contributions which by virtue of their originality have been instrumental in the development of three important aspects of modern biology. Because of this restriction, this compilation is not just a collection of classical papers, although each paper presented is classical. I have selected those few investigations that in my opinion contributed uniquely to the task set, and have omitted many exciting contributions, whose absence does not of course reflect on their value. Moreover, I feel that the field of developmental physiology of insects is still too young, and too active and unsettled, to warrant any definitive collection of classical papers.

This collection falls by design into three parts.

I. EXPERIMENTAL EMBRYOLOGY OF INSECTS

A fascinating new period of developmental biology began at the turn of this century, when comparative descriptive embryology changed into experimental analytical embryology. Called *Entwicklungsmechanik*, this field envisioned by Hans Spemann (1869–1941) and organized by his pupil, Otto Mangold (1891–1962), reached its zenith in Germany in the early twenties. The problem of the embryonic organizers and inductors as well as questions concerning organ determination dominated the thinking of the experimental embryologist at that time. Most of the activity centered around amphibian development, and here the greatest advances were made; but work on such forms as birds, worms, and sea urchins also contributed extensively to our understanding of development.

On the other hand, with a few exceptions, the approach to insect embryology was still mostly descriptive. One reason for this was apparently a

1

lack of appropriate experimental techniques. The insect egg is very small, opaque, and hard-shelled. Thus, the methods of transplantation and extirpation which had been so successfully employed in the experimental analysis of amphibian and other eggs failed in insects. New methods and techniques needed to be invented, and, even more important, the experimental approach to embryogenesis had to be conceptually revised and adapted to the the special organization of the insect egg.

When Friedrich Seidel's famous papers on "The Determination of the Germ Band in Insects" appeared in 1926 and 1928, insect embryology came of age. In its elegance of method and conception, this work of Seidel's gave substance and direction to the experimental embryology of insects. Now it was possible for the first time to make valid comparisons between the casual factors in the development of insects and those established for other animals. Seidel's school prospered, and he and his students enlarged and deepened the field of insect *Entwicklungsmechanik*.

Yet it was not until 1940 that Seidel, in a review article on "The Organization of the Insect Egg," reported on the experiments of one of his students, Eberhard Bock, who had been called into the army. Bock's work was remarkable. He demonstrated the existence of a primary embryonic inductor in insects, which was associated with a specific germ layer, the ectoderm. Inductive stimuli originate in the ectoderm, and the underlying mesoderm responds with specific differentiations.

These findings made important aspects of insect development directly comparable with those, for instance, of amphibians, where the primary inductor, or organizer—in this case the mesoderm—has been known for a long time. The problem of embryonic induction is a vital one, and it is still actively studied today because these early tissue interactions provide the basis for the organization of the embryo.

II. CHEMICAL GENETICS

In the late twenties and early thirties, the problems concerned with the role of genes in development interested an ever-increasing number of geneticists. Richard Goldschmidt (1878–1958), one of the earliest and certainly the most vocal in this group, expressed his thoughts on this aspect of genetics in 1922 in his book, *Physiologische Theorie der Vererbung*. But the most eminent example, elucidating the manner in which hereditary material may control certain aspects of development, was presented by Ernst Caspari in 1933. Working with the flour moth *Ephestia kuhniella*, he provided the best known study of gene-controlled hormone action in development.

Two years later, there began to appear a series of papers on the genetic control of eye color development in *Drosophila*. These investigations by the developmental physiologist Boris Ephrussi, the geneticist George Beadle, and the chemist Edward Tatum, were of brilliant conception and flawless execution. They provided the background for the development of a new area in genetics, then (1935) called physiological genetics, which led to biochemical and finally to modern molecular genetics. From the several early papers available on the *Drosophila* eye-pigment research, we have chosen Beadle and Ephrussi's first publication in English, in which they demonstrated the occurrence in the blood of insects of diffusible substances upon which the normal eye-color development depends. This is followed by two papers: one by Tatum and Beadle, announcing the crystallization of the v+ substance, and the other by Tatum and Haagen-Smit, announcing its identification.

It is of particular interest here to note that the *Drosophila* and not the *Neurospora* work was apparently responsible for the development of the now famous one gene–one enzyme hypothesis. In his Nobel lecture on December 11, 1958, Beadle expressed this as follows:

Although it may not have been stated explicitly, Ephrussi and I had some such concept in mind. A more specific form of the hypothesis was suggested by the fact that of all the 26 known eye-color mutants in *Drosophila*, there was only one that blocked the first of our postulated reactions and one that similarly interrupted the second. Thus it seemed reasonable to assume that the *total* specificity of a particular enzyme might somehow be derived from a single gene. The finding in *Neurospora* that many nutritionally deficient mutant strains can be repaired by supplying single chemical compounds was a verification of our prediction and as such reinforced our belief in the hypothesis, at least in its more general form.

One further contribution which I believe has had a decisive influence on the advancement of developmental genetics is the classical work by Donald Poulson on the chromosomal control of embryogenesis. He clearly demonstrated that the closely coordinated yet separate developmental steps involved in embryogenesis are under the control of specific genes. Moreover, he recognized that mutant genes can be used as valuable tools for the analysis of developmental phenomena. From a series of significant papers on this subject, I have selected the one published in 1945 as outstanding and representative. Even now, more than two decades later, the reader will be impressed by the soundness, foresight, and modesty of his presentation.

III. INSECT ENDOCRINOLOGY

In 1912, Gudernatsch made the astonishing discovery that thyroid tissue, when fed to tadpole or salamander larvae, accelerated the metamorphosis of these creatures. These findings stimulated a new wave of experimentation in vertebrate endocrinology. When it was learned that many vertebrate hormones were not species-specific, their possible effect on invertebrates was studied. The pronounced developmental events associated with the metamorphosis of insects made them a favorite object of such studies, but all attempts failed. Insect metamorphosis could not be influenced by vertebrate hormones.

Now it was remembered that at the turn of the century many investigators had tried in vain to alter the secondary sex characters of insects by exchanging in the larval stage the gonads of the two sexes. The results were also negative when organ-regeneration experiments were combined with gonad transplantations. For instance, a regenerating wing bud in a female caterpillar carrying transplanted male gonads (after removal of its own ovaries) developed into a normal female wing, although it had been under the influence of the male gonad during its entire reconstruction period.

This and other evidence led to the conclusion that the development of the secondary sex characters in insects is, in contrast to vertebrates, autonomous and not dependent upon germ-gland influences. Taken together with the negative results obtained with vertebrate hormones reported above, it appeared that hormones played no part in the development of insects. As a matter of fact, it seemed as if an insect could be defined as a creature having no hormones.

Then, in 1917, the Polish scientist Stefan Kopeć presented to the Academy of Science in Cracow a paper in which he demonstrated with simple clarity that the brain of *Lymantria dispar* L. caterpillars produces a hormone that initiates pupation and maintains pupal development. This work appeared in English for the first time in 1922, and is reproduced here.

For some obscure reason, this epoch-making contribution remained largely unknown for nearly sixteen years. As I recall, two of the first to mention it were Bodenstein in 1933 and Wigglesworth in 1934. Since then, it has gained its deserved place in the sun.

Insect endocrinology began to emerge as a field of its own in the early 1930s. Bodenstein in 1933 reported on leg transplantations on insects and obtained rather convincing evidence that hormones, or hormone-like substances, circulating in the blood of caterpillars control molting and pupation in butterflies.

The following year, Wigglesworth published his first paper on the factors controlling molting and metamorphosis in the tropical bug *Rhodnius*. There are, I believe, not enough superlatives to praise this contribution. It is unequaled in originality, conception, execution, vision, and style. With this paper, insect endocrinology was established. There is no doubt that Wigglesworth must be considered the founder of insect endocrinology, a field that is still actively growing today. Significant contributions have been and are being made by many distinguished scientists in this field, but few can match Wigglesworth's early paper in conception and execution, and none in originality.

From the great number of papers now available in insect endocrinology, I have singled out two contributions for their exceptional merit. One is the discovery of the prothoracic gland by the Japanese scientist Fukuda. This gland has played an important role in the control of and metamorphosis by the endocrine system. The second is the isolation and crystallization of the prothoracic gland hormone, which Butenandt and Karlson named ecdyson. Through this and by his continued work on the biochemistry of insect hormones, Karlson especially has led in the advancement of the new discipline of insect endocrinology.

DIETRICH BODENSTEIN

Charlottesville, Virginia

I

EXPERIMENTAL EMBRYOLOGY OF INSECTS

FRIEDRICH SEIDEL

The determination of the germ band in insects

Friedrich Seidel was born in Lüneburg, Germany, in 1897. He studied at the Universities of Tübingen, Hamburg, and Göttingen, from the last of which he received his Ph.D. in zoology in 1923. He served as Assistant at the Kaiser Wilhelm Institute for Biology, in Berlin, from 1924 to 1925; from 1925 to 1936 he was first Head Assistant in Zoology, then Professor, at the University of Königsberg; the following year he spent at the University of Berlin as Professor and Chairman of the Department of Zoology. In 1945 he returned to the University of Göttingen for three years of research. From 1948 to 1956 he served as head of the Department of Developmental Physiology at the Max Planck Institute, Mariensee. From 1954 to 1969 he was Professor and Chairman of the Department of Biology at the University of Marburg.

His research interests are in the areas of developmental physiology and experimental morphology of insects.

PART I

The embryonic development of insects is typified by a special kind of germ-band formation. Because of the special distribution of formative cytoplasm and yolk in the egg, the germ band is limited to a particular region.

Moreover, not all parts of it are formed at the same time. In the insect body, the ventral part is of special significance, since it is the carrier of the main system of organs; and the ventral part of the embryo is completely established first, the dorsal side developing only afterward.

[Previously published in *Biologisches Zentralblatt*, 46(1926), 321–43, and 48 (1928), 230–351.]

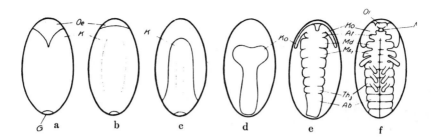

Figure 1. Schematic representation of the embryonic development of insects after the studies by Hirschler on *Donacia* (*Z. wiss. Zool.* 92, 1909). (a) Differentiation of the germ band from the blastoderm, dorsal view. (b) Same, ventral view. (c–f) Ventral view. (c) Fully developed germ band. (d) Germ band with head parts. The posterior portion is embedded in the egg yolk. (e) Segmentation. (f) Segregation of the organ systems. Ab: abdomen. At: antenna. G: sex cell rudiment. K: germ band. Ko: head parts. M: stomodaeum. Md: mandible. Mx₁: first maxilla. Oe: extra-embryonic surface epithelium. Ol: labrum. Th₃: third thoracic segment.

    The essential characteristics of this development can be seen clearly in the Coleopteral embryo. Figure 1 shows these in schematic form in the embryo of the beetle *Donacia crassipes.* Following superficial cleavage, a uniform blastoderm develops on the surface of the egg beneath the chorion. Several of the nuclei which have remained in the interior of the egg serve as vitellophages for the liquefaction of the yolk. Soon visible differentiation can be detected in the blastoderm; the cells, which at first were quite regularly distributed, are now concentrated toward the ventral side. Thus the germ band becomes visible.

    The migration of the blastoderm cells to the ventral side of the egg first becomes noticeable dorsally at the anterior pole of the egg. Here only a few cells remain; they lie flat on the surface of the egg and build a surface epithelium. Figure 1a shows the dorsal side of an egg at the beginning of this differentiation, and Figure 1b the ventral side. The surface epithelium becomes a wedge-shaped area that spreads posteriorly from the anterior pole to the dorsal side of the egg (Figure 1a, Oe). This area enlarges progressively posteriorly and ventrally at the same rate at which the blastoderm cells retract towards the ventral side of the egg. Finally, the germ band lies on the ventral side of the egg in the form of an anteriorly rounded narrow longitudinal strip (Figure 1c, K). The remaining portion of the egg surface is covered by the surface epithelium. The cells of the embryonic rudiment thus formed differ by their predominantly cubic form from the very flat cells of the extra-embryonic epithelium. Very often, as in this case, one can distinguish even at an early stage in development a median portion of the germ band as midplate, and two lateral parts as sideplates.

In some other insect germ bands, one can already recognize at this stage the anlagen of the sex cells at the posterior pole.

Through the differentiation of the anterior portion of the germ band into head parts, and through the invagination of the midplate beneath the merging side plates, the single-layered and well-defined early germ band is transformed into a multilayered definite germ band. Now the segmentation (Figure 1e) and the separation of the organ systems are completed. This results in the complete formation of the ventral side of the embryo (Figure 1f). Between the chorion and the yolk in the interior of the egg one can now distinguish the layers known as ectoderm, mesoderm, and endoderm. In order to complete embryonic development, all three layers grow laterally and dorsally and surround the yolk, thus forming the midgut and the back of the embryo.

From the formation of the germ band up to the dorsal fusion of the embryo, the majority of insects follow the same pattern, though perhaps not always so directly. In addition to the different types of development of embryonic sheaths in different species, the pattern of development is complicated chiefly by changes in the position of the germ band, which may remain on the egg surface (Diptera, Coleoptera, Hymenoptera, Orthoptera), changing size and position several times, or become embedded in the yolk (Lepidoptera), in effect being covered from the sides. During its formation the germ band may be rolled into the interior of the egg, the anterior region first. Embryonic development can then be completed only after the germ has again been rolled out of the yolk (Rhynchota, Odonata). The organization of the germ band always begins with a superficial bilateral thickening of the blastoderm, and after organ formation, the germ band is always located ventrally, and consists of three layers which then surround the remaining yolk and thus form the dorsal side.

The following investigations were concerned with an experimental analysis of the processes of determination in the very young germ band of insects.

It was not clear initially whether determinative events occurred in insect eggs after deposition. Although Hegner's defect experiments (1911) on the egg of the Colorado potato beetle *Leptinotarsa*[1] had demonstrated that the future signifiance of the individual parts of the periplasm was apparently already determined before the cleavage nuclei had entered the periplasm, it was questionable whether this conclusion could be applied to all insects. Comparative morphological considerations urged me to attack this problem again. On the basis of purely descriptively derived criteria (polarity, formation of the blastoderm, type of structural architecture and segmentation, formation of the sex cells, number and yolk content) I tried to demonstrate that the pattern of development is by no means

[1] See also Reith's new experiments with *Muscidae* (1925), which give similar results.

identical in insects (Seidel, 1924). It was, however, possible to construct a series of developmental types, from determinative to nondeterminative, into which all the individual members could be fitted. The Rhynchota (*Pyrrhocoris*) are at the nondeterminative extreme; the Diptera are at the other. Orthoptera and Coleopterare present transitional types. The Orthoptera are related to the Rhynchota, while the Coleoptera (*Hydrophilus, Donacia, Calligrapha*) are closer to the Diptera. Although these observations based on description can say nothing about the developmental possibilities of the individual forms, they nonetheless contain specific indications concerning their developmental behavior, and are therefore helpful in selecting the type needed for the solution of specific problems. If it were possible to observe the determinative event, then the probability of success would be greatest with the egg of an insect of the nondeterminative type.

The eggs of dragonflies possess special advantages for experimental use. In their type of development, they closely resemble the Rhynchota, the representative of the nondeterminative type in the above series. They also show certain similarities to the embryonic movements of this group. Valuable studies concerning the determination of the germ band have been made by using the eggs of the Agrionid *Platycnemis pennipes*.

The egg of *Platycnemis pennipes* is approximately 0.9 mm long and 0.2 mm in diameter. Like other dragonfly eggs, which are deposited on plants, it has a specially formed tip (Figure 3). The egg is bilaterally symmetrical; the dorsal side is rather flat, the ventral side more convex (Fig-

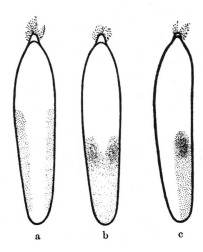

a   b   c

Figure 2. Platycnemis pennipes. Schematic representation of the germ band. (a) Early stage. Anlage comprised of two lateral bands. (Dorsal view) (b) Later stage shortly before the anlage rolls into the yolk. (c) Fusion of the two lateral bands of the anlage. (Dorsal view)

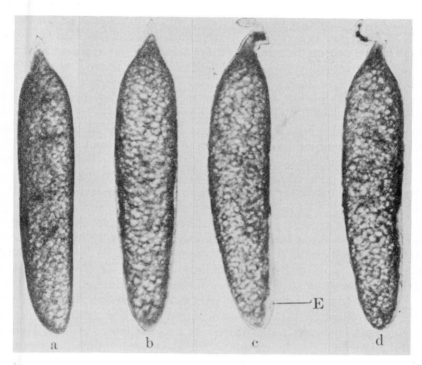

Figure 3. (a) Cleavage 4—cleavage nuclei. (b) Early stage in the formation of the germ band. (c,d) Later stages, shortly before the germ band rolls into the yolk. (c) Lateral view of the germ band. (d) Egg rotated somewhat more than shown in (c). Compare text and Figure 2. (e) Region of egg into which germ band rolls. (Enlarged 91 times.)

ures 2c and 3c). Its orientation according to the axes of the embryo in the later stages therefore creates no difficulties. The egg membranes are very thin, elastic, and extraordinarily transparent. Thus, not only the first cleavage divisions (Figure 3a) but also the formation of the germ band can be observed and photographed in the living egg with little difficulty. A large number of eggs are deposited in a relatively short period (approximately 120 eggs in 30 minutes). Thus many eggs of the same developmental stage are available for the experiment. The long duration of embryonic development (about 20 days at an average temperature of 20.5° C) and the late beginning of the first cleavage (about 9 hours after the depositing of the egg) are highly advantageous factors. The advantages greatly outweigh the disadvantages which are that the egg is very sensitive to pressure and that, owing to the impermeability of the chorion, the egg can be fixed only after being punctured.

The germ band which develops from the blastoderm consists at first of two parts. From the region slightly above the middle of the egg almost to the posterior pole, a light, thin, longitudinal band becomes visible at both sides of the egg (Figure 3b; the dorsal side of the egg faces the observer). It consists of a mass of cells, which at the appearance of the band are not yet easily distinguishable from the surrounding cells. At first, islands appear (see the left side of Figure 3b), which do not always follow the longitudinal direction of the germinal band. They appear in many different ways in different embryos, and no ordered manner of formation is recognizable except that they accumulate in the middle of the egg earlier and more frequently than at the posterior pole. The total picture in the illustrations shows the germinal band as a transparent cellular couplet on the side of the yolk. What the observer sees on the surface of the egg, either above or below the yolk, can be made visible only by turning the egg. The schematic Figure 2 gives a true picture of the surface view.

Gradually the cells of the germinal band concentrate at the posterior end. The parts of the band approach each other, finally merging into a single germ band on the dorsal side of the egg (Figure 2b, c). The bilateral anlagen have completely fused posteriorly. Anteriorly in the head parts a thickening is seen on both sides; this thickening is indicated in Figure 2b, c by heavier dots. It is clear in the photograph of the lateral parts of the germ band (Figure 3d), but is missing in the picture of the median region (Figure 3c). This stage approximates one between those shown in Figures 1c and 1d of the *Donacia* scheme. While in *Donacia* further development takes place mainly on the surface, in our insect the germ band has already started to roll into the yolk (Figure 3c, E). The process is further advanced in Figure 4. (H-posterior end of the germ band, which had rolled into the yolk first). At this point the details of further development are of no special significance for these experiments. It should be mentioned, however, that the first sign of yolk destruction by the vitellophages appears in the area below the middle of the egg and later extends over the entire egg. As a result of further changes, the yolk cleavage gradually bcomes indistinct again, and the yolk particles become smaller, while in the anterior part of the egg there develops some pigment which is used at various times in the development of the embryo.[2]

[2] For the sake of simplicity, we have talked only about the "straight" and the "curved" sides of the egg and not about the dorsal and ventral sides. This has been done because the embryo changes its position relative to the egg sides. The designation "dorsal" for the straight side and "ventral" for the curved side of the egg is justifiable because of the permanent position of the embryo in the egg. The germ band forms on the straight side of the egg and turns its ventral side to the straight (dorsal) side of the egg. During blastokinesis there occurs, contrary to the diagram of Calopteryx by A. Brandt (1869), not just a simple movement in the opposite direction of the rolling-in, but rather a rotation of the embryo before it rolls out. Thus, its ventral side turns to face the curved (ventral) side of the egg, a process which will be described more precisely at another point in the discussion.

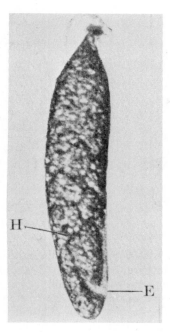

Figure 4. The germ band begins to roll into the yolk. Half of the germ band is still on the surface, while the other half is rolled in. Beginnings of yolk cleavage. E: region at which the rolling-in process begins. H: posterior end of the germ band that has been rolled in. (Enlarged 91 times.)

In order to answer the question whether, before the formation of the blastoderm, the different surface areas of the egg are already determined for the formation of specific parts of the later germ band and embryo, the following experiment was performed. Shortly after the egg had been deposited and after the cleavage of the nuclei had started—but before these had reached the surface of the egg—the contents of the egg were divided into two parts without damaging the chorion, by constricting it with a fine hair from a child.

First a constriction was made in the middle of the presumptive germ band, (see Figure 2a) slightly posterior to the middle of the egg. This ligation was the most difficult of any made in the various regions of the egg, since here the entire amount of the massive yolk has to be divided. Because of the small size of the object, only one knot can be tied in the hair, and this knot often loosens later. Then, too, the chorion cannot always be forced together evenly from all sides so that only the most minute round hole remains to be sealed with the final tightening of the hair. Using a paper cylinder as a model, one can show that when the string is tightened,

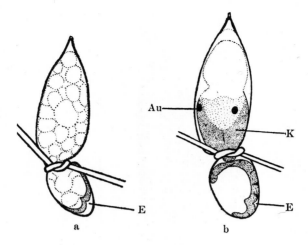

Figure 5. (a) Complete constriction before the formation of the blastoderm: behind the constriction, the germ band and the beginning of invagination (E). In front of the ligature no germ band but yolk cleavage. (b) Incomplete constriction before the formation of the blastoderm: behind the constriction germ band; an attempt of the germ band to roll in (E) and segmentation of the germ band on the egg surface. In front of the ligature the formation of a head part (K) with eye anlagen (Au). Enlarged 62½ times.

the sheath usually becomes entangled in the knot, so that a wide communicating slit, instead of a small hole, must then be closed. Even under microscopic control it was possible only in a very small number of cases, to achieve a perfect constriction. The final and most certain criterion of perfect constriction was the fact that none of the pigment which developed in the initial stage of histological differentiation in the forward part of the egg (see p. 14) leaked from front to back through the knot.

The perfect constriction produced a surprising result. In the posterior part, the germ band developed normally, and the rolling-in process began (see Figure 5a, E). Even though rolling-in could not be completed, because the ligature hindered the germ band's movements, the normal elongation and segmentation of the band took place, and the cells of the band separated into the inner and outer layers. In the anterior part of the egg, however, the germ band did not develop, and no head was formed.

After incomplete constriction at the same egg level (Figure 5) a head part (K) containing eye-anlagen (Au) was formed in the anterior part, showing that in the complete constriction experiment the ligature was not too far forward. Depending upon the condition of the ligature, the head part was smaller or larger, and could contain part of the extremities. In the posterior, where no head was expected, none ever developed.

It was important to know whether the anterior part of the egg, which after complete ligation was unable to form a head part, was still living. That it was shown by the fact that yolk cleavage, which normally occurs at the beginning of the rolling-in process, also took place here, although in several cases belatedly. Furthermore, a plasmatic surface layer developed on all sides of the egg, favoring the dorsal side. This layer developed much later than the germ band normally does, and in its expansion and shape, it bore no resemblance to the germ band, especially in that it did not display the bilateral quality of the early germ anlage (Figure 2a). Histological investigations revealed that this layer was not a thickening of the blastoderm but an accumulation of cytoplasm with only a few nuclei. It appeared at a time when in normal development pigment accumulation would be seen at specific locations in the yolk (see p. 14). As in normal development, the yolk cleavage began to become indistinct during blastokinesis, and the egg increased in size, a process which is obviously related to changes in the yolk. None of these phenomena occurred in dead eggs.

There were thus sufficient nuclei and cytoplasm anterior to the constriction. In experiments 5a and 5b the conditions in the anterior part of

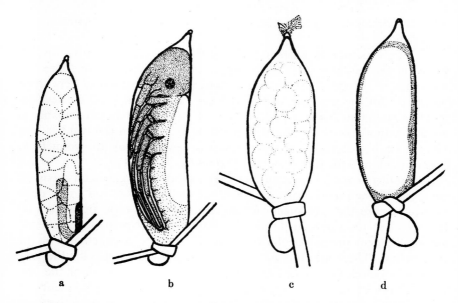

a   b   c   d

Figure 6.   (a,b) Removing by ligation of a very small portion from the posterior end of the egg during cleavage. Formation and development of a germ band. (a) Inrolling process of the germ band and yolk cleavage. (b) Embryo able to emerge. Enlarged 46½ times. (c,d) Removing by ligation a larger egg portion from the posterior end of the egg during cleavage. Germ band formation is prevented. (c) Yolk cleavage in front of ligature. (d) Formation of surface layer. Enlarged 62½ times.

the egg were the same, but in experiment 5a no germ-band formation could occur here, because there was no connection with the posterior portion of the egg. This result demonstrates that at the time of the superficial cleavage the anterior parts of the egg are dependent upon the posterior parts for the formation of the germ band.

.Our next task was to investigate more precisely the place and time of this interdependence. To this end constrictions were made at early developmental stages in different regions of the posterior portion of the egg, and we observed whether or not germ-band development occurred. Figure 6 shows the result of this experiment. The removal of a very small portion from the posterior end of the egg by ligation (Figure 6a), did not prevent the formation of a germ band. The rolling-in process occurred in orderly fashion (compare Figures 6a and 4). The embryo developed and hatched normally (Figure 6b).

When the ligature was placed somewhat more anteriorly, no germ band developed (Figure 6c). Instead, the same characteristics as in the basic experiment appeared in the region anterior to the ligature (p. 16). We observed yolk cleavage, formation of the cytoplasmic surface layer mainly on the dorsal side of the egg, changes in the consistency of the yolk, pigment development, and embedding of the pigment in the surface layer (Figure 6d).

These experiments seem to indicate that the dependence of the anterior on the posterior parts does not extend to the egg pole, since the formation of the germ band is not impeded by the removal of very small portions from the posterior end of the egg (Figure 6a, b). The development of the germ band is possible only if its place of origin remains in contact with a special zone located in the region between the two ligatures (Figure 6a, c)—at the point where, later in development, the germ band begins to roll into the yolk (compare Figures 6a, 3c, and 4).

In order to verify this result with even greater certainty and accuracy, we repeated the experiment, using another method. This had to be done mainly because the very small portion removed by ligation from the posterior end of the egg died during the course of development, thus eliminating pigment migration, the best criterion for the completeness of the constriction. There are, however, several other disadvantages to the constriction method. Owing to the tapering of the posterior end of the egg, the ligature may slip very easily during tightening, thus causing difficulty in removing a piece of definite size. Depending upon the size of the hairs used and variation in folding at the point of constriction, exact measurement of the separated part is rendered impossible by variation in shape and size of the removed tip. For this reason the anterior or posterior regions of the egg may contain different amounts of yolk material, making an exact measurement of the yolk and plasm distribution very difficult. Another objection to the ligation method is that it sometimes prevents an exact analysis of the experimental results. The constriction causes at times a separation of the chorion from the egg material, making it impossible to determine with accuracy whether a germ band has developed at all, or whether it has regressed after its formation.

These disadvantages are avoided when parts of the egg are destroyed with a hot needle. Hegner (1911) was the first to apply this method to insects. I used an electrically heated platinum needle, Peterfi's microthermomocauterizer. Touching the posterior pole of the egg with the needle prevented development of larger or smaller regions of the egg. One special advantage of this method is that approximately half an hour after cauterization a distinct borderline develops between the dead and living areas, perpendicular to the longitudinal axis of the egg, thus making it possible to measure the extent of damage (Figure 7).

With this method it was possible to measure the destroyed part exactly; there was no displacement of cytoplasm and yolk; and the contents of the egg did not separate from the chorion. Therefore, an exact observation

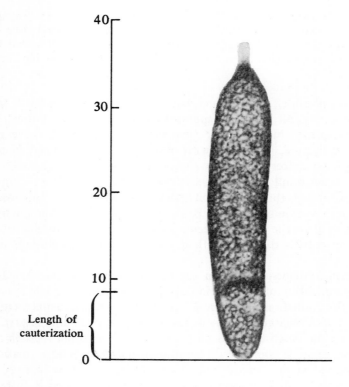

Figure 7.   Effect of cauterization at the posterior part of the egg. Scale: 1 graduation unit equals 24μ. Enlarged 91 times.

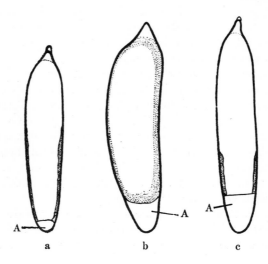

Figure 8. (a) Removal of small regions by cauterizations during cleavage: formation of a germ band. (b) Removal of larger regions by cauterization during cleavage: no germ band; formation of surface epithelium. (c) Removal by cauterization of same region as in (b) after cleavage: Germ band formation. A: destroyed region.

in vivo was possible. This method, by which the posterior part of the egg is destroyed, was all the more applicable here because in contrast to the basic experiment (Figure 5) we were not concerned with the egg parts behind the ligature, but rather with observing what happened in the anterior egg regions after parts of the posterior end had been eliminated.

The same result was obtained through the cauterization (Figure 8a and b) as through the constriction experiments (Figure 6). In those cases where the formation of the germ band was impeded, the same phenomena were observed in the anterior region of the egg. These results, obtained through an entirely different method, corroborate the conclusions reached before.

The measurements taken in the cauterization experiments led to an exact determination of the location of that zone of the egg which is necessary for the formation of the germ band. The measurements were made with an ocular micrometer which was graduated at 24-unit intervals. Depending on the batch that was used, egg length varied between 36 and 40 graduation units. It could be demonstrated that germ-band formation was not prevented in the anterior part when the cauterization in early stages did not exceed 3 to 4 graduation units. (See Figures 7 and 8, distance of cauterization 3–4 graduation units. The graduation units in these and the following figures are measured from the posterior pole of the egg.) The length of this region varied somewhat within the different batches of eggs. In some batches exceptional cases occurred in which cauterization up to the sixth graduation unit was required in order to prevent the formation of germ bands, while in other cases burning of only 2 units did so. Details of these observed variations will be fully reported in a later communication. However, these exceptions do not change the general observation that, in a given batch of eggs, the length of this important region, upon which development depends, does not vary much.

In one example (Pl. 25, T. 26) 48 cauterizations, 42 of which were observed carefully, were performed on one batch during an early stage. The results are summarized in Table 1.

TABLE 1

Length of cauterized area in units	Number of cauterization experiments	
	Germ band formed	Germ band not formed
0–2.9	3	1
3–4	3	3
4.1–5.9	. . .	12
6–7.9	. . .	15
8–9.9	. . .	4
10–12	. . .	1

From four eggs with a defect area of 0–2.9 units, three showed the formation of a germ band and one (2 units) no germ band. Six eggs with a 3–4-unit defect area showed germ-band formation in three cases, and no germ band in three. Thirty-two eggs with defect areas of 4.7–12 units showed no germ-band formation.

The exact region of the egg on which the development of anterior parts depends is thus determined: in an egg approximately 37 units long, the region upon which the formation and development of the germ band depends is located in the area between the third and fourth units, just below the area where at a later stage in development, the germ band begins to roll into the yolk.

The next question was, for how long a period of time in development does this observed dependency for the cleavage stages persist? In other words is there a point in development after which the anterior region no longer needs the posterior parts for initiation of germ band development? To this end defect experiments (Figure 8b) were performed at different times before the appearance of the germ band. They showed that the dependency ceased, when the defect experiments were done at a temperature of 22.5° C, 29–35 hours after egg deposit, i.e., 8–14 hours before the germ band normally becomes visible. The results of an experiment in which 6.5 units were cauterized in an egg 35 hours after egg deposit at

22.5° C is shown in Figure 8c. Anterior embryos develop, smaller or larger depending upon the length of the cauterized area, indicating that from now on development of the different embryonic parts takes place independently of the posterior region. Defect experiments on later stages performed with an ultraviolet microbeam apparatus after Tschachotin verified the above conclusions. (Discrepancies in certain respects, especially with regard to the abdomen, will be more fully explained in later reports.)

The results of the experiments up to this point can be summarized as follows. In its earlier stages—before it becomes visible—the germ band depends for its formation upon a definite region at the posterior end of the egg. This region is located near the place where, at a later stage, the germ band rolls into the yolk. The dependency disappears several hours before the germ band becomes visible. In the head and thoracic region, and independently of each other, the egg parts develop specific portions of the later embryo.

In relation to these results it is necessary to clarify the process of transition from dependent to independent development. In order to express the fact that a rather large part of the egg is dependent for its development on the effects of a rather small region, one may apply the term "center" to designate the importance of this small zone. The nature of the center will be discussed later. The term "center" implies a point from which a specific influence proceeds outward. The application of this term in the described case would be justified if it were proved that the influence of the described zone near the posterior pole of the egg, which causes the anterior egg parts to be independent in their development, proceeds in stepwise fashion from posterior to anterior.

If such a progressive influence is present, one must be able to prove it by defect experiments. A specific time of development, which may be called Z, is the presumed starting point of the center. As development proceeds, it should be possible to eliminate larger and larger parts of the posterior end of the egg without preventing the formation of a germ band. Until time Z, elimination of 3 units or less from the posterior end permits the formation of a germ band. Elimination of 5 units at the same time prevents the formation of a germ band, as shown by the experiments already described (see Figures 6a, 8a). The elimination of 5 units from the posterior end should permit the formation of the germ band if it occurred after time Z; a defect area of more than 7 units at the same developmental time should prevent its formation. At an even later time the cauterization of 7 units should no longer prevent the formation of a germ band, and so on. This was tested by the following experiment.

In order to obtain material as uniform as possible in size and age, eggs of only one batch were used for each experimental series. Moreover, from this batch only those eggs were selected which had passed synchronously the second and fourth cell stages. In such a way it was possible to isolate

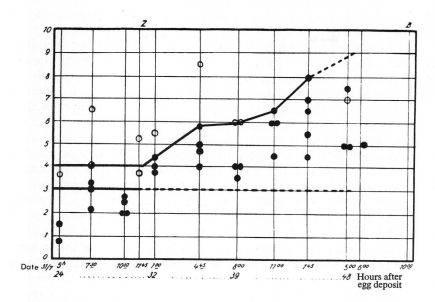

Figure 9.   Graphic representation of the determination process in the egg of *Platycnemis pennipes* before the formation of the germ band—based on cauterization experiments, Pl. 25 T. 25: *Ordinate:* cauterized part at the posterior end of the egg in units (1 unit = 24μ). *Abscissa:* time of operation—average temperature (Compare with figure 11) Z: beginning of activity of the center; B: differentiation of the germ band in control animals.

120 eggs of exactly the same age. The preceding experiments had shown (p. 22) that at 22.5° C the changeover from dependent to independent development occurred approximately 29–35 hours after egg deposition. Therefore, the time Z had to be within this period. At this temperature the germ band of normal eggs becomes visible approximately 43 hours after deposition. Between 24 and 48 hours after deposition, small, medium, and large areas were killed by cauterization at 3-hourly intervals. These regions were measured about half an hour after the operation. During the entire experiment the temperature was registered by a thermograph.

The results of such an experiment (Pl. 25, T. 24) are shown graphically in Figure 9. The ordinate gives the time after egg deposition at which the operations were performed; the abscissa gives the length of the cauterized portions in units (1 unit = 24 μ). The individual experiments are represented as circles; a filled circle indicating that a germ band developed, and an empty one indicating that no germ band was formed. Under the last category only such cases are listed in which the above-mentioned criteria (p. 17) proved that the anterior egg part was not dead. Doubtful cases are designated by circles one- or three-quarters filled, depending upon which of the two categories they seem best to fit. These special cases will be discussed in a later paper.

It first follows from Figure 9 that up to 31 hours after egg deposition the relationships presented on p. 21 were again realized. After the elimination of more than 3–4 units, germ-band formation fails to occur, while the elimination of fewer units allows germ-band development. If the cauterized region reaches into the area between units 3 and 4, half of the cases show germ-band development, and half do not. Thereafter, however, the picture changes. As development progresses, the dependency relationships alter. This is especially well demonstrated by the following observations: Cauterization of 3.8 units 31 hours after egg deposition prevents germ-band formation, while after 32 hours or more, cauterization of the same area does not prevent the formation of a germ band. But 32 hours after egg deposition, germ-band formation is inhibited if the cauterized region consists of 5.5 units, while 35¾ hours after deposition a germ band develops after cauterization of 5.8 units, and 39 hours after deposition, in one instance a questionable germ band developed, while in another case none developed, after cauterization of 6 units. Yet 48 hours after deposition, cauterization of a similar area allowed formation of a germ band in two cases. As the region of cauterization increases in length, the developing germ bands become smaller and smaller, thus giving rise to less and less complete anterior parts, until finally only heads are formed. Heads also were formed by incomplete ligation near the middle of the egg (Figure 5b). The actual time at which the experiments were performed is represented by a continuous line, while the hypothetical extrapolation is shown by a broken line.

It is obvious that the results of the experiments are consistent with the expectations concerning the progressive changes in the dependency relationships in the egg. We can explain these facts by assuming that from a definite time, Z, an effect spreads forward in stepwise fashion from an egg area between units 3 and 4, over anterior egg portions. As a result of which the affected areas can form a germ band independently of the above-mentioned zone. The effect spreads with a certain regular continuity. The limit of its posterior extension is naturally hypothetical.

The necessity of demonstrating a process on a large number of objects of the same age, instead of on an individual case, is a source of error in this experiment. The four-cell stage, which was selected as an age control, lasts about an hour. Thus, the ages of the controlled eggs could still vary by as much as one hour. Because of this, the cauterization times were set 3 hours apart in order to compensate for the variation in age of the controlled experimental eggs. Moreover, in spite of the fact that the eggs were taken from the same egg batch and were cultured in water of the same temperature, the different individuals varied somewhat in their development. This variability explains, presumably, the exceptional case in which 7 units were cauterized 48 hours after egg deposit.

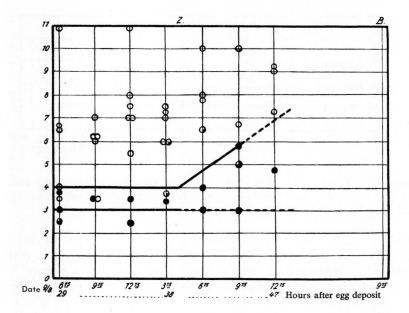

Figure 10: Graphic representation of the determination process in the egg of *Platycnemis pennipes* before the formation of the germ band, based on cauterization experiments, Pl. 25 T. 30. *Ordinate:* length of cauterized area at the posterior end of the egg in units (1 unit = 24μ). *Abscissa:* time of operation—average temperature. Compare with figure 11. Z: beginning of the effect of the center on the anterior egg regions. B: differentiation of the germ band in the control animals.

The exactness with which the shape of the curve can be determined is always somewhat limited by the relatively small number of usable eggs in a batch. Therefore, to make data statistically reliable the experiments had to be repeated several times.

For this reason Figure 10 (Pl. 25, T. 30) represents another experiment of this kind. In this case one cannot demonstrate very clearly the stepwise advance, from time Z, of the influence of the posterior region. But because of the greater number of cases which showed no germ-band formation, this experiment is a very good supplement to the first, demonstrating clearly that the egg parts not influenced by the posterior part are unable to form a germ band.

The process just described, concerning the transition from dependent to independent development, cannot be morphologically identified on the basis of the experiments conducted so far, but its existence must be inferred from them. In order to show that this process takes place at a definite stage in the development of the embryo, its beginning (at time Z)

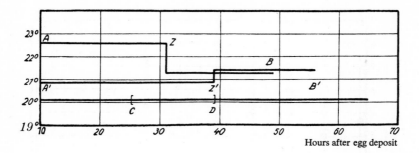

Figure 11. Temperature curves for the experiment shown in figures 9 and 10, and Table 1. *Abscissa:* Time of development. *Ordinate:* Temperature. (For further explanation see text.)

should be placed in relation to other visible differentiations—in this case the visible appearance of the germ band. For this, development of control subjects are needed. It is obvious that there must exist a definite time period between time Z and the first appearance of differentiation, if the beginning of the discovered process is not a chance but a regular occurrence.

The process occurring at time Z appears in the experiment shown in Figure 9 at an earlier developmental time than in that shown in Figure 10. Figure 11 shows that this variation is due to a difference in the prevailing temperature.

The time of egg deposition is shown on the abscissa, and the temperature on the ordinate. The curves indicate the average temperature for the separate experimental phases. For each experiment is given the time between the controlled 4-cell stage (A in Figure 9, A^1 in Figure 10) and time Z (or Z^1); and the time between time Z (Z^1) and the time when the germ band becomes visible in the controls (B_1 or B^1). The average temperatures for phases A–Z and Z–B have been calculated each time at two-hour intervals, according to the temperature data provided by the thermograph.

At a temperature of 22.6° C (Pl. 25, T. 24), time Z is reached 31 hours after egg deposition, while at a temperature of 20.9° C (Pl. 25, T. 30) it is reached 8 hours later. For the experimental phases Z–B or Z^1–B^1, the temperatures and developmental times are approximately the same in both experiments. Thus it is easy to see that the distance between Z and B is the same as between Z^1 and B^1, and that therefore Z always shows a definite time interval from B.

The third curve shows the temperature for the experiment Pl. 25, T. 26, in which the constancy of the position of the posterior zone was investigated at the time C–D (compare Table 1). Because of the prevailing low temperature, time Z should appear at an even later stage of development than the preceding experiment. In this case time Z should not be found in the time interval C–D; this was borne out by the data shown in Table 1.

From the discovered temperature dependency of time Z and the appearance of the germ band the following may be concluded: The experiments have shown the existence of a stepwise process, proceeding from the posterior to the anterior, which is not morphologically visible. In the embryonic development of *Platycnemis*, this process is as determined in time as any other, morphologically visible, phase of development.

It is evident from all the experiments that the egg parts are subject during their development to an influence which proceeds from a special region in the egg, at a certain time, and in a definite manner, from posterior to anterior. Without this influence no germ band can develop. Under its influence however the existing dependency of the germ-band development in the anterior egg region is transformed into an independent development. These results allow one to regard the posterior egg region between units 3 and 4 as a center which is of decisive importance for the development of the germ band, without whose influence germ-band development is impossible.

Up to now this center has been regarded only as a chronological one. In order to obtain some information as to the developmental stage at which the center acts, normal eggs were fixed at each operation time. This procedure showed that the beginning of the center's activity corresponds to that time in development in which the cleavage nuclei reach the surface of the egg.

Objections concerning the interpretation of the experimental results could be made. In particular it may be asked whether the observed results may not have been caused by general injuries related to the method, rather than by inactivating a specific formative factor.

These objections can be dismissed, however, for the following reasons. First, the same results were obtained by using two different experimental methods, ligation and cauterization. Second, it would be astonishing if the failure of germ-band formation in special cases were caused by general injury effects, when one remembers that even the greatest damage, the constriction in the middle of the egg, does not prevent the formation of germ band anteriorly and posteriorly of the ligature. Finally, the results point in the same direction, whether one observes the posterior egg regions under the influence of the center, or follows the developmental behavior of the anterior egg regions after elimination of the center.

There remains the question as to the nature of the center upon whose activity the formation of the germ band depends. Two possibilities exist. One is that the germ band grows anteriorly from a specially defined region at the posterior end of the egg. If this is the case, the center is a germinative one, the processes involved are structural, and nothing definite can be said concerning determination—the fixation of the various egg regions for their final ends—and differentiation—the functional specialization of the already determined regions. The second possibility is that all the material necessary for germ-band formation is already present in the anterior part of the egg, needing only the factor which will activate and direct its development. In this case the center is a determinative one, and there are two possible alternatives: Determination and differentiation can proceed in similar directions at the same time; or they can occur at different times and in different directions. Also, there could exist a differentiation center apart from the determination center.[3]

The following three facts permit a decision about the experiments under consideration:

1. The observed effect of the center occurs before the visible differentiation.

2. The cell accumulations which signal the appearance of the germ band do not appear first at the posterior end of the egg at units 3 and 4, but rather in the middle of the future germ band, between units 10 and 18. The appearance and the fusion of the cell accumulations vary in detail not only in different eggs, but also at the two sides of lateral anlagen in a given egg. Growth of the germ band from posterior to anterior was never observed.

3. A study of the histological sections shows that no accumulation of material, nor appreciable increase in cell number, occurred at the posterior end of the egg. Thus no material from here could have been passed forward, and contributed to the formation of the germ band. On the contrary, the general process of germ-band formation does not differ morphologically from that of other insects studied for this phase of development; in other insects also a blastoderm is formed first, and the germ band develops through an accumulation of the blastoderm nuclei and their surrounding cytoplasm.

It must be concluded from (1) the time difference between the activity of the center and the visible appearance of the germ band, (2) the fact that this region is not a center for the accumulation of material or cell multiplication, and (3) the discrepancy between the direction of influence of the center and the direction of differentiation of the germ band, that the center cannot be considered a growth or a differentiation center. Rather, to the material present at the place of germ-band formation is added a factor which, in early stages, is found in the region where the later germ band begins to roll into the yolk. This factor proceeds forward from here, and in its course determines the material which cannot form a germ band without its activity.

As far as the significance of this factor is concerned, it would be premature to propose a system commenting on its composition and sphere of

[3] For verification of terminology see Spemann 1901–3, 1918, Gräper 1923, von Ubisch 1923, p. 469, Penners 1925, pp. 127–31.

influence before completion of all the planned experiments. However, a few points can be roughly outlined in order to indicate the direction in which further experiments will move.

The effectiveness of the factor is shown by the consequences of its elimination from the conditions of the anterior egg region (p. 16). The nuclei remain evenly distributed over the surface of the egg. They do not increase in number or reach the size of vitellophages. In the course of time nuclei and cytoplasm accumulate at the dorsal side of the egg; but in this case the bilateral arrangement of material characteristic of germ-band formation is missing. Large islands of cytoplasm surround the nuclei. The yolk apparently behaves normally.

After the egg has reached a certain stage of development, the factor causes an increase in cell division; thus the center effects an activation. Beyond this the nature of the determining process is not yet clear. A noteworthy phenomenon is the accumulation of cytoplasm and nuclei (which no longer increase in number) on the dorsal side of the egg, if the formation of the germ band is prevented. This occurs especially at the posterior pole, and often spreads up to the line of cauterization. In normal development the vitellophages work in harmony with the developing germ band in this region. Therefore, the observed accumulations may be a specialized activity of the vitellophages which continue to work normally. It is also possible that the nuclei of the surface layer have accumulated at the dorsal side of the egg. To judge by the morphological structure which they assume here, they exercise a function similar to that of the vitellophages in digesting yolk. Without making a decision in favor of either possibility, one can still say with certainty that a specific condition must be present at the dorsal side of the egg for germ-band development to occur.

The region of germ-band formation in normal development is not the dorsal side of the egg (see Figure 2a) but the lateral regions, which lie 90° on each side from the dorsal median. Such a bilateral organization of the surface layer has never yet been observed in any defect experiment. This suggests that the factor has an influence on the organization of the nuclei. Further experiments will be needed to show whether, in addition to cell multiplication, the factor also influences the distribution of the nuclei. This will involve carefully observing cellular movements during normal development as well as after elimination of the activation center. In addition to the continuation of experiments involving the displacement of the germ band, an ultraviolet-microbeam analysis will be attempted, to determine the advance of the early germ band. This should show how extensive is the range and freedom of action of the assumed determining ability of the factor. On the basis of the experiments performed so far, a few comments can be made as to how the problem of determination fits into the entire course of embryonic development. The constriction experiments in which the ligature was applied at the middle of the presumptive germ band show that the determining influence, as it passes toward the anterior of the egg, fixes on its way the various parts of the forming anlage; at no time was a head formed behind the constriction. The same result was obtained in the cauterization experiments, where defects larger than 4 units prevented the formation of a complete embryo. If we presuppose that the factor advances with constant regularity, we find a remarkable correlation as seen in Figure 9. At the time the germ band appears, the end of the curve is found at unit 10 and not at unit 20, which is the most anterior point of the early germ band. Cell accumulations for the formation of the germ band first appear in the region of units 10–18. Germ-band formation thus begins first at the point reached last by the factor. This region, lying somewhat anterior to the middle of the germ band, is the thorax of the later fully developed embryo.

It appears to be very important that after completion of determination the beginning of differentiation of the germ band occurs in this same area of the germ band in *Pyrrhocoris apterus*. For this insect, whose development is similar to that of *Platycnemis*, it could be further shown that this area remains a center of differentiation until late stages of organogenesis.

It would have been impossible to perform the above-described experiments with such a clear formulation of questions had not Spemann's concept of the organizer in the embryonic development of Triton already existed (Spemann, 1901–03, 1918; Spemann and Mangold, 1924). The fact that both experimental subjects belonged to the indeterminative type of development leads one to expect definite formal similarities in the process of determination. However, the different character of insect and vertebrate development lends different significance in detail to the determination factors. It is difficult to understand fully the determinate factors in insects. Because it is technically impossible to present these factors with indifferent material, one needs first to prove its formative ability. Therefore, one has to use other indirect methods as indicated above. The hope for an exact analysis in the case under discussion is based on the fact that the formation of the germ band in *Platycnemis pennipes* is an easily visible process, in which simple movements of nuclei and cytoplasm are involved.

PART II

The essential result of the first part of this report was the demonstration that the individual parts of the egg of the damselfly (*Platycnemis pennipes*) cannot form the germ band independently of each other. At the posterior end of the egg is located a region which at a certain time exerts an effect on the anterior egg parts. Influenced by this region, the blastoderm nuclei, which are at this time evenly distributed over the egg surface, are stimulated to form the germ band. Without the activity of this region no germ band develops.

The nature of this effect has so far been deduced from negative results obtained in defect experiments. From the fact that after experimental removal of this special region cell division ceased, it was concluded that cell multiplication beyond a certain point depends on a stimulus from this region. Therefore, this region constitutes a focus of activation, an activation center. And from the fact that after the same experiment the nuclei do not, as is normal, accumulate in two bilaterally symmetrical and longitudinal bands, it was concluded that this region has a decisive influence on the distribution of the nuclei during the formation of the germ band.

Statements of this kind, based on negative findings, always remain somewhat uncertain. Developmental processes could fail to occur because their course was not conclusively determined, or because the stimulus for further development of already determined parts was missing. Even if the developmental factors of this center undoubtedly belong to the complex of determining factors (this is the more plausible since the activity of these factors occurs before the visible differentiation of the germ band), it is difficult at this time to be certain whether they influence the quality of the developmental processes, or whether they merely initiate development. An exact decision on this question can be obtained only through experiments yielding positive results. If the processes which occur during the blastoderm stage are merely initiative in nature, experimental interruption of this stage will not cause the embryo to form anything else but organ parts according to their prospective significance. If, however, the quality of the developmental parts is not yet fixed, it should be possible to cause the embryonic regions to form something different from what they would have formed during normal development.

By describing experimentally produced embryonic duplications and polyembryonic formations, we shall demonstrate conclusively that in the egg of the damselfly during the blastoderm stage the fixation of the embryonic regions is not yet completely determined.

In 1926 the formation of the germ band in the normal development of *Platycnemis pennipes* was described, up to the point where it rolls into the yolk with its posterior end forward (Fig. 1 and Fig. 4, 1926). At this time the embryo lies completely surrounded by the yolk. Its posterior end is turned towards the anterior egg pole (Fig. 2). This rolling-in process has nothing to do with the processes of germ layer or organ formation, but is merely a displacement of the embryo within the egg. At the later blastokinesis this process is reversed. Rolling-in and blastokinesis can serve as easily identifiable landmarks of the various periods of embryonic development. We designate, as the first period of normal development,[1] that from the cleavage stages to the formation of the blastoderm, and as the second

[1] See: Heider, "Die Embryonalentwicklung von *Hydrophilus piceus L.*" Jena, 1889.

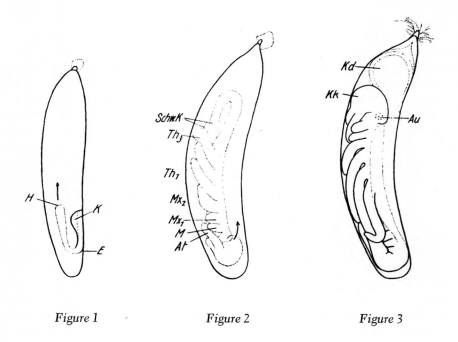

Figure 1   Figure 2   Figure 3

Figure 1. *Platycnemis pennipes.* Normal germ band during the process of roll-ing into the interior of the egg. The head parts (K) and the anterior half of the germ band are still on the surface of the yolk; the other half of the germ band has already rolled (in the direction of the arrow) into the yolk with its anterior end forward. E: Place where the germ band rolls into the yolk; H: posterior end of the germ band. (Enlarged approx. 64 times.)

Figure 2. Normal embryo shortly after rolling out of the yolk. Period of organ formation. One can recognize through the yolk: the head capsule with antennae (At) at posterior pole of the egg; the mandibles (M); the maxillae (Mx$_1$); (two, of which the second are larger than the first); the thoracic extremities (Th $_{1-3}$) (of which the latter shows even at this stage the characteristic flexion of the fully developed leg within the egg); the anlagen of the tail gills (Schw. K). The arrow near the head shows the direction in which the head will turn at the start of blastokinesis. The initial turning shown here combines with a rotation of 180° around the longitudinal axis, so that at the completion of blasto-kinesis the embryo lies as shown in Figure 3. (Enlarged approx. 64 times.)

Figure 3. Normal embryo shortly after blastokinesis. The embryo lies with its ventral side toward the convex side of the egg. Dorsal to the yolk the back has not yet closed. The head capsule (Kk) is still very small because the head yolk (Kd) has not yet been digested. The first anlage of the eyes (Au) become visi-ble (seven facets). The extremities are easily identifiable by the designations in Figure 2. (Enlarged approx. 64 times.)

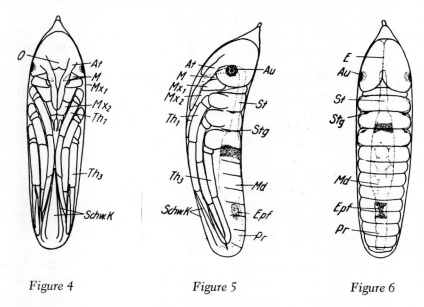

Figure 4   Figure 5   Figure 6

Figures 4–6.   Normal embryo. Stage of histological differentiation. The closure of the back is completed, and the cephalic yolk used up. (Enlarged approx. 64 times.)

Figure 4.   Ventral view. Starting at the head, the extremities appear in the following order; At: antennae; M: mandibles; Mx$_1$, Mx$_2$: maxillae; Th$_1$ to Th$_3$: thoracic extremities; O: labra (the median indentation is characteristic). The mandibles lie with their distal ends below the antennae. The third thoracic leg is bent forward at the tibio-tarsal joint. Schw. K: tail gills, two ventral and one dorsal. (These are bent at their bases toward the anterior egg pole).

Figure 5.   Lateral view. Au: eye with seven facets framed with chitin ridges; Md: mid-intestine; Pr: proctodaeum; St: stomodaeum; Stg: spiracles; Epf: proctodaeal valve at junction of proctodaeum and mid-intestine.
Figure 6.   Dorsal view. The head capsule bears a longitudinal indentation. (E)

that from the formation of the germ band until its rolling into the yolk. The third period is that in which the organ systems separate. It begins at the time when the germ band is embedded in the yolk and its anterior end is towards the posterior pole of the egg, and ends at blastokinesis. The embryo reappears at the surface of the egg, and is now oriented so that its head is turned to the anterior egg pole, while its ventral epidermis and extremities are adjacent to the convex portion of the egg sheath (Fig. 3). It appears at this stage that only the ventral half of the embryo is present. The organs of the dorsal region are located as anlagen at the lateral portions of the embryo. As these parts grow around the yolk, the back of the embryo forms and the yolk is restricted to the mid-intestine. With blasto-

kinesis and the closing of the back begins the fourth period, that of histological differentiation. At this time all parts of the larva can (with some
difficulty) be clearly recognized in their folded state through the chorion
of the egg (Figs. 4–6).

In accordance with the bilateral nature of the germ band, all parts of
the embryo are formed in pairs with the exception of the tail gills, which
are present in triplicate (Figs. 4–7, Schw. K.). On the head the eyes (Au)
protrude conically. Each has seven facets in a typical arrangement as shown
in Fig. 5. Their dark pigment is framed by white borders of chitin. The
number of facets increases only during the molting of the imago. The
antennae (At) appear ventral to the eye on either side. Within the egg
their distal ends join and surround the labra (O). The latter, in accordance
with the paired origin of the head capsule, display a typical indentation in
the center. This indentation can also be recognized in the imago. The
mandibles (M) are short and strong. They lie with their short brownish
tips below the antennae. The first maxillae (Mx_1) are just as short as the
mandibles and have small teeth. The second maxillae (Mx_2) differ from
the mandibles and first maxillae in their length. Later they grow together
and form the prehensile mask of the damselfly larva. This mask is an approximately trapezoidal plate that carries on its free end, on either side, the
articulated palpi. In Fig. 4 one can see the palpi of the second maxillae,
arranged in the same way as the antennae. The basal plate is situated be-

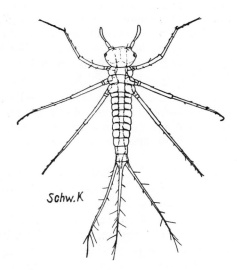

Figure 7.   Dorsal view of normal young larva just after hatching. Schw. K: tail
gills. Course of the tracheal system shown by a dotted line only in the body,
and not in the extremities and appendages. (Enlarged approx. 32 times.)

low the antennae. At hatching, this extended organ flips with its distal end toward the head, and thus assumes the familiar appearance of the functional prehensile mask. The thoracic extremities (Th_1–Th_3) are located in such a way that the two anterior pairs are extended, while the posterior pair is bent forward at the tibio-tarsal joint. The abdomen is divided into ten segments. The last segment carries the three caudal gills, one dorsal and two ventral. Much like the last thoracic extremities, the gills are bent forward at the basal joint, thus lying between the extremities. Like the third pair of legs, the gills also assist the animal during hatching by stretching backward.

After the back of the embryo has been closed, the yolk fills the entire mid-intestine from the head to the end. During this period of histological differentiation, it shows a distinct segmentation and is gradually digested (Fig. 6, Md). At the anterior end, where the fore-intestine joins the mid-intestine, a pigment accumulation occurs from the beginning, stronger than at the posterior end. It represents a center of pigment development. One can observe very clearly how pigment moves from this point to different parts of the body, for instance to the eye and to the back. The stomodaeum extends dorsally from the mouth opening below the labrum to the height of the eyes, and runs from there toward the caudal region. Because of its early dorsal pigmentation, the stomodaeum is clearly visible through the still unpigmented head capsule. One can even observe its peristaltic movements. As development proceeds, observation becomes more difficult. At the junction of mid-intestine and proctodaeum (Pr) the proctodaeal valve (E. Pf.) is formed. Because of its characteristic appearance, it can be used as a reference point for orientation even in embryos that are difficult to analyze. Three thin longitudinal ridges, arranged like the edges of an equilateral prism, develop in the intestinal wall. Closure of the intestine occurs when these ridges, with their apparently elastic ends, come together (compare Fig. 20, Pr). Viewed from the exterior, the chitin of the closed proctodaeal valve appears opal-white through the body (as shown in Figs. 5 and 6). The terminal orifice of the proctodaeum lies between the bases of the dorsal and ventral tail gills.

Before hatching, the body of the embryo is only slightly compressed in the egg. After hatching, the larva expands to double the length of the egg through extension of the extremities and the tail gills.

If the egg is not determined at the blastoderm stage, it is possible that the separation of larger and smaller egg parts from each other at this stage will lead to the development of each part into an independent whole, i.e., that double or multiple formations will occur. Since the factors upon whose influence the formation of the germ band depends are (in *Platycnemis*) located at the posterior end of the egg, and since their effect spreads from this point forward, it is obvious that the isolation procedure must be longitudinal rather than cross partitioning. Longitudinal constriction would be impossible in an egg with a length-to-width ratio of 900:160. Attempts to separate egg material by thermocauterization or ultraviolet microbeam irradiation proved unsuccessful, since too much material was destroyed. The only way so far discovered of separating egg parts along the longitudinal axes without damage has been the production of longitudinal fissures. Fissures of this type resulted initially as undesirable by-products of cauterization experiments, as described in the first report. Every effort was made at the beginning to avoid them, since they prevent exact measurement of the effects of cauterization. Only when a fortunate incident in the summer of 1925 showed their value were attempts made to produce them systematically.

Fissure formations occur through the uneven expansion of the egg material, caused by the unequal heating of the egg. If one side of the egg is touched with a thermocauterizer, after a short period of contraction the egg material expands. This occurs only on the side of the egg which faces the cauterizer. Outside of the defect region caused by burning, longitudinal fissures form in the center of the egg, showing dark in the otherwise clear yolk. After lateral cauterization, fissure formations of this type are usually very large, causing major developmental defects and consequent death of the embryo. On the other hand, much smaller, often scarcely visible, fissures occur after defects are produced with the thermocauterizer at the egg poles. Through such polar defects and through very delicate lateral defects, double and multiple formations are produced. Their individual peculiarities can be traced, in particular cases, back to the form of the fissure. With this type of experiment, one can decide whether to produce fissures anteriorly or posteriorly. However, whether one fissure or more, and hence whether double or multiple formations, occur must be left to chance. At all events it should be possible to influence the direction of the fissure.

The undesirable egg defects necessary for the embryonic duplication experiments do not always lead to embryonic defects. As previously noted (in experiments described in 1926) in early developmental stages one-ninth of the entire egg length can be eliminated from the posterior end of the egg without producing a defect in the embryo. Similarly, at the anterior end approximately one-quarter of the egg can be eliminated without jeopardizing the normal development of the embryo. Lateral defects can also be created without visible effect on later development. The conclusions derived from these facts will be discussed later in another context on the basis of systematically performed experiments. For the present investigation, examination was restricted mainly to polar defects, which produce double and multiple formations in about 3 per cent of the cases, and which could be analyzed to a greater or lesser degree.

Just as embryos with simple defects have difficulties in completing normal blastokinesis, so do embryos with multiple formations. The process of rolling into the yolk occurs without incident in the majority of the cases. Even when a part of the germ band has been eliminated, the remaining part rolls in. Blastokinesis fails more often than the rolling-in process. This is true especially for embryos with defects in the head, or for those showing multiple formations. The embryo lies then in the middle of the yolk with its posterior end turned toward the anterior egg pole (comp. Fig. 2). In such cases there occurs, as a sort of substitute for blastokinesis, a displacement of the embryo from the middle of the yolk to the periphery, with no rotation of the embryo. The closing of the back is completed when the lateral regions of the embryo close around the yolk. Even the histological differentiation of the embryo whose head is turned toward the posterior egg pole progresses further; but an embryo lying in this position is not capable of hatching.

It is an inconvenient fact that in order to obtain double formations one must also simultaneously produce a defect. In addition, development has to proceed in the narrow confines of the egg sheath. Perhaps because of this it was impossible to obtain double formations which were complete in all their parts. In the following, some cases are described which show duplications in various organs. A grouping of the different cases for purposes of comparison can provide an initial survey concerning the prospective potency of the individual parts of the *Platycnemis pennipes* embryo.

Duplication at the Anterior End. A cauterization of the tip shortly before the appearance of the germ band (Pl. 1926, T 79 E_4, about 60 hours after the 4-cell stage at 19.6° C) produced the duplication shown in Figs. 8 and 9. The experimental treatment affected the anterior part of the blastoderm. The germ band rolled normally into the yolk, but was not capable of blastokinesis and thus lay with its head toward the posterior egg pole. The posterior end of the embryo sank into the hollowed out dead material of the cauterized area. The presence of three tail gills, of which the third can be seen in Fig. 8 on the right side (Schw. K), indicates a normally developed abdomen. In addition, sections show that the regular number of eight abdominal ganglia is present. The hind intestine likewise shows no abnormalities.

The thoracic extremities (Th_1–Th_3) display on both the right and left sides normal conditions as to number and position, although they are not completely developed, especially on the left side (Fig. 9). The two maxillae and mandibles, as well as the antenna anlagen, are fully present, although they are not visible on the left side of the embryo and can only be detected in sections.

The head capsule is duplicated. A distinct fissure separates the two heads. The most significant occurrence is the duplication of the eyes (Fig. 9).

Closer observation shows that only head capsule I is joined normally

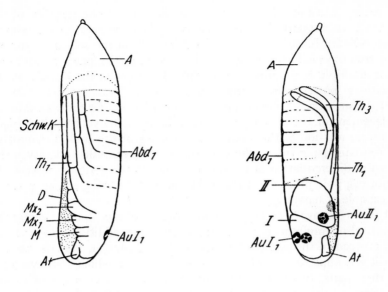

Figure 8   *Figure 9*

Figures 8–9. Duplication at the anterior end, after cauterization at the anterior egg pole in the blastoderm stage. Since the embryo rolled into the yolk but did not accomplish blastokinesis, the embryo lies with its anterior end turned toward the posterior pole of the egg (like the normal embryo in Figure 2). The heads have initiated blastokinetic movements toward the anterior egg pole, in the direction of the arrow in Figure 2, but they could not complete the process. In spite of this abnormal position, further differentiation occurred.

Figure 8. Right side. Antennae (At) and jaws of head I (M: mandibles, Mx_1, Mx_2: maxillae) are visible. Thoracic extremities (Th_1–Th_3) and tail gills (Schw. K) are normally arranged.

Figure 9. Left side of the embryo. Two head capsules, each with two eyes (Au). The head capsules are numbered from left to right in Roman numerals and the eyes of the heads with Arabic numerals. Head capsule II bears no extremities. The jaws of head capsule I are hidden by head capsule II. The antennae of head capsule I (At) are truncated. Abd_1: first abdominal segment. D: the unconsumed yolk lying adjacent to the embryo. A: the destroyed part of the egg. (Enlarged approx. 64 times.)

to the thorax, and head capsule II is almost entirely cut off from the rest of the body. Its upper pharyngeal ganglion has no connection with the ganglia of head I and the abdominal nerve cord. Since the antennal stubs and the jaws are present on head I, it seems possible that the fissure creating the separation cut very far into the side of the egg material. Thus the smaller part apparently was greatly hindered in its development, perhaps as a result of its complete separation from the body. The abdominal nerve cord was also slightly affected by the duplication. The ganglia of the first and second thoracic segments show, instead of the normal twofold division of the fiber masses, a threefold division. This situation will be more clearly demonstrated by other examples. Both head capsules are smaller than normal, and the eyes are closer together than normal.

The following conditions indicate that the heads have initiated blastokinesis in the direction of the arrow shown in Fig. 2. (1) Difference of chitin structure from that of the normal head capsule (which is rough and opal white anteriorly, it is smooth and earlier pigmented posteriorly). (2) The position of the eyes in relation to the location of the antennae. (3) The course of the ganglial chain. The anterior ends of the heads (Figs. 8–9) no longer lie as in Fig. 2 at the posterior egg pole, but have already turned again toward the anterior pole of the egg. Not all the available nutritive matter has been consumed in the differentiation of the heads, as is shown by the unconsumed yolk (D) lying next to the embryo.

Each of the four eyes is smaller than a normal eye, and well rounded. Three eyes are so far advanced in development that the number of facets can be determined. Not all facets are differentiated; nonetheless, there are evidently more facets present in the two eyes than in a single normal eye. In case of an approximately median separation of the head anlage, both eyes of a head might be expected to develop: For instance, eye I_1 with 3 facets and I_2 with 5 facets (Fig. 9) instead of a single eye anlage. In the improbable case of a frontal separation, eye II_1 for instance, with 6 facets, could have been formed either together with eye I_1 (with 3 facets) or with eye I_2 (with 5 facets), instead of each developing just a single anlage. In all of these possible cases the number of facets present in a single normal eye would have been exceeded by the total number of facets (8, or 9, or 11) in each separated part. Thus, in contrast to the normal condition, a new eye anlage was formed, which however could not completely reach its normal number of facets.

The next case (Pl. 1927, T 101 A_{14}) is especially interesting because the type of duplication expected could be predicted soon after the operation was performed. The embryo (at 22.9° C, cauterized at the tip 22 hours after the 4-cell stage) showed after cauterization a very small longitudinal fissure which did not extend to the border of the cauterization zone. During further development the labrum and fore-intestine formed in duplicate, but not the eyes and antennae. A comparison of Figs. 10–12, of this embryo, with the similarly oriented Figs. 4–6, shows the result very clearly. Blastokinesis was easily effected, probably because the head capsule was single. Antennae, number of eye facets, all extremities, tail gills, and the tracheal primordia display no abnormalities. Only the head is a little too small, probably because of the narrow space available for development, and

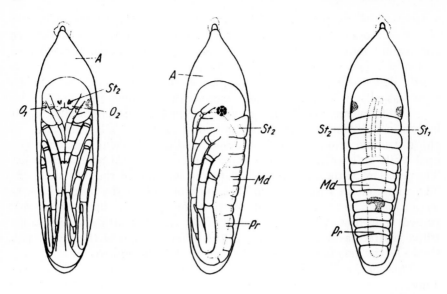

Figure 10. Ventral view.   *Figure 11*. Lateral view.   *Figure 12*. Dorsal view.

Figures 10–12.   Duplication of the labra (O_1, O_2) and stomodaeum (St_1, St_2) after cauterization of the anterior end of the egg in the blastoderm stage. The longitudinal fissure which caused the duplication was visible in the egg at some distance from the border of the cauterization zone. The head capsule is too small, as compared with the normal head capsule (Figures 4–6). Antennae and all extremities are normally developed and well differentiated, and can be compared directly with those of the normal embryo in Figures 4–6. A: destroyed part of the egg. Md: Mid-intestine. Pr: proctodaeum. (Enlarged approx. 64 times.)

because of the destruction of the yolk normally available for the formation of the head.

In spite of this, the division of the labrum anlage led to a complete labrum on each side of the fissure. Each of the two labra (Fig. 10, O_1, O_2) has the indentation characteristic of the normal organ. A fore-intestine opens under each labrum; these intestines are visible through the labra because of their pigmentation (St_1, St_2). The fore-intestines are completely separate as far as the beginning of the mid-intestine (Fig. 12). Since the fore-intestine is formed as an ectodermal invagination, it is understandable that the fore-intestinal duplication extends this far caudally, although the fissure did not extend very far posteriorly, and ventrally only the labrum is duplicated.

In the embryo to be described next (Pl. 1926, T 82 B_3, tip cauterized

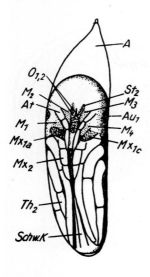

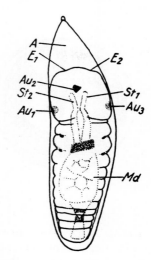

Figure 13.   Ventral view   *Figure 14.*   Dorsal view

Figures 13–14.   Duplications at the head, from the eyes to the first maxillae, after cauterization at the anterior end during the blastoderm stage. Two antennae (At), three eyes (Au_1–Au_3). The apical eye is at its right side slightly sunk into the pharyngeal ganglion and is thus only recognizable on the left. (Compare with cross section in Figure 16.) Two labra (O_1 and O_2), below which open the two stomodaea (St_1, St_2), four mandibles (M_1 and M_4 laterally placed; M_2 and M_3 centrally placed: dotted area), three first maxillae (Mx_{1a}–Mx_{1c}: shaded area); the remaining extremities in normal number and location (compare Figures 4–6). A: destroyed portion of egg; E_1, E_2: indentations in the vertex of the head capsule; Md: mid-intestine; Th_1–Th_3: thoracic legs; Sch.K: tail gills. (Enlarged approx. 64 times.)

at 20.3° C, 36 hours after the 4-cell stage) the duplication extends further. It involves not only the eyes, labra, and intestine, but also the mandibles and the first maxillae. In the middle of the head capsule, where in the normal labrum (Fig. 4), the small indentation usually occurs, a deep cleft is visible (Fig. 13), not large enough, however, to divide the head capsule into two parts. The head capsule is wider than normal; and whereas the vertex of the normal head capsule shows longitudinal—Figure 6, line 1, and Fig. 7 show this indentation—the head of the embryo under discussion is doubly indented (Fig. 14, E_1, E_2). Inside the head capsule, the duplication shows up clearly in the supra-oesophageal ganglion (Figs. 15–16). Normally the supra-oesophageal ganglion consists, as do all ganglia, of two parts. This is particularly obvious for the fiber mass located in the center

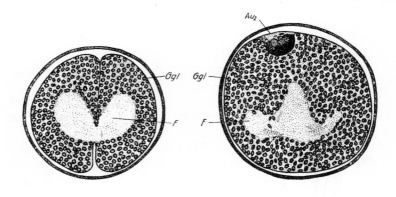

Figure 15   Figure 16

Figures 15–16. Cross sections through the supra-oesophageal ganglion.
Figure 15. Cross section of a normal embryo.
Figure 16. Cross section of the embryo of Figs. 13–14 at the level of the apical eye. The fiber masses (F) of the supra-oesophageal ganglion show a threefold separation, instead of the normal twofold separation, found in the double embryo. The apical eye (Au₂) lies with its right side (at the left in the illustration) somewhat below the surface of the embryo. Ggl: ganglion cells. (Enlarged approx. 280 times.)

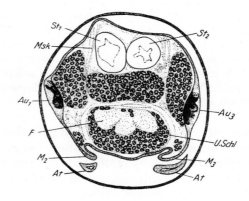

Figure 17. Cross section through the embryo of Figures 13–14 at the level of the posterior eye rim. In correspondence to the partition of the supra-oesophageal ganglion into three parts, the sub-oesophageal ganglion (U. Schl.) also shows this division. Both stomodaea (St₁, St₂) are sectioned transversely. At: antennae; Au₁, Au₃: eyes; F: fiber masses in the interior of the ganglia, M₂, M₃: centrally located mandibles (compare Figure 13); Mxk: muscles. (Enlarged approx. 280 times.)

(F). In the experimental embryo a triply divided configuration of the fiber masses has developed (Fig. 16). The same grouping of ganglia cells appears in the cross-section of the sub-oesophageal ganglion (Fig. 17, U. Schl); and also in the ganglion of the second thoracic segment.

A similar degree of duplication is to be observed in the eyes. Three eyes, developed two lateral (Au_1 and Au_3) and one dorsal (Au_2). Of the lateral eyes, the left is well rounded and has six facets, while the right is less well rounded and has seven facets. The right side of the dorsal eye anlage is sunk slightly below the surface of the embryo (Fig. 14, Au_2; Fig. 16, Au_2, left), so that from the exterior one can discern only three facets with certainty, although to judge from a section, more have been formed. This number is, however, sufficient to determine that in the case of this embryo also the total number of facets exceeds by at least two or three the number found in a normal pair of eyes.

On the ventral side of the head capsule the labra (O_1, O_2) are present in duplicate. One cannot tell whether they bear the typical indentation, since each is half covered by the mandibles (M_2, M_3). Two fore-intestines (St_1, St_2) open under the labra, where they are covered by the mandibles. They proceed in normal fashion (as shown in Fig. 5) between the supra- and sub-oesophageal ganglia toward the dorsal region, where they bend to the posterior. They appear in cross-section in Fig. 17 at the height of the lateral eyes and the pharyngeal ganglion. (The section verifies, quite by chance, the observation that, in the living condition, fore-intestines are capable of carrying out opening and closing movements independently of each other. The left fore-intestine is open, the right almost closed.) The duplication in this case, unlike the previous one, extends to the anterior end of the mid-intestine, which is wider than it would normally be (Fig. 14). In contrast to the normal picture found in the treated embryo (Fig. 6), the yolk cleavage at the anterior end shows different dimensions from those at the posterior end. The proctodaeum is once again single.

Toward the caudal region, instead of two mandibles, there are four (M_1–M_4), lying on each side of the two antennae. They have at their distal ends a brown tip of chitin, as in normal mandibles. The first maxillae (Mx_{1a}, Mv_{1c}), which border on the outer mandibles, are formed normally. And one would not be in error in identifying the broad formation in the median between the two inner mandibles also as a median near placed first maxilla. The tip of this structure is so broadly developed because two rudiments have joined. The second maxillae (Mx_2) have an enlarged basal plate so that the attached palpae diverge. The development of median near palpae did not occur. The differentiation of the palpae is not completed. This is also true of the thoracic extremities, which are present in their normal number. The abdominal segments display no peculiarities, and bear at their ends three tail gills.

The degree of duplication of this embryo differs in the various parts of the body. A maximum exists in the mandibles, with discrete formations of two organs on each side. Toward the posterior there occurs a continuous reduction in duplication from the first maxillae, present in triplicate, to the practically normally developed second maxillae, and to the normally formed thoracic legs. The intestinal system becomes single at the beginning of the mid-intestine. The ventral chain of ganglia becomes normal at the level of the third thoracic segment. In similar fashion, the duplications gradually disappear anteriorly to the mandibles. The labra and fore-intestines, both present in duplicate, are not as far from the median as would have been expected from the position of the mandibles. The antennae are normal. The eyes are not completely duplicated; only three are present.

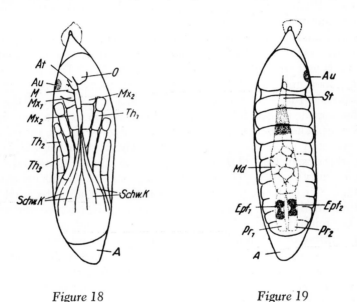

Figure 18   Figure 19

Figures 18–19. Duplication of the proctodaeum (Pr$_1$, Pr$_2$) and the tail gills (Schw. K), after cauterization at the posterior end during the blastoderm stage (A: destroyed portion). Of the tail gills, only those lying on the surface of the egg are visible (compare with cross-section in Figure 21). (Enlarged approx. 64 times.)

Figure 18. Ventral view. The head capsule is too small. The left eye and the left antenna, probably also the left mandible (M) and the first left maxillae (Mx$_1$), are missing. The second maxillae (Mx$_2$) and the thoracic extremities (Th$_1$–Th$_3$) are normally formed.

Figure 19. Dorsal view. The duplication of the proctodaeum is shown especially well in the double arrangement of the proctodaeal valves (Epf$_1$, Epf$_2$) between the mid-intestine and hind-intestine.

Duplications at the Posterior End. An increase in the number of tail gills would allow especially instructive conclusions concerning the potency of the material. Such an instance is shown in experiment Pl. 1925, T 26 D. A cauterization at the posterior end (17 hours after the 4-cell stage, at 19.1° C) resulted in the embryo shown in Figs. 18–19. The abdomen is wider than normal; at the posterior end there are six tail gills instead of three, arranged in clusters of three, each made up of two ventral gills and one dorsal (the surface view of Fig. 18 shows four). As in the normal case, they possess a pigment ring just posterior to their point of attachment. The dorsal gills are turned slightly outward. From the dorsal face of the embryo it can be seen that two hind-intestines (Pr_1, Pr_2) follow the undivided mid-intestine (Md, Fig. 19). Two proctodaeal valves, (Epf_1, Epf_2) instead of one, appear white through the dorsal membrane. Each of the two hind-intestines terminates in an anus, opening under the base of each group of tail gills. Because of the reduced area at the posterior end of the egg caused

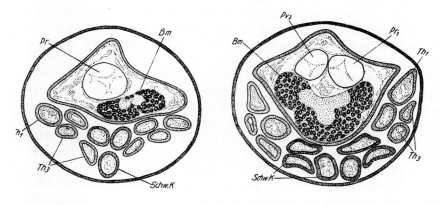

Figure 20   Figure 21

Figures 20–21. Cross sections through the seventh abdominal segment.
Figure 20. Cross section through a normal embryo.
Figure 21. Cross section through the embryos of Figures 18 and 19. The normal embryo can also be compared with the duplicated embryo in regard to the cross sections of the extremities (Th_1, Th_3). In this case, contrary to the normally observed conditions (Figure 4), the tail gills lie very far forward in relation to the extremities, because of the curvature of the abdomen. Of the four cross sections of the extremities (Th_1, Th_3), two belong to the third thoracic leg, bent at the tibio-tarsal joint (compare Figures 4 and 5). The proctodaeum, whose epithelium is thickened on three sides to form the proctodaeal valve, described on p. 234, is duplicated in Figure 21 (Pr_1, Pr_2). The cross section of the abdominal ganglion (Bm) shows three parts instead of the normal two. The number of tail gills (darker stippled) is doubled in Figure 21, as compared with Figure 20. (Enlarged approx. 280 times.)

by the destruction of a portion of yolk (A), the tail gills of the embryo are bent toward the ventral side. In addition, another part of the abdomen has taken part in this bending, so that the tail gills reach very far anteriorly, although they are only as long as the normal gills shown in Fig. 4.

The cross-section (Fig. 21) shows that the duplication has also affected the abdominal nerve cord (Bm). As in the previously described experiment, the supra-oesophageal ganglion has developed the fiber mass in triplicate. Similar masses appear in the last two ganglia, i.e., in the seventh and eighth body segments. In this instance the triple configuration can be clearly recognized also in the external form of the abdominal nerve cord. In this section one can also count six tail gills, thus verifying the observations made in the living embryo. The cross-sections of the gills are shown somewhat darker than those of the extremities. The thickenings on the three sides of the intestinal wall represent the location of the proctodaeal valves (Pr_1, Pr_2) in the two hind-intestines. It was not easy to find a section through a normal embryo comparable to that of a double embryo, because the extremities of the double embryo are bent forward. Therefore a section through the region of the seventh abdominal ganglion of a double embryo shows more extremities than that through the same region of a normal embryo. However, by accident one normal embryo was found in which the tail gills were shifted, as in the double embryo, further forward than usual. A section through this embryo (Fig. 20) can be directly compared with that of the double embryo shown in Fig. 21.

In two cases it was possible to produce by fissures 2 × 3 tail gills on each side. In one of these embryos (T 69 K) the last three abdominal segments were also duplicated. The other embryo (T 150 A) was unable to complete blastokinesis because of head defects.

A duplication in the middle of the embryo also seems possible, although the experiments up to now have not been completely successful. After a lateral defect (Pl. 1927, T 128 M, approximately 46 hours after the 4-cell stage, at 21.3° C) an embryo hatched, which was completely normal except for one outgrowth on the dorsal side of the second and third segments. The outgrowth bore bristles and reached the length of a thoracic extremity, which it also resembled in its chitin structure, so it could reasonably be considered the rudiment of a thoracic extremity.

Triple Formations. With the described method of operation multiple formations can be expected when instead of one fissure several occur in the egg material. Given the narrow room within the egg sheath, triple formations should logically encounter even greater difficulties in their differentiation than the double formations. Sometimes I have seen embryos in which the hind intestine, for example, seemed to be triple, but in these cases differentiation was never completed. Last summer, for the first time, a complete triple formation of the labra and the fore-intestine

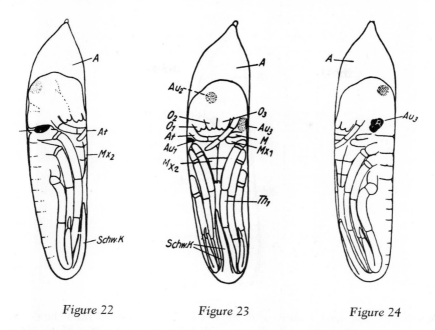

| Figure 22 | Figure 23 | Figure 24 |

Figures 22–24. Triplications of the labrum (and stomodaeum) after tip cauterization in the blastoderm stage.
Figure 22. The embryo from the right side.
Figure 23. The embryo from the lateral side.
Figure 24. The embryo from the left side.
Each of the three labra (O_1–O_3) bears the typical indentation of the normal labrum (Figure 4). Of the three eyes (Au_1–Au_3), the right one (Au_1) faces to the rear, the middle one lies at the dorsal side behind the plane of the drawing, and the left is in a normal position. Mandibles (M) and first maxillae (Mx_1) are present only on the left side. The second maxillae (Mx_2), thoracic extremities ,Th), and tail gills (Schw. K) are located normally. A: destroyed part of the egg. At: antennae. Because of the advancing pigmentation, the course of the intestine can be recognized only in the earlier stages (compare Figure 25). (Enlarged approx. 64 times.)

was obtained (Pl. 1927, T 97 F_{33}; Figs. 22–24). It developed after tip cauterization 41 hours after the 4-cell stage at 21.1° C. The three well-formed labra (Figure 23, O_1–O_3) lie adjacent to each other, each with a small indentation in the middle as in a normal labrum (Fig. 4). Material which was originally destined to form not only the labrum but also the adjacent parts of the head capsule was used in the development of these three complete labra. It is noteworthy also that the three labra taken together occupy a larger area on the surface of the embryo than does the normal

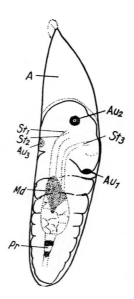

Figure 25. The same embryo as in Figures 22–24, but viewed from the dorsal aspect in an earlier stage, shortly after blastokinesis. Three stomodaea (St_1– St_3). The left and middle stomodaea unite just behind the labra to form one single stomodaeum, which in cross section is approximately twice as large as the right stomodaeum. The duplication extends to the anterior end of the mid-intestine (Md). The proctodaeum (Pr) displays no abnormalities. Au_1–Au_3: eyes. (Enlarged approx. 64 times.)

organ. Both these facts show most convincingly how the fissures cause new formations in each section they create; each new formation is in shape, size, and position more than, and not just a part of, a normal labrum.

A stomodaeum originates under each labrum. The labra can be analyzed only in an advanced stage of chitinization. Since the increasing pigmentation of an older embryo will not permit recognition of the interior, the same embryo is shown from the dorsal aspect in Fig. 25 shortly after completion of blastokinesis. It can be noted—and this is confirmed by sections—that the left and middle stomodaea (St_1, St_2) converge into a common tube slightly posterior to their point of origin, while the right stomodaeum (St_3) remains separate from the others until it reaches the mid-intestine. Although the common tube comprising the middle and left intestine has no double lumen, one can conclude from the cross-section, which is larger—nearly twice as large, in fact, as the lumen of the right stomodaeum—that this tube must have developed in its entire length from a double primordium. Other than an irregularity of the pigment zone at the anterior end of the mid-intestine, the remainder of the intestinal system to the anus is undivided and normally formed.

The extremities are not duplicated. Except for the missing mandible and first maxilla on the right side (Figs. 22–23), everything is normally constructed; even the second maxillae (Mx_2) are scarcely too broad. With continuing development the head capsule regulates by becoming more and more normal. One can confirm this by comparing Fig. 25 with Figs. 22–24. The head capsule shows three eye-primordia (Au_1–Au_3). The left one (Au_3 in Fig. 24) is in normal position, while the middle primordium, as in the embryo shown in Figs. 13–14, is approximately on the vertex (Au_2 in Fig. 25, and below the plane of the drawing in Figs. 21–24). The eye on the right side (Au_1, Fig. 22) looks toward the rear. A central facet is developed in all three eyes. The left eye (Fig. 24) shows in addition that differentiation of the outer facets has started. The antennae have the correct number of segments. The labral region, as a result of its enlargement, is located somewhat out of the normal position.

Only the beginnings of complete twin or multiple formations were found. In most instances the fissures were associated with such great general defects that differentiation could not advance very far. In one case (T 126 K), as the result of a tip cauterization the primordium of a double head capsule was observed, simultaneously with a complete division of the abdomen including two hind-intestines and six tail gills. On another occasion (T 136 B 1), also following a tip cauterization, duplication of the fore and the hind-intestine was observed. Neither case could be analyzed very far. Similarly, after a cauterization at the posterior tip, an embryo developed (T 93 K) in which two proctodaeal valves and four eye primordia could be detected with certainty from among the few slightly advanced differentiations. Considering the difficulty of the experiment, in which duplications are expected to develop in the narrow space within the egg-sheath, one can scarcely imagine that these would ever progress beyond early beginnings.

Nonetheless it was possible to show in different experiments for different organs that certain embryonic regions could develop into other structures than they were normally destined to; that their prospective potency was greater than their prospective significance. Especially instructive were those cases in which both parts of the duplication displayed a form pattern which could not be explained by the simple splitting of an organ and the rounding up of its parts. One must assume that the organ anlage was split and that this caused a regrouping of the determining factors in such a way that each half produced from its own material a complete copy of the organ normally formed by both parts together. If four eyes are formed, of which two together have more facets than one normal eye (p. 39), or if three eyes are formed having in all at least 16 facets (p. 43), then something additional has unquestionably been added. This is especially well illustrated by duplication, or triplication, of the labra, each of which developed into an harmonious organ (Fig. 23). Duplication of the fore-intestine could be explained simply by splitting of the organ. On the other hand, the cell arrangement in the hind-intestine during the formation of the triple proctodaeal valves suggests an independent reformation of each proctodaeal primordium into an harmonious organ. The duplicated tail gills (Figs. 18 and 21), together with the duplicated proctodaea, provide a perfect example of the regrouping of the determining factors.

In this connection, it is extremely important to consider the size relationships. By measuring the surface or the diameter of each of the duplicated organs, it has been found that these valves are always more than half the size of those of the normal organ. This fact can easily be detected as regards the eyes (Figs. 5 and 9), the labra (Figs. 4 and 23), the tail gills (Figs. 4 and 18), and the intestine (Figs. 20 and 21). For any deviation from this general rule, a special reason could always be found. For instance, a lack of material apparently caused the too-small labra shown in Fig. 10. Here the entire head capsule was reduced because the cauterization destroyed too much material. In order to provide an approximate basis for the dimensions to be expected, let us compare the eggs and their embryos with ellipsoids. Assuming that the volumes of two embryos are 1:2, or 1:3, and that their longitudinal axes remain unchanged, then the surface dimensions of the two embryos will be respectively, *mutatis mutandis*, 1:1.4 (1:2) and 1:7 (1:3). Thus, double or triple organs must show surface dimensions which exceed one-half or one-third the dimensions of the normal organs, as in fact appears in the above mentioned measurements. Thus, the observation concerning the size of the developed organs supports the conclusion (based on form comparison) that harmonious organs develop from separated embryonic parts.

Only large-scale measurements of normal and duplicated organs in equal condition (expansion, contraction, fixation effects) and developmental stage can determine to what degree every part may be harmoniously reduced in relation to the normal organs. Single measurements of organs which are subject to fewer changes, such as eyes and labra, allow us to anticipate that the reduction in size takes place on a harmonious scale.

Harmoniously reduced dwarfs develop after sagittal splitting of the germ material. As shown especially by the triple formations, the blastoderm of *Platycnemis pennipes* possesses the same characteristics in the dorsal-ventral axis as equipotential systems possess in each axial direction.

The fact that the relationships are different in the longitudinal axis is shown by constriction and defect experiments in which the anterior and posterior ends of embryos were isolated from each other in the early blastoderm stage (1926). The development of the anterior parts is dependent on factors located in the posterior region. The following conditions must have been met if a harmonious dwarf develops from parts of a cross segment: First, at the time of the experiment, determination had not yet begun in all parts of the cross segment, at least their final destiny had not yet been fixed. Furthermore, all factors important for the determination of this segment must have been present, or at least their route to the different parts must not be blocked by the fissures. After transverse constriction, the latter supposition applies to the anterior end, which cannot develop after a constriction in the middle of the egg. One would have to be able to transplant in order to overcome this obstacle to analysis. It is also to be noted, however, that the posterior part of the egg never developed a harmonious embryo, but only a posterior end. Thus there can be no doubt that the egg reacts differently in the longitudinal than it does in the transverse axis.

This difference may be caused by the peculiar nature of the determination process, which apparently proceeds in stepwise fashion from posterior to anterior, so that the parts which it affects in its course are no longer capable of any regulation. The difference, however, may also be due to a general predetermination of the longitudinal axis in the blastoderm stage, which has already been described in the first report as a specific disposition of the egg parts for the formation of the germ band.

For the dorsal-ventral axis, too, a similar predetermination could be present. However, it may not be as precise and unalterable as that of the longitudinal axis. If it were present, the effect of the experiment would consist in a division of the organ primordium and a subsequent regrouping of the determining factors. If it were not present, a division of the primordium cannot be considered. The determining factors would find a divided germ material and would act in such a manner that the parts of the material would produce a harmonious whole.

We must then restrict our conclusion to the following:

The experiment which caused the development of these double and triple formations was performed before the externally visible differentiation of the germ band, probably during the time of action of the developmental factors described in 1926. Through the production of double and multiple formations, it has been established that at the beginning of the action of these factors the determination of the germ band has not yet been completed. The factors, which operate from the posterior end toward the anterior end, find the egg parts in a not-yet-determined state.

REFERENCES

Brandt, A. (1869), *Mém. Acad. St. Péterbourg* (7), 13: Figs. 1–19.
Gräper, (1923), *Arch. Entw. Mech.* 98:469.
Hegner, R. W. (1911), Experiments with Chysomelid beetles. III. The effects of killing parts of the eggs of *Leptinotarsa decemlineata*. *Biol. Bull.*, 20:237–51.

Seidel, F. (1924), Die Geschlechtsorgane in der embryonalen Entwicklung von *Pyrrho-coris apterus* L. Z. *wiss. Biol.*, A1:429–506.

Spemann, H. (1901–3), Entwicklungsphysiologische Studien am Tritonei. I–III. *Arch. Entwicklungsmech. Organismen*, 14–16.

Spemann, H. (1918), Über die Determination der ersten Organanlagen des Amphibien-embryo. I–IV. *Arch. Entwicklungsmech. Organismen*, 43:448–555.

Spemann, H., and Mangold, H. (1924), Über Induktion vom Embryonalanlagen durch Implantation artfremder Organisatoren. *Arch. Entwicklungsmech. Organismen*, 100: 599–638.

Penners,   (1925), Z. *wiss. Zool.* 127.

Reith,   (1925), Z. *wiss. Zool.* 126:181–238.

Ubisch,   von (1923), *Arch. Entw. Mech.* 98:469.

FRIEDRICH SEIDEL, EBERHARD BOCK, and GERHARD KRAUSE

The organization of the insect egg (reaction and induction processes; egg types)

Eberhard Bock was born in Plauen Voightland, Germany, in 1909. He apparently studied at the universities of Königsberg, Jena, and Rostock from about 1929 to 1934, and was awarded a Ph.D. in zoology from Königsberg or Berlin about 1939. By this time he seems to have been already in the German army; and the possibility of further work ended with his death in action on the Russian front in 1942.

Gerhard Krause was born in 1906, and received his Ph.D. in zoology from the University of Königsberg. He has held the posts of Professor of Zoology and Comparative Anatomy at the University of Würzburg, and Director of the Zoological Institute, also at Würzburg.

Even today it is difficult and in many cases virtually impossible to give a clear characterization of the developmental physiology of the large animal groups. The reason is that the investigations on the various groups were often made with different methods, on research levels not suitable for comparison, and above all during varying stages of development. For example, the experiments on amphibians by Spemann, Vogt, and their students were concerned mainly with the development of organs. The developmental centers and factors discovered there displayed activities between different tissue layers, or from one germ layer to another. A comparison of these factors and centers with those found in the early developmental stages of

[Previously published in *Sonderdruck aus die Naturwissenschaften*, 28 (1940), 433–46.]

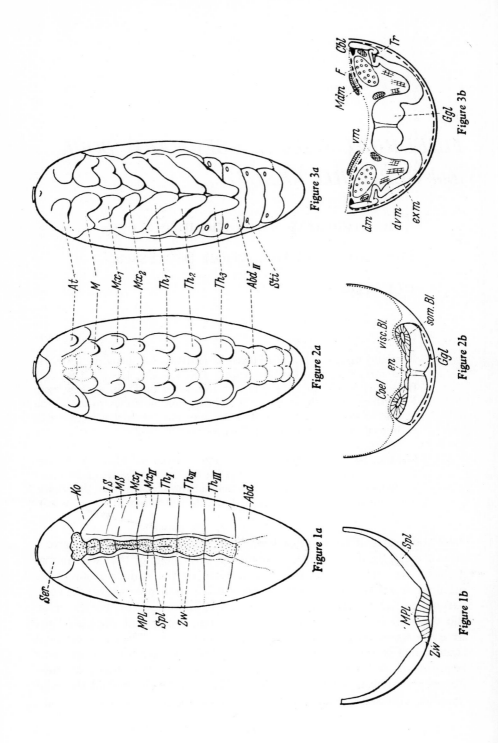

Figure 1a

Figure 2a

Figure 3a

Figure 1b

Figure 2b

Figure 3b

insects could be made only on a purely formal basis and with some reservation. Only after Eberhard Bock found also in insects relationships between the germ layers and certain developmental reactions was it possible to work out more clearly similarities and differences in developmental physiology between amphibians and insects. Some of these reactions, because of the method used for their characterization, and because of their mode of action, could be considered inductive processes similar to those found in amphibians.

To make the following experiments more readily understandable, several supplementary details should be given concerning the normal development of the germ layers and organs of the golden-eyed fly, Chrysopa (Neuroptera). Figures 1–3 show the Chrysopa embryo in three consecutive stages of development. . . . The first stage (Fig. 1a) is that of germ layer formation, the second (Fig. 2a) that of the completion of the basic body form, the third (Fig. 3a) that of the completed organ differentiation. In the process of germ layer formation, one median plate (mesentoderm) and two lateral plates (ectoderm) develop through cellular differentiation. At the stage of the completed basic body form, all parts of the embryo are established in their basic form. In the following stage, the different organic rudiments become visible within the body parts. The added cross-section figures (Fig. 1b–3b) give a picture of the morphological relationship between the germ layers in the respective stages. At first, the germ layers lie next to each other in one plane (Fig. 1b). In the second stage, each is still an unsegmented morphological entity; however, they are connected with each other at all points (Fig. 2b). Then the different germ layers divide into organ rudiments (Fig. 3b). The events leading from the first to the second stage are called organ segregation. The process starts with the invagination of the midplate and ends with the formation of the coelomic epithelia. After the invagination of the midplate, the mesoderm cells are

Figures 1–3.   Chrysopa perla (Neuroptera), Normal development.
Figure 1.   Stage of germ layer segregation
Figure 2.   Stage of completed basic body form
Figure 3.   Stage of completed organ differentiation
Each stage is represented by (a) a view of the germ band from the ventral side of a thoracic segment.
Abd: Abdominal segments. Amn: Amnion. At: Antenna. Cbl: Cardioblasts. Coel: Coelom. deg.Z.: Degenerated cells. dm: Dorsal muscles. dvm: Dorsoventral muscles. en: Entoderm. exm. Muscle of extremities. F: Fat body. Ggl: Ganglion. IS: Intercalar segment. Ko: Head parts. Md: Mid-intestinal anlage. Mdm: Mid-intestinal muscle cells. M: Mandible. Ms: Mandible segment. Mpl: Midplate. $Mx_{I,II}$: Maxillary segments. $Mx_{1,2}$: Maxillae. som.Bl.: Somatic layer. Spl: Lateral plates. Sti: Stigma. $Th_{I,II}$: Thoracic segments. $Th_{1,2}$: Thoracic extremities. Tr: Tracheae. vm: Ventral muscle. visc.Bl.: Visceral layer. Zw: Border between mid- and lateral plates (Bock).

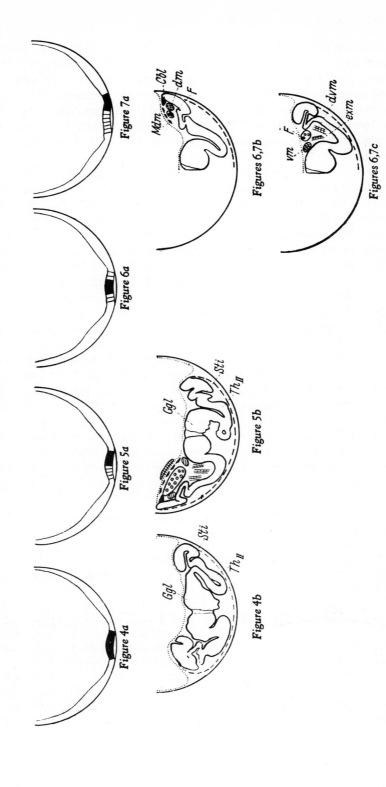

Figure 4a

Figure 5a

Figure 6a

Figure 7a

Figure 4b

Figure 5b

Figures 6,7b

Figures 6,7c

located in three layers below the median portion of the germ band. While the two lower layers expand toward both sides, the cells slowly unite into a compact epithelium (Fig. 2b). A lower epithelium forms the visceral (visc. Bl.); and an upper one the somatic layer of the coelum (som. Bl.). The formation of an epithelium is the basis for organ segregation. The germ layers grow in width in such a way that the relative position of all parts remains the same. We can trace the internal group of organs back to the visceral and the external group back to the somatic layer. The visceral layer differentiates and forms the fat body (F) and the muscles of the mid-intestines (Mdm). The somatic layer gives rise to the ventral muscles (VM), the muscles of the extremities (exm), the dorso-ventral (dvm) and the dorsal muscles (dm). The region of transition between the two coelomic layers lies below the edge of the ectoderm. Here the cardioblasts (Cbl) differentiate. Within each segment differentiation proceeds with the same space and time dependency. Until organ segregation is completed, a morphological gradient of differentiation is visible in the right-left axis, in the ectoderm and in both layers of the mesoderm. During their separation, the individual organs develop in all germ layers, one after the other, from medial to lateral, in the same sequence as they later appear.

The interrelations between the germ layers can be investigated by defect experiments in which parts of a germ layer are destroyed at the stage of its formation, while the other layer remains intact. The parts were removed by cauterization. In living condition during the formation of the germ layers every single cell is visible. This made it possible to remove with

Figures 4–7. Chrysopa perla (Neuroptera): mesodermal defects.
Figures 4a–7. Operation in the stage of germ layer formation represented by cross section diagrams. Destroyed areas are black. (Compare with Fig. 1b.)
Figures 4b–7b. Developmental results at the stage of completed organic differentiation, represented in cross section diagrams. (Compare with Figure 3b.)
Figure 4a. Complete destruction of the midplate.
Figure 4b. Result: Ectoderm has formed abnormally, but it is histologically normally differentiated.
Figure 5a. Cauterization of one-half of the midplate in one segment.
Figure 5b. Result: The defective germ half is without mesoderm; the opposite one is normal.
Figure 6a. Cauterization of a small median portion of the midplate; lateral mesoderm remains.
Figure 7a. Cauterization of a small lateral portion of the midplate; medial mesoderm remains.
Figures 6,7b. Results: Differentiation of medial and lateral mesoderm remnants with nonretarded migration.
Figures 6,7c. With retarded migration.
The mesoderm always differentiates according to its location and independent of its origin.
Abbreviations: Compare Figures 1–3 (Bock).

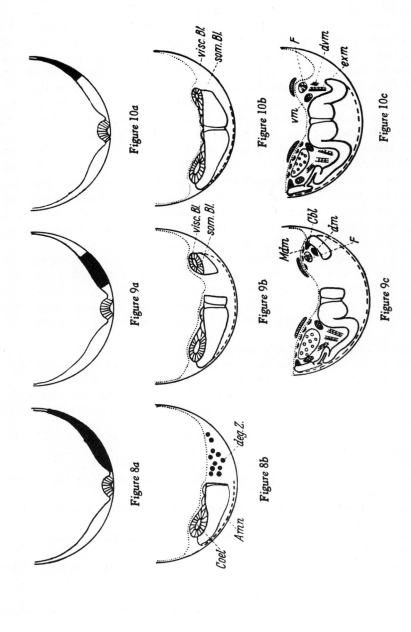

Figure 8a

Figure 9a

Figure 10a

Figure 8b

Figure 9b

Figure 10b

Figure 9c

Figure 10c

great accuracy small areas and to detect the presence or absence of even a few cells.

In order to test the developmental capacity of the ectoderm independent of the mesoderm, the latter was completely removed in the first experimental group (Fig. 4a). The results were as follows: Embryos without mesoderm were able to differentiate histologically to completion all ectodermal organs. However, both the single organs and the entire body were misshapen (Fig. 4b). Thus the ectoderm needs the mesodermal substratum for the normal shaping of the organs it produces. Yet, as in the case of *Platycnemis*, the ectoderm differentiates independently of the mesoderm and must be regarded as a self-differentiating system.

In order to test the capacity of various regions in the midplate to replace each other, a second group of experiments was designed. When one half of the midplate of one segment was destroyed the remaining half was not able to replace the missing part (Fig. 5a, b). Therefore the movement of the underlying material is system limited laterally and cannot cross the median line. In a large series of experiments small regions not quite as large as the diameter of the midplate were killed by cauterization within one mesodermal half-segment. In some cases the defect was placed on the median of the midplate, in others somewhat to the side (Figs. 6, 7a). In each case the remaining mesoderm retained its original direction of movement and spread below the lateral ectoderm. Whether, as in the case of the median defects, this remaining mesoderm was of lateral origin (Fig. 6a) or, as in the case of the paramedian defects, of medial origin (Fig. 7a),

Figures 8–10. Chrysopa perla (Neuroptera): ectodermal defects. The representation of experiments and results corresponds to Figures 4–7.
Figures 8a–10a. Cauterization in the stage of the germ-layer segregation.
Figures 8b–10c. Developmental results: (b) in the stage of the completed body form; (c) in the stage of the completed organ differentiation.
Figure 8a. Cauterization of the entire side plate at one side of a thoracic segment.
Figure 8b. Result: Mesoderm underlies lateral regions but does not differentiate.
Figures 9–10. Cauterization of parts of the ectodermal side plate at one side of a thoracic segment.
Figure 9a. Cauterization of the medial portion of the side plate. The lateral portion remains.
Figure 10a. Cauterization of the lateral portion of the side plate. Medial portion remains.
Figures 9b–10b. Result: Harmoniously shortened coelom epithelium (Fig. 9b) below lateral ectoderm remnant; (Fig. 10b) below medial ectoderm remnant. The shortened coelom epithelia of the same origin differentiate below the lateral ectoderm remnant (Fig. 9c) differently from below the medial ectoderm remnant (Fig. 10c) but in each case according to the location.
Abbreviation: Compare Figures 3–5 (Bock).

it underlay in every case the ectodermal edge. According to its new location, it formed here cardioblasts and muscles of the mid-intestine (Fig. 6, 7b). When similar experiments are performed with larger cauterized regions, an arrangement of germ layers results which can be used as control experiments, since the underlying process decreases as the cauterization area increases. In such cases not even lateral mesoderm cells can reach the ectoderm edge, but migrate, in contrast to their prospective significance, only to the region below the medial ectoderm, and differentiate there, according to their new location, into muscles and fat tissues (Fig. 6, 7c); cardioblasts and mid-intestine muscles are missing.

These experiments lead to two important conclusions: 1. Within one half of a segment, medial cells of the midplate can migrate into lateral germ parts and vice versa. Thus under changed experimental conditions the cells can be displaced similar to a self-transplantation. 2. Independent of their origin, the mesoderm cells always develop according to their location. Thus all cells of the midplate must be considered.

The result of the first group of experiments implies that the ectoderm is a self-differentiating system. It might therefore be concluded that the differentiation of the mesoderm is under the influence of the ectoderm. This possibility could be tested by removal of ectoderm regions. Accordingly, in a third and fourth group of experiments, ectoderm was either completely (Fig. 8) or partially (Figs. 9, 10) removed from one half of a segment.

Destruction of the entire ectoderm (Fig. 8a) at one side of the segment did not prevent the mesoderm from spreading into the ectoderm-free area, but it failed to differentiate (Fig. 8b). It degenerated at the time when it normally would differentiate into an epithelium. The spreading movement of the mesoderm is thus to a certain degree independent of the ectoderm. The epithelization of the mesoderm is, however, in some way dependent on the ectoderm. The question arises whether the ectoderm, in addition to the epithelization of the mesoderm, also influences its further differentiation.

To test this, a fourth group of experiments was designed. Within one side of the segment, progressively larger regions of the ectoderm were destroyed, either from the medial to lateral, or in the opposite direction. The mesoderm below both the lateral (Fig. 9b) and the medial remains of the ectoderm (Fig. 10b), formed coelom epithelium of diminished proportions corresponding to the reduced ectoderm portions above, in spite of the fact that the mesodermal material was not reduced. Independent of their harmonious proportions, these epithelia always differentiated according to their position into mesodermal structures. The mesoderm below the lateral ectoderm remnant differentiated into cardioblasts (Cl) and into intestinal muscles (Mdm) (Fig. 9c); these did not develop below the medial ectoderm remnant (Fig. 10c). In both groups of experiments the mesoderm always formed below the ectodermal remnants an epithelium-like structure; only the type of ectodermal remnant was different. Since according to the experiments discussed above the mesoderm must be considered isopotent, it may be concluded that: The lateral ectoderm contains factors which are necessary for the formation of cardioblasts and intestinal muscles. These factors are absent in the medial ectodermal portion. Because the migrating isopotent mesoderm cells underlie ectodermal regions which they normally do not underlie, this brings them under the influence of different ectodermal factors. This represents a kind of self-transplantation. Therefore, if we seek a comparable physiological occurrence for the process of change in the ectoderm edge, we can speak here, even in the strictest sense of Spemann's definition, of an *induction*.

If we now apply to these reaction processes a conception generally attributed to amphibia embryos, a comparison of the organizing events between amphibians and insects is possible. For triton as well as for *Chrysopa*, the decisive factors for the organization of the embryo are located in both forms in a definite germ layer: In triton they are found in the mesoderm, in *Chrysopa*, in the ectoderm. The inducting material in triton enjoys great freedom of movement. The extent of these movements determines to a large degree the size and proportion of the induced structures (neural plate). Contrary to this, in the insect *Chrysopa* the inductor, the ectoderm, is a relatively rigid system, which is endowed with a mosaic of inductive potencies. The mesoderm underlies this system and responds to the stimulus emanating from it. The movements of the embryonic material, different as they are in the two animals, undoubtedly have the same basic significance. They bring together for the purpose of interaction developmental systems that provide the basis for the organization of the embryo.

It is important to note that the germ layers can have completely different functions in different organizational types. The means by which nature develops its organic forms may be essentially the same. However, the manner in which they are incorporated into the whole developmental sequence is as different as are the types of organization and the various body forms.

II

CHEMICAL
GENETICS

ERNST CASPARI

The action of a pleiotropic gene in the
flour moth *Ephestia Kuhniella* Zeller

Ernst Wolfgang Caspari was born in Charlottenburg, Germany, in 1909. He studied at the Universities of Freiburg, Berlin, and Frankfurt, and received his Ph.D. in zoology from the University of Göttingen in 1933. For the next two years he served at Göttingen as Assistant in Zoology. From 1935 to 1938 he was in Istanbul, working in microbiology. In 1938 he came to the United States as a Fellow in Biology at Lafayette College, becoming an Assistant Professor in 1941. He went to the University of Rochester in 1944 as Research Associate in Zoology. In 1946 he became Associate Professor of Biology at Wesleyan University, and from 1949 to 1960 he was on the staff of the Carnegie Institution at Cold Spring Harbor as Research Associate in Genetics. In 1960 he returned to the University of Rochester as Professor and Chairman of the Department of Biology.

His research interests lie in the areas of physiological genetics and genetics of behavior.

INTRODUCTION AND DEFINITION OF THE PROBLEM

In previous attempts to establish the mode of action of genes, developmental investigations have been combined primarily with genetic experiments.

Dobzhansky was the first to point out that the so-called pleiotropic genes, that is, genes each of which influences several outward characters,

I wish to thank my honored teacher, Professor Kühn, who stimulated my undertaking this study, and Dr. Henke, for their interest in the investigations. I am indebted as well to Mr. Frieling for Figs. 2d–f. (Author's note.)
[Previously published in Wilhelm Roux' *Archiv für Entwicklungsmechanik der Organismen*, Volume 130, 1933, pp. 353–81. Reprinted by permission of publisher and author.]

are very favorable for solving the question of the mode of action of genes. To this end he studied a series of mutants of *Drosophila* and the most varied bodily characteristics, and found that each mutant has its well-defined expression elsewhere also, for instance in the sexual apparatus—in other words that all the genes he studied are pleiotropic. He feels that by investigating the relationship between the various phenotypic characteristics controlled by a single gene, one may obtain insight into its physiological role in development. Other authors, such as Plunkett, have studied the influence of external conditions and accessory genes on the degree of expression of phenotypic characteristics determined by a single gene and have on this basis formed conceptions of the mode of action of genes. A broadly developed hypothesis as to the action of genes is presented by Goldschmidt in his "Physiological Theory of Inheritance." Here he weaves together extensive observations concerning sex determination, obtained partly from pure genetic and partly from evolutionary studies, into a co-ordinated picture of the mode of action of genes. Some very concrete notions as to the problem were obtained by Sturtevant and Dobzhansky through studies of gynandromorphs and mosaic specimens. Here in some instances it was possible to detect a mutual influence of genetically different body parts and to analyze more closely the nature of this influence.

Hitherto no one has attempted to attack the question as to the mode of action of genes via the method elsewhere most customary in the physiological study of development, namely, by means of experimental surgery. No doubt that is in part because the animals that are most useful for the study of genetic problems are not readily operable. The flour moth, *Ephestia kühniella* Zeller, proved to be suitable for both genetic and surgical investigations. On the one hand, it can be reared easily and at all seasons; on the other, it is large enough for surgical experimentation. Furthermore, Kühn and Henke have identified a large number of mutations in it.

Hence, it was decided to use the flour moth in order, by combining the various experimental methods, to penetrate deeper into the processes whereby a single gene evokes a certain outward characteristic. For this purpose was chosen the *red-eyed mutation* gene A (Fig. 2c), whose inheritance had been described by Kühn and Henke (1930, 1932). They showed that this is a monohybrid, Mendelian, recessive mutation. This gene seemed especially favorable because it determines other characteristics in addition to the red eye color. As Kühn and Henke showed, this hereditary factor, when homozygous, is expressed also in lower vitality and in a reduction of the rate of development. Besides, the coloration of the testes and the body color of the caterpillar are also affected by gene A (Kühn 1932). First the degree of correlation between the various characteristics controlled by the same gene was tested. Then transplantations were made, between races, of those tissues that are influenced by gene A.

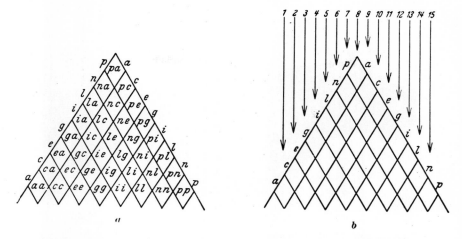

Figures 1a–b.   Color sheet from Ostwald's color charts. (*a*) Designation of the areas: *pa* is a pure hue, *aa–pp* a gray scale running from white to black. (*b*) Designation of the saturation intervals.

The insect cultures were maintained according to the methods indicated by Kühn and Henke (1929, p. 27).

Coloration of testes and eyes was determined with Ostwald's color-charts. These are 24 triangular charts, the baseline of which consists of a gray scale running from white to black, and the apex of which is a pure color (Fig. 1a). The rest of the areas are occupied by shades of color that consist of graded mixtures of a pure color with white and black. Thus the hue of any pigment may be identified as to its pure color by the number of the chart on which it appears or by the numbers of two charts, between which the hue lies; and as to its content of white and black by its co-ordinates in the triangle. Areas which are on the same horizontal line thus possess the same degree of purity of color but differ in their black and white content. Areas lying vertically above and below one another have the same saturation. Since the pigmentation of the testes was basically a matter of saturation, the lines of equal saturation were given successive numbers from 1 to 15, so that 1 = pure white, 15 = pure black (Fig. 1b). These were then divided into classes according to need.

I. TESTIS COLOR IN THE BLACK-EYED AND RED-EYED RACES

a. The Black-Eyed Races

Dobzhansky studied the gonads of various *Drosophila* mutants. He found that the testes are colorless and transparent in a large number of mutants, whereas they are bright yellow in the wild type and in some other races.

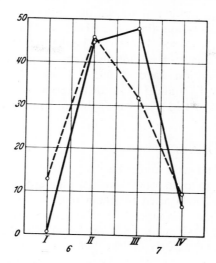

Figure 3.   Saturation of the testis color in AA (– – –) and Aa (———) spec-imens. Abscissa: saturation of the testis color, in Classes. Ordinate: per cent of specimens. Number of animals: $n_{AA} = 415$; $n_{Aa} = 192$.

In wild type *Ephestia*, as in many Lepidoptera, the testicular sheath is brightly varicolored. The general impression is mainly of a brownish violet, which varies greatly. On closer observation, the color is seen not to be uniform (Figs. 2d,e and 6b). It is produced by the combined effect of a rather light-colored background and an overlay of stronger pigment. The latter consists of spiraling lines that run together to a focal point. In addition, the space between the lines is filled out with irregular spots of evenly dark pigment.

Testes were taken from freshly emerged specimens. Their coloration was measured under the binoculars in physiological saline or, frequently, in 70 percent alcohol also. A series of comparative determinations showed that the measured value is the same in both media. In order to obtain a uniform color for the entire testis, the binoculars were not focused sharply during measurement, so that the markings blended with the background.

For the most part the color of the testes was found on Sheet 7 of the Ostwald color charts (first red). Very light testes were to be found in the light areas of Sheet 6 (third), darker ones on the dark areas of Sheet 8 (second red). This difference in hue did not need to be taken into con-sideration; rather, testing the degree of saturation was sufficient. In making

Figures 2a–h.   (a) Moth of the black-eyed race AA. (b) Moth of the *aa* race, with coffee-brown eyes. (c) Red-eyed moth of the *aa* race. (d–e) Imaginal testes of flour moths of the AA race. (g) Full-grown caterpillar of the *aa* race. (h) Full-grown caterpillar of the AA race, with testis showing through.

calculations it proved practical to combine into one class each two successive stages of saturation from the chart, so that altogether there resulted four saturation classes (Fig. 1b). Then all testes that belonged in the sixth and seventh stages of saturation were counted in Class I. Class II corresponds to saturation stages 8 and 9, Class III to stages 10 and 11, Class IV to stages 12 and 13. The distribution of all AA specimens is shown in the curve of Fig. 3 and in Table 6. The mean was found to be $M = 2.38 \pm 0.04$.

b. The Red-Eyed Races

The testes of the red-eyed moths vary a great deal. Some are totally unpigmented, others are more or less strongly pigmented. A different category of classification had to be used for them than for the testes of the black-eyed specimens. Their completely colorless testes look yellowish, very light and transparent (Fig. 2f); they fall on Sheet 2 (second yellow) of the Ostwald color charts, namely on the light areas *ca, ec* and *gc* (Fig. 1). With weakly colored testes the background is yellowish, and only in the spiral lines already described for the black-eyed moths does violet pigment occur. In the Ostwald color charts this is not expressed in a displacement of the saturation value, but only in the fact that, depending on the strength of pigmentation, more or less pink is admixed with the yellow coloring, so that the hue is diplaced toward orange. Thus, weakly pigmented testes are not distinguished from completely colorless ones by saturation value, but only in hue, that is in the number of the color sheet. But the more strongly pigmented testes, which lie on Sheets 6 and 7, differ in saturation value, so that this too must be taken into account in classification. Hence the categories were chosen in such a way that for the lighter testes only their assignment to a color sheet was decisive; Classes 1, 2, 3 and 4 comprise the testes falling on Sheets 2, 3, 4 and 5, respectively. For testes that fell on Sheets 6 and 7 only the degree of saturation was evaluated. They were divided into three classes: Class 5 includes the degrees of saturation 2–5 (see Fig. 1b), that do not occur with the black-eyed moths. Class 6 corresponds to degrees of saturation 6–9; Class 7 comprises all testes that are darker. Hence Class 6 corresponds to Classes I and II, Class 7 to Classes III and IV, of the scale that was used for the testes of the black-eyed moths. In the graphs both categories of classes have been indicated—the more extensive category for the testes of the red-eyed strains by means of Arabic numbers, the shorter category for the black-eyed moths by means of Roman numbers.

The curve of Fig. 4 shows the distribution of the testes of the red-eyed moths in these seven classes. The curves show also the testes of the black-eyed moths, according to this same classification. The latter are only in Classes 6 and 7. The two curves intergrade only slightly and are clearly distinct. This is expressed also in the very different mean values. With the AA specimens the mean is 6.41 ± 0.02, with the *aa* specimens 2.22 ± 0.07.

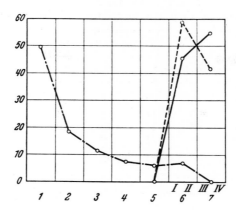

Figure 4. Saturation of testis color in AA (– – – – –), Aa (————), and *aa* (– · – · – · – · –) specimens. Abscissa: saturation of testis color, in classes. Ordinate: percent of specimens. Number of specimens: $n_{AA} = 415$, $n_{Aa} = 192$, $n_{aa} = 569$.

Thus, the black-eyed specimens have significantly more strongly pigmented testes than the red-eyed ones.

But the parallelism between eye color and testis color goes farther. The eye color of the red-eyed specimens varies a great deal. Kühn and Henke found that their range of variation extends from bright yellow to coffee brown (Kühn and Henke, 1932, Table VIII, Figs. 4–9). As was determined by several workers in the laboratory here, this variability depends in part on the presence of different hereditary factors and in part on modifications resulting from different conditions of culture.

Now an attempt was made to correlate the intensity of eye pigmentation with testis color. For this purpose the eye colors of specimens from different colonies were likewise determined under the binoculars. They were then classified according to the degree of saturation. As classes, the simple saturation stages of the Ostwald color charts were selected.

The result for all red-eyed moths taken together is shown in Table 1 in the form of a correlation table.

The distribution of values shows a clear positive correlation, which is also expressed in the high correlation coefficient ($r = 0.60 \pm 0.03$). Thus, on the average, specimens with lighter eyes also have more weakly colored testes than specimens with dark eyes.

The nature of this correlation may be analyzed further. The material used belongs to various strains that Engelhardt had selected over several generations for light eye color. Some of the specimens were reared under constant conditions at 18° and some at 25°.

TABLE 1

Correlation between eye color and testis color in red-eyed moths

Eye color in saturation stages	Testis color in classes							
	1	2	3	4	5	6	7	x
6	18	1	...	...	...	...	...	19
7	81	11	5	...	...	...	...	99
8	100	29	11	4	2	5	...	151
9	75	45	21	19	10	6	...	176
10	9	20	22	9	13	7	...	80
11	...	1	5	8	5	11	...	30
12	...	...	...	2	3	7	...	12
13	...	...	...	...	...	2	...	2
y	283	107	64	42	34	39	...	569

$r = 0.60 \pm 0.03$

Table 2 shows the percentage distribution of eye color in cultures of two strains, which I designate as R_1 and R_2 at both rearing temperatures.

Strain R_1 had been selected for light eye color for several generations. At 18°, the eyes on the average are medium light ($M = 8.30 \pm 0.09$). At 25°, the eyes are even lighter. The mean value is 7.76 ± 0.09. Thus, the limits of three standard deviations for the mean values of eye coloration at 18° and 25° are identical. If we consider the relatively small amount of experimental material, the difference may be regarded as certain.

TABLE 2

Eye color of red-eyed specimens from different cultures and temperatures, in percent; absolute number n and mean value M with three standard deviations m

Strain	Saturation classes								n	M	m	$M \pm 3m$
	6	7	8	9	10	11	12	13				
R_1 at 18°	2.8	19.7	33.8	32.4	10.6	0.7	...	...	142	8.30	0.09	8.03– 8.57
R_1 at 25°	2.5	36.7	43.0	17.7	...	...	...	...	79	7.76	0.09	7.49– 8.03
R_2 at 18°	...	1.8	8.1	27.0	35.1	17.1	9.0	1.8	111	9.92	0.11	9.59–10.25
R_2 at 25°	7.4	29.8	33.3	22.2	7.4	...	...	...	54	7.93	0.14	7.51– 8.35

Strain R_2 is a strain selected for dark red eye color. At 18°, the eyes often look coffee brown (saturation stages 11–13). The table shows that at 18° the eyes are clearly darker than those of strain R_1. But at a rearing temperature of 25°, they are approximately as light as those of strain R_1.

Table 3 shows the distribution, over the seven classes of testis pigmentation, of testis color for these same strains at the same rearing temperatures.

TABLE 3

Testis pigmentation of red-eyed specimens from different cultures and temperatures, in percent; absolute number n and mean M with three standard deviations m

Strain	Saturation classes							n	M	m	$M \pm 3m$
	1	2	3	4	5	6	7				
R_1 at 18^0	43.0	33.1	16.2	6.3	1.4	...	...	142	1.90	0.05	1.75–2.05
R_1 at 25^0	97.5	2.5	...	...	...	...	...	79	1.03	0.02	1.00–1.09
R_2 at 18^0	12.6	14.4	9.9	18.9	18.9	25.3	...	111	3.93	0.21	3.30–4.56
R_2 at 25^0	92.6	7.4	...	...	...	...	...	54	1.07	0.04	1.00–1.19

The picture is altogether similar to that for eye color. At 25° the specimens from strain R_1 have lighter testes than at 18°. At 25° the testes are almost wholly colorless; only a small percentage are weakly tinted. At 25° the specimens from strain R_2 are not to be distinguished from those of strain R_1; for the most part they too have colorless testes. At 18° they are darker than the testes of strain R_1 at this same temperature and overlap into the area of the black-eyed races.

The testes and eyes react alike not only to the hereditary factors in which strains R_1 and R_2 differ, and to different temperatures; they also display similar responses to other environmental influences that have not been examined singly. This may be seen best in the tables of correlation between eye and testis coloration at the two rearing temperatures for the individual cultures just described (Tables 4 and 5).

At 18°, strain R_1 shows a rather high correlation. The correlation coefficient $r = 0.65 \pm 0.05$ is approximately as large as that for the entire ex-

TABLE 4

Correlation between eye and testis color in R_1 at 18°

Eye color in saturation classes	Testis color in classes							x
	1	2	3	4	5	6	7	
6	3	1	...	...	...	...	...	4
7	17	8	3	...	...	...	...	28
8	25	13	7	2	1	...	...	48
9	16	19	5	6	...	...	...	46
10	...	6	7	1	1	...	...	15
11	...	...	1	...	...	...	...	1
12	...	...	...	...	...	...	...	...
13	...	...	...	...	...	...	...	...
y	61	47	23	9	2	...	...	142

$r = 0.65 \pm 0.05$

TABLE 5

Correlation between eye and testis color in R_2 at 18°

Eye color in classes saturation	Testis color in classes							x
	1	2	3	4	5	6	7	
6	...	...	...	...	...	...	...	...
7	2	...	...	...	...	...	...	2
8	4	1	...	1	1	2	...	9
9	7	8	1	4	6	4	...	30
10	1	7	9	7	9	6	...	39
11	...	...	1	7	3	8	...	19
12	...	...	...	2	2	6	...	10
13	...	...	...	...	...	2	...	2
y	14	16	11	21	21	28	...	111

$r = 0.51 \pm 0.07$

perimental material. With strain R_2 also, one sees a clear correlation between eye and testis color at 18° ($r = 0.51 \pm 0.07$). Since at 25° the testes are almost always completely colorless and scarcely vary (Table 3), no possibility of correlation can be examined at this temperature.

Thus, analysis shows that eye color and testis color are modified in the same direction by temperature; at lower temperature both eyes and testes are pigmented more strongly than at higher temperature. Further, in different selected strains eye and testis coloration show the same direction of variation. Besides, there is even within a single strain at a given temperature of rearing a clear correlation between the pigmentation of the eyes and that of the testes. Thus both characteristics respond similarly to all influences.

c. Crosses

According to Kühn and Henke (1930, 1932), in F_1 the characteristic "black-eyed," which is determined by gene A, is dominant over "red-eyed," a. Hence the eyes of an F_1 between a black-eyed and a red-eyed specimen are black. The testes of the F_1 are strongly colored, like those of the black-eyed specimen. They too are mostly on Ostwald Sheet 7. In Fig. 4 the distribution of the testes of the F_1 over the seven classes for testis pigmentation is shown together with the corresponding curves for the AA and aa specimens. The testes of the Aa specimens are found only in Classes 6 and 7; that is, they are colored like those of the homozygous black-eyed animals, and intergrade only a little with the testes of the red-eyed strains. Thus the strong pigmentation of the testes in the black-eyed specimens is dominant over the lack of color, or weak coloration, found among the red-eyed moths. Hence eye and testis coloration behave similarly in the hybrids.

TABLE 6
Saturation of testis color in all AA and Aa specimens

Number of specimens, %	Saturation classes				n	$M \pm {}^3m$		σ	σm
	I	II	III	IV					
AA	12.8	45.8	31.8	9.6	415	2.38	0.12	0.63	0.02
Aa	0.5	44.8	47.9	6.8	192	2.61	0.12	0.84	0.03

In Table 6 the testis colors of the F_1 and the homozygous black-eyed moths are given The four classes that had already been used for the homozygous black-eyed moths were employed as categories.

No weight can be given to the fact that the testes of the Aa specimens are even darker, on the average, than those of the pure black-eyed specimens, since the AA and aa moths were not from the same cultures and hence had not been reared under fully identical conditions. Among the AA specimens the scatter is greater also.

In the F_2, as Kühn and Henke (1930, 1932) have shown, one obtains a pure monohybrid segregation. The testis color of the black-eyed and red-eyed specimens from several F_2 cultures was examined. Table 7 shows the result.

TABLE 7
Saturation of testis color in specimens from several F_2 cultures

	Saturation classes							n	M	m
	1	2	3	4	5	6	7			
Black-eyed specimens, %	...	...	...	...	0.7	69.1	30.2	136	6.30	0.04
Red-eyed specimens, %	81.1	8.9	4.0	5.0	1.0	...	...	101	1.36	.0.09

The testes of the black-eyed specimens are almost all in Classes 6 and 7. In all respects they are colored just like the testes of the black-eyed moths of the curve in Fig. 4. The testes of the red-eyed specimens display a considerable scatter. But their degree of pigmentation never reaches the intensity of Class 6, and thus lies completely within the range of variation of the aa moths of Fig. 4. In the cultures studied, therefore, the testis color has in no instance been separated from the appropriate eye color.

d. The Transparent-Eyed Races

Kühn and Henke (1932, Table 8, Fig. 10) have described yet another eye-color race of flour moth, which they characterize as "transparent-eyed." It is evoked by a recessive factor, designated as t, which is expressed only

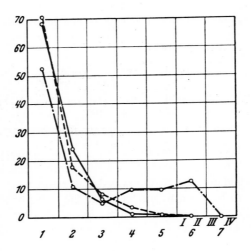

Figure 5. Saturation of testis color in *aaT* specimens of races R_1 (– – – – –) and R_2 (– · – · – · – ·) and of the *aatt* specimens (————). Abscissa: saturation of testis color, in classes. Ordinate: percent of specimens. Number of specimens: $n_{R_1} = 221$, $n_{R_2} = 165$, $n_{aatt} = 228$.

in the presence of *aa*. In specimens that contain the factor A and that therefore are phenotypically black-eyed, it remains without effect even if it is present in homozygous form.

When tested with the Ostwald color charts, the testes of the transparent-eyed moths are seen to be predominantly light-colored. Therefore, the same division of classes was chosen as with the red-eyed moths. The result is shown in the curve of Fig. 5. With a mean value of $M = 1.41 \pm 0.05$, they do not diverge much from the red-eyed specimens. The influence of temperature is also demonstrable (Table 8).

TABLE 8

Testis pigmentation of transparent-eyed specimens at different rearing temperatures, in percent; absolute number n, mean M, and three standard deviations, $3m$

Number in %	Saturation classes							n	$M \pm 3m$
	1	2	3	4	5	6	7		
At 18°	42.9	43.6	11.1	1.6	0.8	...	...	126	1.74 ± 0.21
At 25°	100	...	...	...	...	...	...	102	1.0

Whereas at 25° the testes are all in Class 1, that is to say, are without color, at 18° they display not inconsiderable scatter and a definitely significant mean value. In all, the picture is very similar to that of a light-colored red-eyed strain, such as R_1 (see also Fig. 5).

e. Discussion

Thus it has transpired that the red-eyed strains are distinguished from the black-eyed ones by a lesser pigmentation of the testes. The crossing experiment shows that the two characteristics (pigmentation of eyes and testes) are inseparable. In formal Mendelian terms, it is therefore justifiable to regard the two outward characteristics as being determined by a single hereditary factor. In agreement with this is the fact that both characteristics—red eyes and light-colored testes—apparently came into being simultaneously, for the light-colored testes are found in all red-eyed races descended from the first mutant specimen. In the black-eyed strain, on the other hand, in which this specimen appeared and which was maintained thenceforth by inbreeding at 18°, the testes are pigmented as in other black-eyed flour moths. Therefore, the gene A, or a, in the flour moth is a pleiotropic gene. At present we know the following characteristics to be determined by the gene in homozygous condition: red eyes, light-colored testes, decreased developmental rate (Kühn and Henke 1930, 1932) and reduced viability (Kühn 1932; Kühn and Henke 1932).

Among the red-eyed moths, the testis color and eye color varied under the influence of genetic factors, temperature, and other less clearly identified external conditions. Here it was possible to determine a clear positive correlation between the lightness of the eyes and the degree of pigmentation of the testes.

Such a correlation is not always manifested in attributes that are determined by a given pleiotropic gene. Thus, H. A. Timoféef-Ressovsky investigated the degree of expression of five characteristics evoked in *Drosophila funebris* by the gene "polyphan." When the variations took place under the influence of undefined conditions, a clear positive correlation could be found for only two pairs of characteristics. Also, the individual attributes did not respond equally to the influence of rearing temperature.

A positive correlation such as we find in the flour moth between eye color and testis color may rest on the fact that these two outward characteristics depend on the same ontogenetic process. If eye color and testis color are dependent in the same way on temperature, it is tempting to suspect that a single temperature-dependent developmental process influences the pigmentation of both the testis and the eyes. The positive correlation of testis color and eye color in AA, Aa, and aa specimens, as well as in the two red-eyed strains selected for degree of lightness of eye color, may indicate that different hereditary factors are also affecting the same ontogenetic process. Transplantation experiments seemed appropriate for probing further into this possibility of the mode of action of A.

II. COLOR OF CATERPILLARS OF THE BLACK-EYED
AND RED-EYED RACES

A further attribute upon which gene *a* exerts an influence is the body color of the caterpillars. In all larval stages, caterpillars of the black-eyed races, which contain gene A, are variously pink, flesh-colored, or waxy yellow. Contrariwise, caterpillars of the red-eyed strains, that is, *aa* caterpillars, are always completely pale and transparent-whitish, often with a slight tinge of greenish. Figs. 2g and 2h show two full-grown caterpillars from the last larval stage. In them is seen also the difference in the coloration of the testis, which shows through the dorsum of the fifth abdominal segment in the AA specimens, for the testis of the black-eyed flour moth begins to become colored as early as this stage. It is generally unrecognizable in caterpillars of red-eyed moths, since for the most part it remains colorless or becomes only lightly colored. The difference in the body color of the larvae is due to a coloration of the exoskeleton in the black-eyed individuals that is lacking in the red-eyed ones. If a piece of skin is clipped from the body of an AA caterpillar and examined in Ringer's solution under the binoculars, it is seen to be covered over and over with fine splashes of a pink pigment. Under the same circumstances the skin of *aa* caterpillars looks pure white and transparent.

In order to test whether the color difference of the larval skin is definitely associated with eye color, the following procedure was used: Caterpillars of the same age from black-eyed and red-eyed cultures were kept in a single beaker. When the specimens were in the last larval stage, they were picked out of the food and the pink ones separated from the pale white ones. Both were thereafter reared separately. When the imagines emerged, the numbers of specimens with red or black compound eyes were counted for each of these rearings. The result is recorded in Table 9.

TABLE 9

Relationships between larval color and eye color

	Pink larvae		White larvae	
	Black-eyed	Red-eyed	Black-eyed	Red-eyed
Absolute number:	153	1	4	377

From this one sees that the two kinds of caterpillar actually correspond to the black-eyed and red-eyed specimens. The exceptions amount only to 0.9 percent and thus are slight. Also, they are easily explained. Before molting the AA caterpillars undergo a change in coloring. During this time the above-mentioned pigment largely disappears; an excised piece of skin then looks white in Ringer's solution. Consequently, the AA caterpillars cannot be distinguished from the aa caterpillars shortly before a molt. This resemblance is most striking before pupation. The AA prepupae lose their pigment, and simultaneously both the AA and aa prepupae take on a greenish color. According to W. Köhler, this is to be attributed to the color of the hemolymph. Hence it is impossible to distinguish AA caterpillars from aa caterpillars in the prepupal stage.

If AA specimens and aa specimens are crossed, the Aa caterpillars of the F_1 have a pink color that cannot be distinguished from that of the AA specimens. Gene A thus is fully dominant over a in respect to larval color also.

The question arose whether in crosses the larval color, like the testis color, is inseparable from the eye color, or whether these two characteristics might be to a degree freely combinable. In order to decide this, selections were made by the method described above from a number of F_2 cultures, F_3 cultures, and backcrosses with the recessive starting race R_1. The pink or white larvae were then reared separately to maturation. Table 10

TABLE 10

Relationships between larval color and eye color in crosses

	Pink larvae		White larvae	
	Black-eyed	Red-eyed	Black-eyed	Red-eyed
F_3	548	5	2	156
F_2	289	...	2	116
R_1	76	...	...	74
Total	913	5	4	346

shows the result.

Thus, larval color cannot be separated from eye color in a crossing experiment. The error in selection from the cultures of crossed insects is just as slight as that with the mixed cultures of homozygous specimens in Table 9. As there, it is to be explained by the similarity of the stages transitional to the prepupa in both races. Hence, light larval color is firmly connected with the possession of red eyes. Since the mutation of larval color appeared simultaneously with eye coloration and testis coloration, all these characteristics depend on the same gene a.

Thus, gene a in the homozygous state is not expressed only in the imago, and does not first come into action at metamorphosis. Rather, it is effective during the entire period of development and exerts an influence on definite developmental processes. This influence becomes noticeable even during embryonic life, for the aa caterpillars at hatching from the egg are already distinguishable in color from the A caterpillars. The difference in testis color begins to appear first in the last larval stage, in which the testes of the A caterpillars start to become pigmented. Finally, the difference in eye color appears first in the pupa.

III. TESTIS TRANSPLANTS

a. Methods

In order to obtain further insight into the mode of action of genes A and *a*, transplantations of testes that contained A or *aa* were undertaken. These transplantations had to be carried out before the gene had produced its effect on the external characteristics that were the last to appear, i.e., before pigmentation of eyes and testes.

In the transplantation experiments, cultures of *aa* constitution were taken only from the R_1 stock, and all specimens were reared at 25°, for, as shown above, the differences as to both testes and eyes in the A and *aa* specimens are greater at a rearing temperature of 25° and never intergrade there. In some instances, a transparent-eyed stock was also used.

The transplantation technique was patterned after the methods of Meisenheimer, Kopeć, and Klatt, who had previously transplanted lepidopterous testes successfully in connection with other problems. Meisenheimer has summarized their methods in Abderhalden's *Handbuch der biologischen Arbeitsmethoden.*

For operation, the specimens were anesthetized with ether. Chloroform and chloroethyl ether did not prove satisfactory, because the specimens went into tonic convulsions, so that they lost much blood during the operation. The operations were performed with the forceps-scissors of R. G. Harrison, of Walb-Heidelberg, a pair of watchmaker's forceps, and two pins. With a dorsal incision at the level of the fifth abdominal segment, in which the gonads lie, the testes were freed and removed with scissors and forceps. The testes were then placed in Ringer's solution isotonic for the flour moth. This solution was prepared by monitoring the reaction of spermatocysts of the flour moth in it. Lepidopterous spermatocysts are very sensitive to changes in osmotic pressure. A salt solution in which they did not change shape could be regarded as adequately isotonic. The composition of this solution was: NaCl 0.7 percent, KCl 0.02 percent, $CaCl_2$ 0.02 percent, $NaHCO_3$ 0.004 percent. In this solution the tissues could be kept for a long time. On one occasion, a testis that had stood in this Ringer's solution for over an hour was induced to grow on transplantation. Calyces and calyx regenerates often showed movement in it for four hours after they had been removed from the body.

The donor caterpillars from which the testes were taken were of various ages. Most of them were in the last larval stage, but many were in

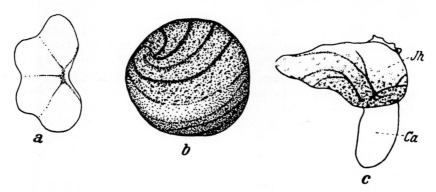

Figures 6a–c. (*a*) Slightly colored testis of an AA caterpillar. (*b*) Thoroughly colored testis of an imago, formed from two larval testes that have grown together. (*c*) Mature implant, formed from a single larval testis. *Ca:* calyx regenerate; *Ih:* implanted testis. (Enlarged 56½ times.)

the next to last. Fig. 6a shows a testis in the stage at which most of the testes were transplanted. The testis consists of four follicles, in which the spermatocysts lie. The follicles are separated from one another by walls. With the A specimens, pigment appears earliest in the follicle walls. In the testis illustrated, the follicle walls have become slightly tinted. The transplanted testes differed in their coloration, some being still wholly colorless, some already lightly tinted like the one drawn. The difference did not depend on the absolute age, for at the time of the last molt only some of the testes have started to become pigmented, while others are still wholly colorless. The larva has two testes that, as De Cunha has determined in our laboratory, unite after pupation and then rotate about their long axis. Thus, from two testes such as are shown in Fig. 6 a, there arises the rounded testicular body of the imago, which is pictured in Fig. 6b.

The recipients were approximately the same age as the donors. They were reared under similar conditions at 25°. Some males and some females were used as hosts. Their own gonads, whether male or female, were left in the hosts.

Before the operation, the recipient was anesthetized with ether for as short a time as possible. Then a small incision was made with scissors in the skin of the fourth abdominal segment. Any hemolymph that leaked out was blotted up with a small piece of filter paper. The testis to be implanted was then fished out of the Ringer's solution with a pin and carefully pushed by the latter into the skin wound. Invariably only a single testis was implanted. The pin used for implantation had been dulled at the tip in order to avoid injuries as far as possible. The wound was closed with collodion. The operated animals were placed in small dishes 3 cm in diameter and were kept there singly in sterile food at 25°.

After the specimens recovered from narcosis, they began to spin cocoons. For this reason, the larval color of the operated specimens could not be followed, because if they were taken out of the web, the animals, damaged in any event by the operation, invariably died. At the end of the first week after the operation, there was great mortality. Further, many additional specimens died during pupation and as pupae. Consequently, total mortality was very high. Of 1,023 operated specimens, only 213, i.e. 20.8 percent, were able to develop into imagines. In addition there were 18 specimens that were killed for examination while they were still pupae. Thus, a total of 231 specimens, i.e. 22.6 percent of the entire material, were worked up.

To what the high mortality should be attributed is uncertain. There was no question of infection of the wounds, for seventy operations done under absolutely sterile conditions had no better success. Klatt assumes that damage to the gut during implantation was the cause of mortality in his experiments. In support of this he cites the fact that in his material the smallest specimens, with which the danger of damaging the gut is naturally the greatest, had the greatest mortality. This might also be true of operations on the flour moth, since the operated stages are only 1.0–1.5 cm long, thus being smaller than the smallest *Lymantria* larvae that Klatt operated on. But it must also be taken into account that flour moths are quite generally sensitive to mechanical damage. Even when a number of

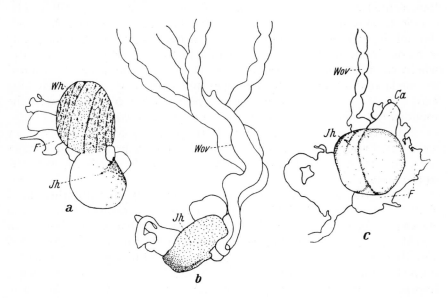

Figures 7a–c. (*a*) Implant grown together with the host testis. (*b–c*) Implants grown together with the host ovaries. *Ih:* implanted testis; *Wh:* host testis; *Wov:* host ovary; *Ca:* calyx regenerate; *F:* fatbody. (Enlarged 46 times.)

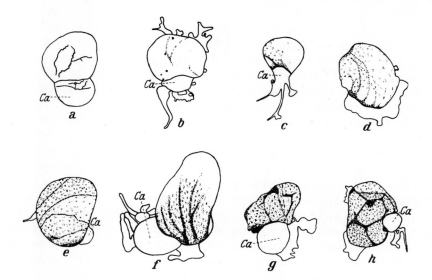

Figures 8a–h. Implants of various intensities of pigmentation. (*a–b*) Class 1. (*c*) Class 2. (*d*) Class 3. (*e*) Class 4. (*f*) Class 5. (*g*) Class 6. (*h*) Class 7. Ca: Calyx regenerate. (Enlarged 46 times.)

flour moth larvae are picked up from their food with fine spring forceps, as was necessary, for example, in determining the larval color, a not inconsiderable percentage of the selected specimens die.

The eyes of the imagines that emerged were measured with the Ostwald color charts. Next the specimens were dissected under Ringer's solution, and the gonads and any implants were located and removed. Then the color of the testes and implants were determined with the color charts. In addition, the outline of the implants was drawn with the camera lucida, and the location and intensity of their pigmentation was indicated on the sketch. Protocol drawings of this kind are reproduced in Figs. 6c, 7, and 8.

Finally the testes, implants, and heads were fixed in Bouin-Allen mixture or in Bouin-DuBosq-Brasil for histological treatment and were imbedded in paraffin via methylbenzoate-celloidin.

b. General Consequences of the Operation

Some of the resulting imagines had been severely damaged by the operation. A few were totally unable to emerge spontaneously, and had to be freed manually from the pupal case. In many that did emerge, the wings were severely crippled. Such deformation of the wings had also been observed by Kopeć in the specimens he operated on. Also, my specimens were mostly smaller than their unoperated sibs.

In dissection the host gonads were seen to be normally developed. The implants were developed to a very variable extent. In Fig. 6c a fully developed implant is pictured. Comparison with the initially implanted larval testis (Fig. 6a) shows clear differences. Though it has grown but little, its form has changed greatly. The pigmentation will be discussed in precise detail later. Here we may mention only that, as in the fully pigmented imaginal testes, more strongly colored lines stand out against a more weakly pigmented background. Frequently these lines are twisted spirally. Perhaps this is an indication that the unaided implants complete the torsion about themselves that the gonads normally carry out when the growing together of the two larval testes into a single organ has taken place. This might play a part in the striking change of form in comparison with the larval testis. A rather large, colorless, transparent vesicle is often attached to the implant. Its shape and the histological picture make it certain that this is the structure called by Kopeć the calyx regenerate. The calyx is the first enlargement in the vas efferens. Hence Kopeć concludes that the uppermost portion of the vas efferens is regenerated from the transplanted testis. In Ringer's solution these calyx regenerates, as Kopeć has already described, display rhythmic contractions and movements that often last for hours. The calyces of the normal sexual apparatus behave similarly and likewise contract rhythmically in Ringer's solution.

The size of the implants differed greatly, yet they never reached the dimensions of normal testes, like some that Kopeć occasionally saw. In general they did not go far beyond the size of the larval testes.

This agrees well with the supposition put forward by Meisenheimer and Kopeć for the dimensions of the implants. These workers adduce reasons for the view that the growth in size of an implant is controlled basically by the amount of space available to it. As Meisenheimer's and Kopeć had previously castrated the hosts, the implants in their experiments had appreciably more room than did the ones described here.

In many experiments, however, the implants were significantly smaller than the larval testes that had been inserted, being often so indistinct that they could be found only with difficulty. This, too, has been known since the time of Kopeć and Klatt. Kopeć thinks this may be connected with damage that the implant suffers at operation. Only unharmed follicles could be preserved; damaged ones would be resorbed.

In many instances no implant whatever was found in the operated specimens, as Kopeć and Klatt also report. It must be assumed that in these cases the implants were resorbed by the body of the host. A lucky finding verified this possibility. In place of the implant, a dark brown, necrotic-appearing object was found in the body cavity of an operated specimen. In histological section the object proved to be unquestionably a testis degenerated into connective tissue.

Such degeneration into connective tissue was seen and described by Kopeć in his transplantations from one species into another. Implants into a host of a different species first became necrotic, then were pervaded with connective tissue, and later were dissolved and resorbed. With the flour moth imagines, this process seems already to have reached completion in our cases. Only in one instance was resorption not finished, so that its occurrence could be witnessed.

A very high percentage of the implants were resorbed. Among the 213 imagines that emerged, no implant could be found in 67, i.e., in 31.5 percent. Specimens without a demonstrable implant are, of course, for the most part valueless for analysis.

Only rarely were the implants lying free in the body cavity. They have a tendency to grow together with all sorts of other organs. Most often, of course, this occurs with the fat body. Frequently, too, they are found to have become attached firmly to the hypodermis, or to have coalesced the host gonads. Fig. 7a shows an implant that has grown together with the host testis. In such instances the host testis and the implant can be distinguished by their color. Also, the implant is invariably smaller. Figs. 7b and c show two implants that have grown together with the host ovaries. Similar instances of coalescence of male and female sex organs are described also by Meisenheimer and Kopeć.

Before the implant becomes firmly attached, it often seems to pass through marked shifts in location. The operation was made in the third or fourth abdominal segment. The pin that inserted the implant was pushed forward into the wound from behind, so that the implant came to lie in the second through the fourth abdominal segment. Yet in many instances it was found much further toward the posterior. In a few specimens it even lay beside the hindgut vesicle in the seventh abdominal segment.

The operation scar remained visible throughout the entire time of development. It was often to be recognized as an indentation in the fourth abdominal segment. In the imago it frequently had a pink color.

c. Coloration of the Implants and of the Host Testis

Four experimental series were done: (1) testes of aa specimens were transplanted into AA specimens; (2) testes of AA specimens were transplanted into aa specimens; (3) AA and (4) aa testes were transplanted into specimens of the same genotype. As shown above, the aa tests would have remained colorless in their natural environment, while the AA testes would have become deeply colored. Table 11 shows the pigmentation attained by the implants and by the host testes under the experimental conditions.

The testes and implants were measured with the color charts and arranged in the seven classes set up for the pigmentation of the testes of the aa specimens. Fig. 8 gives examples of the form and intensity of pigmentation for the several classes. Figs. 8a and b show a totally colorless and a very lightly pigmented implant, which belong to Class 1. The pigmenta-

TABLE 11

Pigmentation of the host testes and implants after transplantation. Number of experimental animals in percent, absolute number n, mean with three standard deviations $M \pm 3m$.

Experimental group	Type of testes	Pigmentation classes							n	$M \pm 3m$
		1	2	3	4	5	6	7		
AA specimens (controls)	AA testes	...	...	...	...	...	51.8	48.2	166	6.48 ± 0.12
AA testes in AA specimens	AA implants	4.0	8.0	...	12.0	12.0	48.0	16.0	25	5.28 ± 0.96
	AA host testes	...	...	...	...	...	33.3	66.7	12	6.67 ± 0.42
aa testes in AA specimens	aa implants	2.1	8.5	10.6	29.8	23.4	25.5	...	47	4.40 ± 0.57
	AA host testes	...	...	...	...	...	28.6	71.4	21	6.71 ± 0.30
AA testes in aa specimens	AA implants	8.5	8.5	16.9	16.9	16.9	32.2	...	59	4.22 ± 0.63
	aa host testes	...	7.7	26.9	15.4	3.8	42.3	3.8	26	4.58 ± 0.90
AA testes in aa specimens resorbed	aa host testes	50.0	8.3	16.7	8.3	...	16.7	...	12	2.50 ± 1.59
aa testes in aa specimens	aa implants	100	...	...	...	...	...	...	19	1.00
	aa host testes	100	...	...	...	...	...	...	12	1.00
aa specimens (controls)	aa testes	97.5	2.5	...	...	...	...	...	79	1.03 ± 0.06

tion in Fig. 8 is so slight that it cannot affect the measured value. Each of the other drawings presents an example of the six other classes.

As the illustrations show and as has already been mentioned above, with all their differences in shape and size the implants nevertheless display a quite characteristic marking pattern. For the most part, the background remains pale; only in a very few instances is it lightly colored. Above this colored background rests a pattern of lines that are mostly somewhat curved. The space between the lines is often sown with irregular spots of pigment, between which the colorless background is visible. But in many implants (Figs. 8c, f) broad stretches of the surface are totally unpigmented. By means of inexact focusing of the binoculars, these zones, too, were included in the value measured. The color of the lines and spots may be either brown-violet or pinkish.

When aa testes are transplanted into AA specimens, one sees, as the table shows, an influence of the host on the implant. The aa testis contains in homozygous condition the gene a, which determines absence of color; in its normal environment in the aa specimen, the testis would not have developed color. But the aa testes transplanted into an AA specimen do become colored, even though to very different degrees. Although the scatter is very large—the implants are distributed over six classes—and consequently the standard deviation is very high, nevertheless, the mean value of pigment intensity for the aa testes transplanted into AA specimens, as indicated by three standard deviations, differs significantly from that for the testes of the AA specimens. The AA testes of the host have the pigmentation normal for A testes. No influence of the implant on them is to be discerned.

The number of AA testes measured is much smaller than the number of implants because many of the implants were into female hosts. These implants, too, became pigmented. Table 12 shows the pigmentation developed by implants in males or in females. The ranges of the true means overlap; hence, both kinds of implants may be considered equally strongly pigmented.

A host that contains AA thus stimulates an aa testis to become pigmented. Yet the implant does not attain the full intensity of the AA testes. Both sexes of host have an equal influence on the testis implant.

TABLE 12

Pigmentation of aa implants into AA males and into AA females, in percent

Sex of host	Saturation classes							n	$M \pm m$
	1	2	3	4	5	6	7		
♂	5.0	10.0	15.0	30.0	20.0	20.0	. . .	20	4.10 ± 0.23
♀	. . .	7.4	7.4	29.6	26.0	29.6	. . .	27	4.63 ± 0.31

With the opposite implantation, of AA testes into *aa* specimens, the reverse occurs—an influence of the implant on the host. The AA implant becomes pigmented in accordance with its own genetic constitution. It does not develop the complete intensity of color of an A testis, but stops at about the degree of pigmentation of *aa* implants in AA specimens. But AA testes not only differentiate as befits their origin when implanted into *aa* specimens; they also exert an influence on the host's *aa* testes, which without the operation would have remained colorless. When AA testes are implanted, the testes of the *aa* hosts all develop more or less color. They, too, show variation of the same degree as the implants. The mean value of pigment intensity of the testes of the *aa* hosts is not statistically different from that of *aa* implants into AA specimens and of AA implants into *aa* specimens; it clearly differs from normal testes, both *aa* and AA. Thus an influence of the operation on the testes of the *aa* hosts is certainly present.

In order to demonstrate that the influence is to be attributed to the A nature of the implant and is not general consequence of the operation, a control experiment was undertaken: *aa* testes were implanted into *aa* specimens. In this case both the implants and the host testes all remained colorless. This shows that the coloration of *aa* testes after implantation of AA testes does not depend on the operation itself but on the specific character of the implant. Since the two kinds of implant differ by the genes AA and *aa*, it is the gene A whose action shifts the pigmentation of the testes of the *aa* host toward the A phenotype.

As already mentioned, the implants are frequently resorbed. But in this case, too, they have often exerted an influence. This is shown by line 8 of Table 11. Even though no implant could be found in the 12 *aa* specimens of line 8, in about half of them the testes are pigmented, some of them quite intensely. The numbers are too small to be statistically valid, but it is certainly a result of the operation when *aa* specimens at 25° display testes that belong to pigment Classes 3, 4, and 6. As line 11 shows, the great majority of the testes of *aa* specimens fall in Class 1, only exceptionally in Class 2. Since the operation as such does not increase the degree of pigmentation, it seems clear that when in the experiment more intense pigment levels are found in relatively high proportion, this must be ascribed to the influence of the resorbed AA implant.

The broad scatter shown by all implants as well as by the *aa* testes under the influence of AA implants is striking, as is that the implants as well as the host testes pigmented through their influence do not become colored to the full intensity of AA testes.

Two possible reasons why the AA testes in the *aa* specimens do not on the average develop the full color intensity of the normal A testes might be, first, an influence of the *aa* environment, and second, an effect of treatment during the operation and of the possibly more unfavorable conditions to which the testis is exposed as an implant. In order to test these possibilities, AA testes were implanted into AA specimens. Table 11 shows the result in lines 2 and 3. The implanted AA testes became colored in the AA specimens but definitely not to the full intensity of the normal AA testis; the significance of the difference is demonstrated to three standard deviations. Thus, it appears that implanted testes tend to display a weaker coloration than they do in the normal situation. However the AA implants into AA specimens also exhibit a quite considerable difference from the AA testes that were transplanted into aa specimens; even though on account of the large scatter it is not guaranteed to three standard deviations, it is rendered probable to two standard deviations. That would then point further toward an influence of the AA or aa environment.

Similar reasons could explain why the testes of the aa hosts, which become colored because of the action of AA implants, yet do not attain the full intensity of pigmentation of normal AA testes. In the first place, the implants, being subject to less favorable conditions, might be unable to exert their full effect. But, secondly, the aa environment might inhibit similarly the development of color in the host testis and in the implant. In both cases one could expect a positive correlation between the intensity of pigmentation of the aa host testes and the AA implants. Table 13 shows

TABLE 13

Correlation between intensity of pigmentation of aa host testes and that of AA implants

		AA implants in pigmentation classes						
		1	2	3	4	5	6	7
aa host testes in pigmentation classes:	1	...	...	...	...	...	...	...
	2	...	2	...	...	...	...	...
	3	2	...	4	...	...	...	...
	4	...	2	...	1	...	1	...
	5	...	...	...	...	...	1	...
	6	...	...	1	2	1	3	...
	7	...	...	...	2	1	2	...

$r = 0.70 \pm 0.10$

this correlation. The numbers are too small to furnish definite proof, but the arrangement in the table corresponds to a positive correlation ($r = 0.70 \pm 0.10$).

It remains to note that in all experimental groups there were among the aa specimens some that carried the gene t in homozygous condition. They responded exactly like the aa specimens, so that they may be counted without hesitation as pure aa specimens. The gene tt has no influence on the effect of an A implant.

The statement holds, then, that presence of AA testes in the organism brings about coloration of *aa* testes, i.e., causes a change toward the A phenotype. In every instance, the dominant gene A prevails.

d. Coloration of the Eyes

The difference between A and *aa* specimens is not limited to the color of the testes. The larval color, and the eye color of the mature moths, are also different in the two races. For reasons already mentioned, the influence of testis transplantation on larval color was not studied: removal from the web is too damaging to the insect, already harmed by the operation. However, the effect of testis transplantation on eye color could be established.

For this purpose, the entire experimental material was divided into three classes according to eye color: red-eyed, black-eyed, and a transitional stage that may be designated brown-eyed (Fig. 2b). This last class contains saturation stages 11–13 on Sheet 6 of the color charts (see Fig. 1), and thus includes those specimens that Kühn and Henke designated "coffee brown." In stock R_1, which was used for the operations, they never occurred at a rearing temperature of 25°. Table 14 shows the distribution of the normal and operated flour moths in these three classes.

Ordinary *aa* specimens always belong to Class 1, that is, are always red-eyed. Ordinary AA specimens always belong to Class 3, and are thus black-eyed. The latter are unchanged by the operation. AA specimens al-

TABLE 14
Pigmentation of the eyes after transplantation, number of experimental animals in percent and absolute number

	Pigmentation classes of the eyes			n
Experimental group	1 (red)	2 (brown)	3 (black)	
AA specimens (controls)	...	...	100	415
Transplantation: AA testes into AA specimens	...	...	100	25
aa testes into AA specimens	...	...	100	47
AA testes into *aa* specimens	...	10.3	89.7	58
AA testes into *aa* specimens (resorbed)	76.9	15.4	7.7	26
aa testes into *aa* specimens	100	...	...	19
aa specimens (controls)	100	...	...	79

ways remain black-eyed, no matter whether an AA or an *aa* testis is implanted into them.

With the *aa* specimens it is different. Implantation of AA testes clearly shifts their eye color toward black. The majority progress so far in this direction that they must be designated as black. Only a small fraction were coffee brown; red-eyed specimens did not occur at all.

Specimens in which the implant had been resorbed remained red-eyed for the most part, but a not inconsiderable percentage became coffee brown. Since otherwise coffee brown specimens never occur at 25°, this must be referred to the influence of the resorbed implant. Two specimens became black-eyed. Possibly a very small implant may have been overlooked in these cases.

In order to exclude the simple effects of operation, once again experiments were used in which *aa* testes had been implanted into *aa* specimens. Here the imagines were invariably red-eyed, whether the implant had taken or not. Consequently here too, as with the testes, the change in color of the eyes must be imputed to the A nature of the implant. Here also the transparent-eyed specimens, which possess the constitution *aatt*, have been counted in with the *aa* specimens. The factor *tt* was in no way expressed: transparent-eyed specimens, too, were changed into black-eyed ones by implantation of an AA testis. Only the "brown" specimens in Class 2 showed a difference in comparison with the corresponding *aa*T specimens. They possessed a color that had previously been unknown in the flour moth—dark brown with a hint of bluish, so that in Ostwald's color charts they lie on the dark areas of Chart 7. Additionally they have a slight gleam and are slightly transparent.

Thus, for eye color, too, the statement holds: The effect of the dominant gene always prevails. An A implant is capable of impressing the phenotype of an A specimen on the *aa* eyes of its host.

e. Offspring of Specimens Whose Eye Coloration Was Developed as a Result of Implants

As already mentioned, the hosts were left in possession of their own gonads. Thus, *aa* specimens that had become black-eyed because of the influence of an AA implant had functional gonads that produced *a*-containing sperm and eggs. If such a phenotypically black-eyed specimen could be crossed with a normal one, the descendants ought to develop red eyes.

Great technical difficulties hindered this experiment. The operated specimens had been severely damaged by the operation and therefore had little inclination to mate. Nevertheless, the experiment finally succeeded in two instances. On one occasion, a black-eyed female from a transparent-eyed stock, which should therefore have had the genotype *aatt*, laid eggs from which hatched caterpillars of the pale white type of *aa* larvae. There were obtained 59 moths, all of which had transparent eyes. Thus, the phenotypically black-eyed mother had had the constitution *aatt*. In a second instance a black-eyed male, that had the constitution *aaT* and thus would have been red-eyed except for the operation mated with a red-eyed female. Here too whitish caterpillars hatched from the egg, yielding 75 moths. All were red-eyed and thus had the genotype *aa*. With these results it is thus shown incontestably, by genetic means as well, that the black coloration of the eyes of an *aa* specimen had occurred because of the testis transplant.

f. Discussion

To my knowledge, an influencing of the host toward the racial characteristics of the transplant has not been observed previously. The transplantation experiments with the flour moth afford a glimpse into the mode of action of genes A and *a*. A implants have the property of impressing the A phenotype on *aa* tissues in the same organism. Since the implants frequently lie free in the body cavity, distant from testes and eyes, there can be no question of a contact action. Hence, it is only in agreement with our current physiological knowledge to infer that the A testis delivers into the blood a substance that has the property of causing the strong production of pigment by testes and eyes whose cells lack the gene A. But this substance is given off not only by AA testes, for *aa* testes become colored in AA females, too. Thus, in them some other organ, perhaps the ovary, must serve to produce this material. But it is also possible that still other or possibly even all tissues that contain the gene A have the capacity to secrete this substance that causes the strong pigmentation of the eyes and testes. Some findings of Dobzhansky, to which we shall return later, make it probable that in *Drosophila* the ovary, oviduct, and eye produce a similar substance. The normal pigmentation of the eyes and testes of the A specimens would then have its source in the effectiveness of this substance.

With lesser activity of the A substance, in 10 percent of the cases with preserved transplants and in 15 percent of the cases with resorbed transplants, coffee-brown-eyed specimens of the lighter colored strain R_1 were obtained at 25°. Since specimens with coffee brown eyes otherwise occur only in strain R_2 at 18°, it is possible that the difference between the two red-eyed strains with differing degrees of light coloration also depends upon a substance that differs either quantitatively or qualitatively from the A substance. But the demonstration of such a substance can be achieved only with transplantation experiments.

This result is unexpected, particularly since it comes from an insect. The opinion is generally held that for insects the phenotypic characteristics of each cell are determined by its own genome. This was concluded from transplantations between male and female Lepidoptera performed by Meisenheimer and Kopeć, and from the frequently appearing mosaic individuals in which no influence on one another of genetically different regions could be determined. Yet there are also long-known exceptions to this rule, which Sturtevant described in *Drosophila melanogaster*. With gynandromorphs an eye that contains the "vermilion" gene may not develop the corresponding eye color if the normal allele for "vermilion" is present in the other eye. Likewise, the expression of the "bar" character of an eye in mosaic individuals is influenced by neighboring tissues that possess the normal allele for "bar." Thus an effect of proximity is surely present here.

A significantly greater similarity with the results of the transplantation experiments here described is exhibited in the descriptions given by Dobzhansky of some gynandromorphs of *Drosophila simulans*. Dobzhansky produced gynandromorphs the male portions of which contained the "yellow" and "white" genes while the female parts possessed the wild-type dominant alleles. Now, as already mentioned above, Dobzhansky had shown that the yellowish-white specimens have colorless, transparent testes and vasa efferentia, while the testes and vasa efferentia of wild-type specimens are a brilliant yellow. Thus, in Dobzhansky's gynandromorphs, the testes and vasa efferentia, as male organs that contained "yellow" and "white," should be colorless. And for the most part they were so. Only when an ovary had grown together with a vas efferens or lay close by it were the parts of the vas efferens that were nearest the ovary colored yellow. A testis that lay near an oviduct responded similarly. Thus here there is an effect of proximity, just as in Sturtevant's two cases. Further, Dobzhansky observed that the light-colored testes and vasa efferentia of these gynandromorphs finally became colored yellow, too; however, this did not occur until later imaginal stages, i.e., appreciably later than with testes that were genetically of the wild type. This late development of color in yellow-white testes was accelerated when the eyes of the specimen in question were of the wild type. Thus there is present here action at a distance, as in the transplantation experiments in *Ephestia*. Here, however, the effect is reversed, in that the eyes act on the testes. On the basis of these findings, Dobzhansky suspects that the normal alleles of the yellow and white genes exert their effect via a substance that is given off to the blood by yellow-white tissue. For the gene A of the flour moth such a concept has been demonstrated experimentally.

SUMMARY

1. The testes of black-eyed flour moths are colored.
2. The testes of red-eyed flour moths are colorless or only weakly colored.
3. With the *aa* specimens there is a positive correlation between the light coloration of the eyes and the intensity of pigmentation of the testes. Specifically, the pigmentation of the eyes and testes responds by variation in the same direction to temperature and other external influences. Furthermore, a stock selected for dark red eye color also has darker testes than a light red strain.

4. Among Aa specimens in the F_1, the A coloration of the testes proves to be dominant over the a lack of color.

5. In the F_2, eye color and testis color always go together. Thus they are determined by the same gene.

6. The transparent-eyed $aatt$ strain behaves with respect to testis color like a light-colored red-eyed strain.

7. AA specimens have pink caterpillars, while aa larvae are white. The pink color proved to be dominant in the F_1. In the F_2, larval color and eye color were always allied and thus determined by the same gene. Hence, genes A and a are already manifest in the larval stage.

8. If aa testes are transplanted into an AA specimen, the aa implant becomes colored, though not to the full intensity normal for an A testis. The eyes and testes of the AA host develop normal coloration.

9. If AA testes are transplanted into an aa specimen, the AA implant develops color in accordance with its origin, though not to full intensity. The host's aa testis also develops color but does not attain the full intensity of an A testis. The host's aa eyes develop pigmentation to the extent of becoming black, or in a few instances coffee brown.

10. If aa testes are transplanted into an aa specimen, both implant and host testes remain colorless, the eyes red. Thus, the change in coloration after implantation of AA testes is dependent on the A nature of the implant.

11. If AA testes are implanted in an AA specimen, the implant becomes colored, though not to the full intensity of a normally located AA testis. The testes and eyes of the AA host remain normally pigmented.

12. In AA females, aa testes develop coloration.

13. An aa specimen that has become black-eyed through implantation, if mated with a normal aa specimen, produces offspring that are pure red-eyed and thus aa.

REFERENCES

Dobzhansky, T. Über den Bau des Geschlechtsapparates einiger Mutanten von *Drosophila melanogaster*. Z. *Abstammgslehre 34* (1924).

———— Studies on the manifold effect of certain genes in *Drosophila melanogaster*. Z. *Abstammgslehre 43* (1927).

———— Interaction between female and male parts of gynandromorphs of *Drosophila simulans*. *Arch. Entw. mechan. 123* (1931).

Goldschmidt, R. Physiologische Theorie der Vererbung. Berlin 1927.

Klatt, B. Keimdrüsentransplantationen beim Schwammspinner. Z. Abstammgslehre 22 (1919).

Köhler, W. Die Entwicklung der Flügel bei der Mehlmotte *Ephestia kühniella* mit besonderer Berücksichtigung des Zeichnungsmusters. Z. *Morph. Ökol. Tiere 24* (1932).

Kopeć, S. Untersuchungen über Kastration und Transplantation bei Schmetterlingen. *Arch. Entw. mechan. 33* (1911).

Korschelt, E. "Regeneration und Transplantation. II. Transplantation." Berlin 1931.

Kühn, A. Entwicklungsphysiologische Wirkungen einiger Gene von *Ephestia kühniella*. *Naturwiss. 20* (1932).

Kühn, A., and Henke K. Genetische und entwicklungsphysiologische Untersuchungen an der Mehlmotte *Ephestia kühniella.* I–VII. *Abh. Ges. Wiss. Göttingen 15,* 1 (1929).

———— Genetische und entwicklungsphysiologische Untersuchungen an der Mehlmotte *Ephestia kühniella.* VIII–XII. *Abh. Ges. Wiss. Göttingen 15,* 2 (1932).

———— Eine Mutation der Augenfarbe und der Entwicklungsgeschwindigkeit bei der Mehlmotte *Ephestia kühniella. Arch. Entw. mechan. 122* (1930).

Meisenheimer, J. "Experimentelle Studien zur Soma- und Geschlechtsdifferenzierung. I. Beitrag. Über den Zusammenhang primärer und sekundärer Geschlechtsmerkmale bei den Schmetterlingen und den übrigen Gliedertieren." Jena 1909.

———— Kastration und Gonadentransplantation bei Insekten. *Abderhaldens Handbuch der biologischen Arbeitsmethoden,* IX, 4, H. 1. 1922.

Ostwald, W. Der Farbkörper. Die Farbenfibel. Leipzig 1922.

Plunkett, C. The interaction of genetic and environmental factors in development. *J. Exper. Zool.* 46 (1926).

Sturtevant, A. H. The vermilion gene and gynandromorphism. *Proc. Soc. Exper. Biol. Med.* 17 (1920).

———— The effect of the bar gene of Drosophila in mosaic eyes. *J. Exper. Zool.* 46 (1927).

Timoféeff-Ressovsky, H. Über phänotypische Manifestierung der polytopen (pleiotropen) Genovariation „Polyphän" von *Drosophila funebris. Naturwiss.* 19 (1931).

G. W. BEADLE and BORIS EPHRUSSI

The differentiation of eye pigments in *Drosophila* as studied by transplantation

George Wells Beadle was born in 1903 in Wahoo, Nebraska. He received his M.S. from Cornell University in 1927, and his Ph.D. in genetics from the same university in 1931. He served as an assistant at the New York State College of Agriculture at Cornell from 1928 to 1931. From 1931 to 1936 he was at the California Institute of Technology, first as National Research Council Fellow in Biology, then as Institute Fellow and as an instructor. He was an assistant professor of genetics at Harvard University, 1936–1937, Professor of Biology at Stanford University 1937–1946, and Professor and Chairman of the Division of Biology, California Institute of Technology, 1946–1961. In 1961 he became President and Professor of Biology at the University of Chicago.

His research interests have included the cytology and genetics of maize, the physiological genetics of *Drosophila*, and the chemical genetics of *Neurospora*.

He was awarded the Nobel Prize in Medicine and Physiology in 1958, and is a member of the National Academy of Science.

Boris Ephrussi was born in Moscow in 1901. He studied at the University of Paris where he received his Sc.D. degree in 1932. From 1941 to 1944 he was Associate Professor of Biology at The Johns Hopkins University. In 1946 he returned to France as Professor of Genetics at the University of Paris, and Director of the Laboratory of Physiological Genetics of the Centre Nationale de Recherches Scientifiques. 1956 saw him back in the United States for a semester as Exchange Professor at Harvard University, and in 1959 he held the same post at the California Institute of Technology. Since 1961 he has been Distinguished Professor of Biology at Western Reserve University. He is a member of the Royal Danish Academy, and a Foreign Associate of the National Academy of Science.

His research interests are in developmental physiology and biochemical genetics.

INTRODUCTION

Prominent among the problems confronting present day geneticists are
those concerning the nature of the action of specific genes—when, where
and by what mechanisms are they active in developmental processes? De-
spite the recognized importance of such questions as these, relatively little
has been done toward answering them, a situation not at all surprising
considering the difficulty of getting at these problems experimentally. Even
so, promising beginnings are being made; from the gene end by the methods
of genetics, and from the character end by biochemical methods. Probably
the one factor which has played the most significant role in retarding progress in this field is the fact that relatively little is known from a developmental point of view about those organisms that have been studied most
thoroughly from the genetic point of view, and, on the other hand, little
is known genetically in those organisms that have been most studied from
the developmental point of view. One of the two obvious (and alternative)
ways of overcoming this difficulty would be to study development in a
genetically well known organism. *Drosophila*, with its numerous mutant
types, offers a favorable opportunity for a study of this kind. Several facts
have led us to begin such a study on the differentiation of eye color pigments. Many eye color mutants are known, pigments have many advantages
for chemical studies, and interactions between tissues of different genetic
constitutions with respect to eye pigmentation are already known from
studies of mosaics.

In this paper we shall present the detailed results of preliminary investigations (Ephrussi and Beadle, 1935a, 1935b, 1935c; Beadle and Ephrussi, 1935a, 1935b) which we hope will serve to point out the lines along
which further studies will be profitable.

MATERIAL AND METHODS

The technique used in making transplantations in *Drosophila* has been
described elsewhere (Ephrussi and Beadle, 1936). In brief, the desired
organ or imaginal disc, removed from one larva, the donor, is drawn into
a micro-pipette and injected into the body cavity of the host. As a rule,

Work done at the Institut de Biologie physico-chimique, Paris, and the Station Bio-
logique de Roscoff.
[Previously published in *Genetics*, 21 (May 1936): 225–47. Reproduced by permission
of publisher and author.]

operations were made on larvae cultured at 25°C for three days after hatching from the eggs. At this time they are ordinarily about ready to pupate. Some of the stocks developed at slower rates than others, and larvae from these were sometimes used on the fourth day after hatching. In most cases the host larvae pupated within 24 hours after the operation. It is clear, from the above, that the stage of development at the time of operations was not controlled in a very precise way. However, since repetition of experiments at different times and, in some cases, with quite different stocks have given consistent results, we can be reasonably sure that the small differences in stage of development which may have existed between host and implant have not played any significant part.

The reasons for the choice of that stage of development reached shortly before puparium formation as "standard" for the studies reported here are largely those of convenience. At this time the optic discs are of a convenient size for transplantation, injections are readily made, and the host larvae require no more food.

As will be discussed below, implanted optic discs develop in a manner somewhat different from that characteristic of the same disc in its normal position. Because of this, it is not always desirable to compare the pigmentation of an implanted eye with that of a normal one. By dissecting the two eyes, normal and implanted, and observing fragments of the pigmented tissue, one can usually make a god comparison. However, to avoid all difficulty, which becomes important where slight differences are involved, we have practically always made comparisons only between implanted eyes. Thus, a vermilion eye disc implanted in a claret host gives rise to an eye with vermilion pigmentation. This conclusion is reached by comparing the implanted eye with an implanted eye known to be vermilion, obtained by implanting vermilion discs in vermilion larvae. Further comparisons with wild type and with claret control implants enable one to say definitely that the eye in question is vermilion, not wild type and not claret.

List of Mutants

A list of the eye color mutants used in the studies reported in this paper is given together with their standard symbols. These mutant types and the genes which differentiate them from wild type will be referred to by symbol only. Other mutant genes were also carried by certain of the stocks used.

bo —bordeaux	Hn^r—Henna-recessive	se —sepia
bw —brown	lt —light	sed —sepiaoid
ca —claret	ma —maroon	sf^2 —safranin-2
car —carnation	p^p —peach	st —scarlet
cd —cardinal	pd —purpleoid	v —vermilion
cl —clot	pn —prune	w —white
cm —carmine	pr —purple	w^a —apricot
cn —cinnabar	ras —raspberry	w^e —eosin
g^2 —garnet-2	rb —ruby	

These are indicated in the tables by symbol only since they presumably have no bearing on the results. These symbols are used generally in *Drosophila* work; their significance can be found in Morgan, Bridges and Sturtevant (1925).

DEVELOPMENT OF IMPLANTED EYES

When an eye transplant is made, the eye disc is injected into the body cavity of the host larva. The implanted disc continues development in the body cavity, and at maturity of the host usually comes to lie in the abdominal cavity. Occasionally, it may lie in the thorax but such cases are exceptional. The location of the implanted eye in the adult fly seems to be determined by purely mechanical factors; it is pushed into that part of the body cavity of the developing individual where the normal organs are least crowded. Usually injections are made toward the posterior end of the larva, but they have also been made near the anterior end, and this seems to have no effect on the final position of the eye. The implanted eye may lie just under the body wall of the adult fly where it is readily visible in the living fly, or it may lie deeply imbedded, in which case it may not be visible without dissection or clearing.

Very often the implanted eye becomes attached to other organs during its developement. In females, it is often attached to one of the ovaries. This appears to be brought about mainly by the growth of tracheal tubes. In males the implanted eye may be attached to a testis. Males with an implanted eye sometimes have one testis which retains the ellipsoid shape which is characteristic of a testis at a much earlier stage of development. Such "inhibited" testes may have their sheaths normally pigmented but whether they contain viable spermatozoa is not known.

An implanted eye, which has developed within the body cavity of the host, is inverted as compared with an eye in its normal position. The normal eye has the shape of the head of a mushroom, the outer surface of the eye being represented by the top or convex surface of the mushroom head. An implanted eye disc is detached from its optic ganglion and, after development, its curvature is reversed in such a way that the facets are on the inside and the basement membrane on the outer convex surface. In other respects implanted eyes appear to be perfectly developed and differentiated; particularly, there seems to be no difference in the pigmentation of an implanted and a normal eye.

The optic and antennal imaginal discs in the larval stage are attached to each other. In removing an optic disc for transplantation, the antennal disc is usually left attached and implanted with the optic disc. This is not necessary but is done in routine procedure because it facilitates handling the discs and in most experiments does no harm. In special experiments where it may be desirable to do so, it is easy to remove the antennal disc and implant the optic disc alone. If the antenna disc is not removed and is not injured during dissection, it develops with the implanted eye and gives rise to an antenna, complete with an arista, attached to the eye by the chitinous head parts mentioned below. In most instances antennae developing with implanted eyes are normally everted.

The optic disc gives rise also to certain head parts when it is implanted, and presumably also in its development in the normal position. The exact extent of these head parts which arise from the optic disc has not been determined but they completely surround what would normally be the periphery of the eye and have normally developed bristles. As the developed implanted eye is inverted, these chitinous head parts form a kind of rim around the concave facet-side of the eye with the bristles on the inside.

In very exceptional cases an implanted eye disc may give rise to an external eye. This has happened only four times in about 1200 cases. In one of these, the eye was nearly normal, the facets were on the exterior convex surface, and there was a normally developed antenna attached to the eye by chitinous head parts. In all four cases the supplementary eye was attached to the abdominal wall of the adult fly, presumably at the point of injection. These cases are unusual and probably arise when the optic and antennal discs "plug," in a special way, the hole through which the pipette was inserted.

EXPERIMENTAL RESULTS

Because of the rather complex interrelations of the different types of data to be presented in this paper, they cannot be discussed efficiently until all the data have been presented.

In the following tables the various sex combinations of implant and host are given. In only one case, which will be specifically mentioned, does the sex of either the donor or the host appear to influence the result.

Mutant Eye Discs in Wild-Type Hosts

As a beginning in the study of the differentiation of eye pigment of implanted eyes, it is desirable to know how many eye color mutants are autonomous in their pigment development when implanted in wild type hosts. For the late larval stage, with which we are chiefly concerned in this paper, the data on this point are presented in table 1. These data show that most of the eye color mutants are autonomous in their pigmentation. The only clearly exceptional cases are those of v and cn. When implanted in wild type or in heterozygous v, the pigmentation of both of these is that characteristic of a wild type eye. In the case of bo, the result is not clear because the visible difference between an implant with bo pigmentation and one with wild type pigmentation is very slight. This is also true of the two eye

TABLE 1

Data on the differentiation of mutant eye implants in wild type hosts. Eye color mutant symbols are distinguished from symbols of incidental mutants present in the stocks by being printed in italics. In this and following tables, under the heading "number of individuals," are given the four sex combinations and the total in the following order: female in female, male in female, female in male, male in male, and total.

IMPLANT	HOST	NUMBER OF INDIVIDUALS	PHENOTYPE OF IMPLANT	IMPLANT	HOST	NUMBER OF INDIVIDUALS	PHENOTYPE OF IMPLANT
bo	+	3, 1, 1, 1; 6	?	pd	+	2, 0, 2,* 2; 6	pd
bw	+	4, 2, 2, 0; 8	bw	y pn	+	1, 1, 4, 0; 6	pn
ca	+	7, 0, 5, 2; 14	ca	b pr	+	4, 0, 1, 0; 5	pr
car	+	5, 0, 6, 0; 11	car	sc ras	+	2,‡ 0, 0, 0; 2	ras
cd	+	4, 0, 0, 0; 4	cd	rb cv	+	2, 0, 3, 0; 5	rb
cl	+	2, 2, 0, 1; 5	,cl	se wo	+	5, 6, 5, 4; 20	se
cm	+	1, 0, 2, 1; 4	cm	sr sed	+	2, 2, 0, 6; 10	sed
cn	+/v	5, 3, 2, 0; 10	+	tk sf² abb	+	0, 2, 1, 1; 4	sf²
cn	+	2, 0, 2, 0; 4	+	st	+	3, 0, 0, 2; 5	st
g²	+	1, 1, 0, 0; 2	g²	v	+/v	11, 6, 8, 5; 30	+
jv Hnʳ h	+	0, 0, 1, 0; 1	Hnʳ	w	+	1, 0, 0, 0; 1	+
lt c	+	0, 1, 2, 1; 4	ll	wᵃ	+	0, 0, 3, 0; 3	wᵃ
ma	+	2, 2, 2, 2; 8	ma				
pᵖ	+	2, 0, 1, 1; 4	pᵖ				

* One fly in this class had an implanted eye with wild type pigmentation—presumably because of a mistake in the selection of the donor.

‡ One host in this class dissected as mature pupa.

TABLE 2

Data on the differentiation of wild type eye implants in eye color mutant hosts. Arrangement as in Table 1.

IMPLANT	HOST	NUMBER OF INDIVIDUALS	PHENOTYPE OF IMPLANT	IMPLANT	HOST	NUMBER OF INDIVIDUALS	PHENOTYPE OF IMPLANT
+	bo	0, 0, 0, 1; 1	?	+	p^p	3,* 2,* 0, 0; 5	+
+	bw	2, 1, 1, 0; 4	+	+	pd	2, 0, 6, 0; 8	+
+	ca	2, 2, 2, 0; 6,* 1*; 13	ca	+	$y\ pn$	2, 4, 0, 1; 7	+
+	car	1, 0, 1,‡ 0; 2	+	+	$b\ pr$	3, 1, 4, 1; 9	+
+	cd	4, 1, 0, 0; 5	+	+	$sc\ ras$	1, 1, 1, 1; 4	+
+	cl	2, 2, 5, 1; 10	+	+	$rb\ cv$	1,‡ 0, 2, 1; 4	+
+	cm	2, 1, 0, 0; 3	+	+	$se\ wo$	5, 1, 8, 1; 15	+
+	cn	3,* 1,* 0, 0; 4	+	+	$sr\ sed$	2, 3, 0, 0; 5	+
+	g^2	1,* 0, 0, 0; 1	+	+	$tk\ sf^2\ abb$	1, 0, 1, 2; 4	+
+	jv Hnr h	4, 1, 1, 6; 12	+	+	st	1, 1, 1, 0; 3	+
+	lt c	2, 1, 0, 0; 3	+	+	v	3, 2, 5, 2; 12	+
+	ma	2, 2, 5, 7; 16	+	+	w	6, 0, 0, 0; 6	+

* Sex of donor not determined.
‡ Host dissected as mature pupa.

102

color types as seen in normal eyes. Special experiments using other mutants as "intensifiers" of the difference between *bo* and wild type will probably be necessary to determine the behavior of *bo*.

Wild Type Discs in Mutant Hosts

Knowing the behavior of the various mutant eye color discs implanted in wild type hosts, the reciprocals of these offer points of interest. The data are summarized in table 2.

It is evident that a wild type disc gives rise to an eye with wild type pigmentation when implanted in any of the mutants except *ca* and possibly *bo*. As in the reciprocal transplant, the result with *bo* is not clear. The significance of this exceptional behavior of + in *ca* transplants will be discussed later.

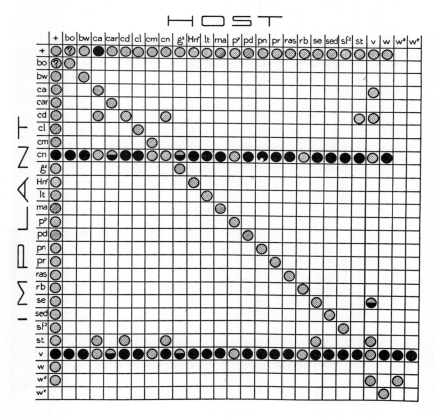

Figure 1. Diagrammatic representation of the results of eye transplants. Shaded circles indicate autonomous development of the pigmentation of the implant. Black circles indicate nonautonomous development of pigmentation. Circles half black and half shaded indicate nonautonomous development of such a nature that the resulting implant is intermediate in color between two controls.

TABLE 3

Data on the differentiation of v eye implants in eye color mutant hosts.
Arrangement as in Table 1.

IMPLANT	HOST	NUMBER OF INDIVIDUALS	PHENOTYPE OF IMPLANT	IMPLANT	HOST	NUMBER OF INDIVIDUALS	PHENOTYPE OF IMPLANT
v	bo	0, 0, 0, 1; 1	+	v	pd	2, 1, 1, 0; 4	+
v	bw	7, 0, 2, 1; 10	+	v	$y\ pn$	2, 0, 1, 1; 4	+
v	ca	4, 4, 3, 2, 3,* 2*; 18	v	v	$b\ pr$	2, 0, 1, 1; 4	+
v	car	5, 0, 2, 1; 8	Interm.	v	$sc\ ras$	0, 1, 0, 1; 2	+
v	cd	2, 1, 4, 1; 8	+	v	$rb\ cv$	2,‡ 1, 1, 0; 4	v
v	cl	2, 3, 1, 0; 6	+	v	$se\ wo$	4, 4, 6, 1; 15	+
v	cm	7, 0, 1, 2; 10	v	v	$sr\ sed$	0, 1,‡ 0, 0; 1	+
v	cn	6, 1, 3, 3; 13	+	v	$tk\ sf^2\ abb$	3, 0, 0, 1; 4	+
v	g^2	2, 0, 3, 2; 7	Interm.	v	st	3, 0, 3, 2; 8	+
v	$jv\ Hnr\ h$	1, 0, 2, 1; 4	+	v	w	8, 2, 2, 1; 13	+
v	$lt\ c$	2, 0, 0, 0; 2	+	v	w^a	0, 0, 0, 1; 1	+
v	ma	3, 0, 0, 3; 6	+	v	w^e	0, 1, 0, 0; 1	+
v	p^p	3,* 2,* 0, 0; 5	v				

* Sex of donor not determined.
‡ One host dissected as mature pupa.

TABLE 4

Data on the differentiation of *cn* eye implants in eye color mutant hosts.
Arrangement as in Table 1.

IMPLANT	HOST	NUMBER OF INDIVIDUALS	PHENOTYPE OF IMPLANT	IMPLANT	HOST	NUMBER OF INDIVIDUALS	PHENOTYPE OF IMPLANT
cn	*bo*	1, 1, 2, 0; 4	+	*cn*	*pd*	1,† 0, 5, 1; 7	+
cn	*bw*	3, 0, 0, 3; 6	+	*cn*	*y pn*	3, 0, 0, 0; 3	+
cn	*ca*	2, 0, 1, 0; 3	*cn*	*cn*	*b pr*	0, 1, 2, 0; 3	+
cn	*car*	2, 0, 5, 3; 10	Interm.	*cn*	*sc ras*	0, 0, 0, 1; 1	+
cn	*cd*	3, 3, 2, 2; 10	+	*cn*	*rb cv*	1, 0, 2, 1; 4	*cn*
cn	*cl*	2, 0, 1, 2; 5	+	*cn*	*se wo*	3, 3, 2, 3; 11	+
cn	*cm*	1, 2, 3, 1; 7	*cn*	*cn*	*sr sed*	0, 3, 2, 0; 5	+
cn	*g²*	5, 1, 1, 2; 9	Interm.	*cn*	*tk sf² abb*	3, 0, 3, 0; 6	+
cn	*jv Hnr* h	1, 0, 3, 0; 4	+	*cn*	*st*	3, 2, 2, 2; 9	+
cn	*lt* c	0, 0, 2, 1; 3	+	*cn*	*v*	2, 4, 5, 1; 12	*cn*
cn	*ma*	1, 2, 1, 1; 5	+	*cn*	*w*	0, 2, 1, 0; 3	+
cn	*pp*	5,* 3,* 0, 0; 8	*cn*				

* Sex of donor not determined.
† Host dissected as mature pupa.

105

Vermilion Discs in Mutant Hosts

In the case of a *v* disc implanted into a wild type host, the developing eye is affected by the host in such a way that the final pigmentation is like that of a wild type eye. Before discussing the factor responsible for this change in more detail and its relation to the factor responsible for the fact that a *cn* eye disc implanted into a wild type host develops wild type pigmentation, data should be considered which bear on the question of whether other eye color mutants have anything to do with this "body-to-eye" phase of the *v* reaction. This question can be answered by implanting *v* eye discs into hosts which differ from wild type by various eye color mutants. Such data are given in table 3.

These data show that, when implanted in certain mutant hosts (*bo, bw, cd, cl, cn, Hn^r, lt, ma, pd, pn, pr, ras, se, sed, sf^2, st,* and *w*), a *v* optic disc gives rise to a wild type eye; in others (*ca, cm, p^p,* and *rb*), it gives an eye with *v* pigmentation. In *car* and *g^2* hosts, a *v* disc gives an eye with pigmentation intermediate between *v* and wild type. Discussion of these relations will be deferred until other evidence is considered.

Cinnabar Discs in Mutant Hosts

Since a *cn* disc implanted in a wild type host gives a result of the same type as the comparable implant of a *v* disc, namely, a wild type eye, the same question arises concerning *cn* as the one stated above for *v*. Data showing the results obtained by implanting *cn* eye discs in eye color mutant hosts are given in table 4. The results, excluding *cn* and *v* hosts, are the same as those for *v*, that is, a *cn* disc gives a wild type eye in the same mutant hosts in which a *v* disc gave a wild type eye, and gives a *cn* eye in the same hosts in which a *v* disc gave a *v* eye. Table 3 shows that a *v* disc in a *cn* host gives a wild type eye. Table 4 shows that the reciprocal transplant does not give this result, that is, a *cn* disc in a *v* host gives a *cn* eye.

Experiments Concerning v, cn, *and* ca

From the data present above, it is seen that, in the cases of *cn* in wild type, *v* in wild type, and wild type in *ca*, the developing eye implant is influenced in its pigmentation by something that either comes or fails to come from some part or parts of the host. Just what this is, whether or not, for example, it is of the nature of a hormone, we cannot yet say. We shall therefore refer to it by the noncommittal term "substance."

Certain obvious questions at once arise concerning the substances concerned in these three cases. For example, is there only one substance? If not, are the different substances related and in what way? What is their relation to the genes concerned in their production? Before attempting to discuss these and related questions, we shall consider additional data which bear on the problem.

Behavior of v in Combination with Other Eye Color Mutants

By studying the differentiation of pigment implants which differ from the host tissues by two eye color characters, one autonomous, the other non-autonomous in development, it might be possible to learn something about the interaction of the genes concerned. Data of this nature are summarized in table 5A for the combinations of *v*, *w^a^v* and *v car*. It is seen that the behavior of *v* is here the same as that observed in transplants in which *v* is the only mutant gene concerned. Likewise, *car* and *w^a* behave in the same way as in simple transplants involving only these mutant genes. This result tells us only that, so far as its behavior in transplants goes, the interaction of the *v* allelomorph with *car* or *w^a* plus the normal allelomorphs of all the other genes concerned with eye pigmentation is not different from its interaction with *car^+* or *w^+* under the same conditions. The same kind of result was observed by Sturtevant (1932) in studies of early cleavage mosaics in *D. simulans* in which the individuals were made up of *v^+g^+* and *v g* tissue; here the *v* character is, under certain conditions, not autonomous, but the g character is always autonomous.

The Relation of Bar and Vermilion

In studies of the differentiation of Bar (*B*) eye discs implanted in not-*B* hosts, it was observed that a *v^+B* disc implanted in a *v* host gives rise to a B eye[1] with *v* pigmentation.

This experiment was repeated several times varying both the *v* stocks used as hosts and the *B* stocks which furnished the implants. The result was in all cases the same, indicating that the *B* gene, in addition to influencing the size of the eye in a characteristic way, has an effect closely related to the *v* reaction. The data from the various experiments involving the *v* and *B* mutants, as well as appropriate controls are given in table 5B. It is seen that only in case the host is *v*, does the *B* implant develop *v* pigmentation. An eye disc heterozygous for the *B* gene implanted in a *v* host gives an eye with wild type pigmentation. It follows that, whatever its action may be, the *B* gene effect is recessive in this interaction with *v*. These results suggested that the condition of some process in the B eye disc at or after the time of transplantation might be retarded relative to the state of other developmental reactions, and led to experiments in which eye discs from young wild type larvae were implanted in older *v* larvae.

In table 6 data are given from transplants of this kind. In the first ex-

---

[1] It is clear that a B disc implanted in a not-B host is B but whether or not there is any modification of the B character such as is observed in mosaics (Sturtevant, 1932), we have not yet determined.

TABLE 5

Data on various eye implants. Explanations in text.

IMPLANT	HOST	NUMBER OF INDIVIDUALS	PHENOTYPE OF IMPLANT
		PART A	
sc v f car	$+$	14, 7, 4, 2; 27	car
$+$	sc v f car	1, 0, 2, 0; 3	$+$
sc v f car	v	2, 2, 1, 0; 5	v car
v	sc v f car	2, 0, 4, 1; 7	v
sc v f car	cn	1, 3, 3, 2; 9	car
$w^a v$	$+$	0, 0, 1, 1; 2	w^a
$+$	$w^a v$	6, 4, 2, 0; 12	$+$
$w^a v$	v	0, 0, 1, 1; 2	$w^a v$
v	$w^a v$	0, 2, 0, 4, 6,* 3*; 15	v
$w^a v$	cn	0, 0, 2, 0; 2	w^a
cn	$w^a v$	4, 5, 1, 2; 12	cn (host eyes w^a)
$w^a v$	wa^3	0, 0, 7, 0; 7	w^a
		PART B	
B	y v f	0, 0, 3, 0; 3	v B
B	v	2, 0, 1, 1; 4	v B
g^2 f B	v	0, 0, 3, 2, 5	v $g^2 B$
$B/+$	v	3, 2, 0, 0, 5	$B/+$
B	$+$	0, 0, 3, 0; 3	B
B	B	0, 0, 0, 1; 1	B
se wo	v	6, 1, 5, 5; 17	se Interm. v (sex diff.-text)
		PART C	
cd	cn	2, 0, 0, 0; 2	cd
cd	st	3, 2, 6, 2; 13	cd
cd	v	2, 0, 3, 0; 5	cd
st	cd	0, 4, 1, 3; 8	st
st	cn	4, 3, 2, 3; 12	st
st	v	3, 0, 2, 0; 5	st
st	se wo	3, 0, 1, 0; 4	st
B	st	0, 0, 1, 2; 3	B
g^2 f B	st	0, 0, 1, 0; 1	$g^2 B$
se wo	cn	4, 1, 1, 1, 7	se
cd	ca	3, 2, 5, 1; 11	cd
st	ca	1, 1, 0, 0; 2	st

* Sex of donor not determined.

periment, only two transplants were successful in the sense that the implanted discs gave rise to differentiated eyes. Here the age difference between implant and host, at the time of transplantation, was about 28 hours. One of the two implanted eyes showed v-like pigmentation, the

TABLE 6

Data on the differentiation of wild type eye discs from young larvae implanted in older v larvae. Arrangement under heading "Number of individuals" same as in previous tables.

| IMPLANT | | HOST | | NUMBER OF INDIVIDUALS | PHENOTYPE OF IMPLANT |
CONSTITUTION	AGE AFTER HATCHING (HRS.)	CONSTI-TUTION	AGE AFTER HATCHING (HRS.)		
+	44 to 48	v	80±	1, 1, 0, 0; 2	♀ v (?) ♂ + (?)
+	43 to 46	v	80±	3, 1, 3, 1; 8	Interm. between + and v
+	44 to 47	+	80±	4, 0, 1, 0; 5	+

TABLE 7

Data on transplants of non-v ovaries to v hosts

| CONSTITUTION | | NUMBER OF DEVELOPED IMPLANT OVARIES | NUMBER OF INDIVIDUALS | | PHENOTYPE OF HOST |
IMPLANT	HOST		FEMALE	MALE	
+	v	1	17	7	v
ca	v	1	4		v
+	$w^a v$	1	29	5	$w^a v$
cn	$w^a v$	1	1		$w^a v$
+	v	2	5	2	v
+	$y\,v\,f$	3	2		v

other more nearly wild type pigmentation. Unfortunately, in this experiment, there were no satisfactory controls. Later, an experiment was made in which young wild type discs were implanted in older v larvae, and at the same time, for a control, wild type discs of the same age and from the same culture dish of larvae were implanted in older wild type larvae. The data (table 6) show that, with an age difference of about 28 hours, the wild type discs implanted in v hosts did indeed give eyes with pigmentation approaching in color that of control v in v implants. The wild type in wild type controls with a similar age difference gave eyes with pigment of the same type as did known wild type control implants. In all cases the young discs implanted in older hosts gave rise to eyes markedly smaller than implanted eyes from transplants where little or no age difference exists between implant and host.

From the data so far discussed, it might be assumed that the difference between B in v and wild type in v transplants is determined merely by the smaller size of the B implants. The behavior of young wild type implants in older v hosts could then be interpreted in the same way. But there are two arguments against this interpretation. In the first place, we have often obtained, from wild type in v transplants where there was no age difference, small fragments of eyes resulting from breakage of the disc during the operation of transplantation. In all cases these "small eyes" had wild type pigmentation. Many of these fragments were smaller than the eyes obtained in the "young in old" transplants. Further, it is known from mosaics that small patches of v^+ tissue in an otherwise v eye have wild type pigmentation (Sturtevant, unpublished). The second argument is one from analogy with the behavior of se in v transplants discussed below, in which there was little or no age difference between implant and host, but in which the implanted eyes were intermediate between v and v^+ (actually intermediate between se and v se, since se is autonomous in its development). Here the implanted eyes were "normal" in size since the se gene does not affect eye size.

Actually, then, it appears probable that the behavior of B in v implants will find its explanation in terms of the states of certain eye reactions, influenced by the B gene, relative to the states of certain developmental reactions in other parts of the organism. Such a situation can, of course, following Goldschmidt, be expressed in terms of rates of certain eye reactions relative to the rates of other developmental reactions. What the nature of this eye reaction (or reactions) might be, we have, at present, no way of knowing. We shall return later to a consideration of its possible relation to the action of the v gene.

The experiments on se in v transplants mentioned above are summarized in table 5B. Actually these data are the result of three separate experiments, all of which gave the same result. Two se stocks were used, the second obtained by outcrossing the first to a v stock and recovering *se* flies in the backcross to the *se wo* stock. There was a definite difference between eyes developed from implants of discs from male and female donors; the male discs gave eyes with pigmentation more closely approaching v *se* control implants (v *se* in v *se*) than did female discs. Speculation concerning this effect of *se*, which may be of the same kind as the effect of B, will be more profitable when more data are at hand. The nature of the observed sex difference also needs further investigation.

Influence of Eye Implants on Host Eye Pigmentation

In the above experiments in which $w^a v$, stocks were used, it was observed that $w^a v$ flies in which implanted cn eyes had developed, had normal eyes with w^a rather than $w^a v$ pigmentation. Since the $w^a v$ stock used had been recently made up, it was at first thought that this stock might not be pure. However, the same experiment was later repeated with adequate controls and the same result obtained. A cn eye implant, then, furnishes something to a $w^a v$ host fly which changes the course of eye pigment formation in such a way that the result is, in effect, v^+ and not v pigmentation. Since no such action of wild type or cn eye implants on the normal eyes of v hosts had been observed previously, a series of transplants was made to check this point carefully. The results were as follows:

Implanted eye disc	Host	Pigmentation of	
		Implant	Host
$+$	v	$+$	v
cn	v	cn	v
v	v	v	v
$+$	$w^a v$	$+$	$w^a v$
cn	$w^a v$	cn	w^a
$w^a v$	$w^a v$	$w^a v$	$w^a v$

These results suggest two obvious questions. The first is, why are the eyes of a $w_a v$ host changed by cn eye implants to w_a (from v to v^+) while the eyes of a v host are unaffected by such an implant? This change in the $w^a v$ eyes seems to be complete in many cases, that is, the modified eyes show no difference from stock w^a flies. Hence it seems clear that the same proportionate change does not occur in the two cases, detectable in $w^a v$ and not in v hosts. A more probable interpretation assumes that a cn eye implant releases into the blood of the host a certain quantity of some substance, presumably the same as that which changes the pigmentation of a v implant in a wild type host, and that this substance is only sufficient in amount to result in the change of a limited amount of pigment from v to v^+. The $w^a v$ eyes have little pigment and this can all be changed, by the available substance, from v to v^+. The normal eyes of a v host, on the other hand, have such a large amount of pigment that the limited supply of substance does not produce a detectable change, even though it may result in a change of the same absolute of pigment as in the case of the eyes of a $w^a v$ host. This interpretation obviously can be tested by relatively simple experiments. In fact, we have already observed that, in case the cn eye implant is small, the change in $w^a v$ is not complete.

A second question that is apparent from these results is, why is a cn eye implant effective whereas a wild type implant has no effect? Both types of eye implants of course have the v^+ gene, and presumably the production of v^+ substance goes on in both. It seems from the data that the cn gene produces a change such that the substance in question is released from the implant.

In connection with the influence of an eye implant on the eye color of the host, it is known, from studies of $w^{+} = w$ gynandromorphs in *D. simulans* (Dobzhansky, 1931; Sturtevant, 1932), that rate of testis sheath pigmentation is correlated with the amount of w^+ eye tissue present. The substance responsible for the pigmentation of the testis sheath very probably is formed by w^+ eye tissue—if so, it must be able to diffuse from the eye.

Implantation of Gonads

In his studies of v-v^+ early cleavage mosaics in *D. simulans*, Sturtevant (1932) was able to demonstrate clearly a strong correlation between the autonomous or non-autonomous pigmentation of genotypically v eye tissue and the constitution of the gonads with respect to the v gene. Here, if both gonads are v^+ (and female), genetically v eye tissue show v^+ pigmentation in practically all instances. If, on the other hand, both gonads are v (and male), genetically v eye tissue shows v or intermediate pigmentation in all cases. We have pointed out in a preliminary paper (Ephrussi and Beadle, 1935a) that it is the constitution of the gonads with respect to the v gene and not with respect to sex that is important. In these experiments of Sturtevant, there were some exceptions which led him to conclude that, in addition to the gonads, some other organ or part of the fly must be involved in the differentiation of v eye tissue in mosaics.

On the basis of Sturtevant's results we have made transplants of wild type ovaries in v hosts to see whether we could influence the pigmentation of the eyes of the host. Such ovary implants develop quite normally and are even capable of forming functional connections with the oviducts of the host (Ephrussi and Beadle, 1935b). The results of such experiments with ovary transplants, and which bear on the v case, are summarized in table 7.

It is seen that one or two wild type ovaries in a v male host or one, two, or even three such ovaries in a v female host, have no detectable effect on the v color of the eyes of the host. Likewise, neither an implanted wild type nor an implanted cn ovary has any influence on the normal eyes of a $w^a v$ host, male or female. These results, then, are entirely negative. Since in all these cases normal v ovaries or testes were present in the host, it could be argued that they account for the fact that implanted ovaries are without effect on the host eyes. However, this seems rather improbable as it would involve the assumption that the implanted ovaries produce the necessary substance but that something else produced by either v ovaries or v testes acts as an inactivating agent on the v^+ substance.

Taken in connection with the results of Sturtevant which show quite definitely that wild type ovaries do have something to do with the production of the substance which changes the course of pigment formation in v eye tissue, our results only corroborate his conclusion that some other organ or part of the body plays an essential role in the production of this substance, i.e., gonads plus an unknown part of the body interact in its formation. Our studies give no clue as to what this unknown might be, but Sturtevant has shown that it is not closely related in terms of cell lineage to any surface part of the body, and does not lie in the abdomen (1932).

These results of gonad transplantation in Drosophila show certain obvious differences from those obtained by Caspari (1933) and Kühn, Caspari, and Plagge (1935) in gonad transplants in *Ephestia kühniella*, likewise made in connection with studies on eye pigmentation. These workers have shown that wild type testes or ovaries implanted in larvae of the red-eyed mutant race a modify the eye pigmentation toward wild type. Here, then, the substance concerned, which they refer to as a hormone, can evidently be formed by the gonads from a wild type race in the absence of other organs or tissues of a^+ constitution. In this case, the substance has an effect on pigmentation in several parts of the organism, in larval skin, larval eyes, eyes of the imago, and in the gonads themselves. The substance can evidently be produced in other parts of the body since a wild type brain implanted in an a host modifies, under certain conditions, the pigmentation of the host.

Special Experiments with the v-Like Group of Mutants

The four mutants, v, cn, st, and cd, are very much alike in their phenotypic appearance. Furthermore, Schultz (1935) has shown that in the development of their pigmentation, they show rather marked similarities and, as a group, are distinct from other mutants. In fact, on the basis of these similarities, he was led to suggest that they might all be found to show the v-type of behavior in mosaics. It has already been shown that, although v and cn are not autonomous in their pigment development in certain kinds of transplants, st and cd do show autonomous development in eye transplants in wild type hosts. Because of the similarity of st and cd to each other and to v and cn, we have used them in certain transplants in which other mutants have not been used (table 5). These data need little discussion. It is evident that both st and cd show autonomous development of pigment in all the combinations in which they are involved.

It is clear that the v-like group of mutants is not homogenous as regards developmental behavior. In this respect v and cn are obviously related but not the same, as will be pointed out in more detail below, and st and cd are different from either v or cn.

The ca Case

As shown by the data already referred to, a wild type eye disc implanted in a ca host gives an eye with ca-like pigmentation. To account for this result, we must assume that in the development of wild type pigment something must come to the eye from another part or other parts of the body and that this substance is not formed in a fly homozygous for the ca gene. But the data given in tables 3 and 4 show that a v eye disc implanted in a ca host gives a v eye, i.e., not v ca, therefore ca^+, and that, similarly, a cn disc implanted in a ca host gives a cn ca^+ eye. Data given in table 5 show that a similar result is obtained if a st or a cd disc is implanted in a ca host, namely, a st ca^+ or a cd ca^+ eye results. Summary of these results:

$+$ disc implanted in a ca host gives a ca eye
v disc implanted in a ca host gives a v ca^+ eye
cn disc implanted in a ca host gives a cn ca^+ eye
st disc implanted in a ca host gives a st ca^+ eye
cd disc implanted in a ca host gives a cd ca^+ eye

In determining that the last four of these results were really v, cn, st and cd and not v ca, cn ca, st ca, and cd ca respectively, the appropriate double recessive controls were not available, but comparisons were made with v, cn, st, and cd control transplants and no differences could be detected. Since v ca and st ca are both known to be readily separable from v and st respectively, there is little chance of error in the determinations. The question, of course, is, why is the development of ca^+ pigmentation not autonomous in the first case listed and autonomous in the remaining cases studied? Possibly the four genes v, cn, st and cd act, in the implant, in such a way that no ca^+ substance is necessary to give ca^+ pigmentation; that is, a v^+ca^+ implant requires ca^+ substance from the host to develop ca^+ pigmentation, but a v ca^+ implant does not require this substance to develop v ca^+ pigmentation.

DISCUSSION

From the experimental results considered above, several hypotheses can be suggested concerning the nature of certain of the eye color mutants and the action of the genes which differentiate them from wild type. Alternative hypotheses are obviously possible, and it should be emphasized that those presented are tentative.

The Vermilion Character

Since the pigmentation of a genetically v eye can be modified to v^+ by transplanting it to a host which supplies it with what may be called the v^+ substance, it follows that v differs from wild type by the absence of this substance. Evidently there is no change in the v eye itself which prevents its pigmentation from assuming wild type characteristics. It follows that the mutation $v^+ \rightarrow v$ has resulted in a change such that v^+ substance is no longer formed. Since a cn eye disc implanted in a v host remains cn, the $v^+ \rightarrow v$ mutation has resulted also in preventing the formation of cn^+ substance. The v^+ gene plays an essential part in the formation of the v^+ and cn^+ substances, but it does not form them directly since any one of several other gene mutations (ca, cm, p^p, and rb) may result in the absence of them. According to this scheme, v^+ substance is necessary for wild type pigmentation. The question then arises, why does a wild type eye disc implanted in a v host, which can supply no v^+ substance, develop wild type pigmentation? Two answers are possible; either the v^+ substance has already acted at the time of transplantation or this substance is produced by the eye itself. The fact that, in mosaics, a small patch of v^+ eye tissue in an effectively v individual has wild type pigmentation (Sturtevant, unpublished), shows that the first of these answers cannot be correct, for in this case, the v^+ tissue has been in a v tissue environment almost from the beginning of development. We must then conclude that the substance is produced in the eye itself. Actually we have been able to demonstrate that it is produced by a cn eye (modification of normal $w^a v$ eyes by an implanted cn eye). But, it may be asked, why was it not possible to demonstrate that it is produced by a wild type eye? The answer may be that the substance is produced but cannot get out of the eye, i.e., one of the effects of the cn gene is to make eye cells permeable to v^+ substance. The difference in behavior between a wild type and a B eye implanted in a v host may be accounted for by assuming that one of the effects of the B gene is to prevent the formation of v^+ substance in the eye, but not in other parts of the body. This assumption is not necessarily an alternative to the assumption previously suggested that the action of the B gene may be explained "in terms of the states of certain eye reactions, influenced by the B gene, relative to the states of certain developmental reactions in other parts of the organism." It may well be that it is the formation of v^+ substance that is retarded (in an extreme way) in the eye relative to its formation in other parts of the body. The "young in old" experiments can be formally explained in the same terms. In young wild type discs implanted in older v larvae, the time during which v^+ substance can be formed in the implanted eye is much reduced. In a similar way, in a se eye, v^+ substance is formed in the eye at a rate so low that, when implanted in a host without v^+ substance, pigmentation intermediate between v^+ and v results.

The Cinnabar Character

The evidence for the existence of a cn^+ substance is the same in kind as that for v^+ substance. It is already evident and will be pointed out in more detail below that the cn^+ substance is different from the v^+ substance. By the same kind of arguments as were presented in the above discussion of the v character, it may be concluded that the mutation $cn^+ \rightarrow cn$ produces a change such that cn^+ substance is no longer formed. According to this interpretation, as in the interpretation of v, it is assumed that a wild type eye produces cn^+ substance in its own cells. This would account for the fact that a wild type eye implanted in a cn host gives wild type pigmentation.

The Claret Character

In contrast to the v and cn cases, two phases of the action of the ca gene can be distinguished. First, since a genetically wild type eye cannot develop wild type pigmentation unless some other part of the organism is ca^+, it is concluded that a ca^+ substance is necessary for the formation of wild type pigmentation. This is not formed in the eye itself but comes from some other part of the body. Secondly, since by supplying a ca eye with the necessary ca^+ substance by implanting it in a wild type host, we do not produce a change to wild type pigmentation, it is postulated that there is a change in a ca eye of such a kind that the addition of ca^+ substance is not sufficient to give wild type pigmentation.

Other Eye Color Mutant Characters

By implanting v and cn eye disc in other eye color mutant hosts, it has been demonstrated that the mutants cm, p^p, and rb are characterized by lack of both the v^+ and cn^+ substances. In these three mutant types, as in ca, there must be two phases of gene action, (1) the failure of the formation of the v^+ and cn^+ substances, and (2) an action in the eye itself, since supplying the two substances by transplantation does not produce a change. The genes car and g^2 must be placed in the same class, but in these two cases the formation of v^+ and cn^+ substances is not prevented but only limited.

The other mutants with which we have worked, *bo, bw, cd, cl, Hn^r, lt, ma, pd, pn, pr, ras, se, sed, sf^2, st,* and *w^a* are characterized by the presence of all the three substances postulated. It cannot be concluded that the normal allelomorphs of the genes differentiating these characters have nothing to do with the production of v^+, cn^+ and ca^+ substances. There is no justification in assuming that, if a given gene concerned with the production of a substance such as we are considering mutates, the particular mutant allelomorph resulting will be of such a nature as to result in the absence of the substance. Kühn, Caspari, and Plagge (1935) come to such an unjustified conclusion with regard to the t^+ gene in *Ephestia.*

Relation of the v^+, cn^+, and ca^+ Substances

It has been shown from the difference in reciprocal transplants between *v* and *cn* that the v^+ and cn^+ substances are different (Beadle and Ephrussi, 1935a). At the same time, it was concluded from the fact that a *v* fly lacks both substances, that the two substances are related. This conclusion is corroborated by the more extensive data presented in this paper. The strongest indication that two substances are concerned is the fact that a *v* eye disc implanted in a *cn* host gives rise to an eye with wild type pigment. Two other facts strengthen the supposition of two substances: (1) A *B* eye disc implanted in a *v* host gives an eye with *v* pigmentation, but, implanted in a *cn* host, gives wild type pigmentation. (2) A *se* eye disc implanted in a *v* host gives a *se*, partially *v*, eye, but, implanted in a *cn* host, gives a straight *se* eye.

The fact that these substances, although not the same, are developmentally—and presumably chemically—related, is shown by the fact that, if a given mutant is characterized by the absence of one of these substances, it will probably be characterized by the absence of the other also.

Considering the relation of the ca^+ substance to the other two, it is clear that it is different from either for it may be present in the absence of both the others. The fact that the *ca* gene prevents the formation of all three substances (*v* or *cn* discs implanted in *ca* hosts are not modified in their pigmentation) indicates that ca^+ substance is related to the other two.

It may be asked whether, from the relations discussed above, anything can be inferred as to (1) how the v^+, cn^+, and ca^+ substances are related in terms of development, and (2) how the mutant forms of the genes known to be concerned with the production of the three substances produce their effects? A simple, and, it seems to us, plausible, hypothesis may be of help in answering these questions. Such an hypothesis assumes that the ca^+, v^+, and cn^+ substances are successive products in a chain reaction. The relations of these substances can be indicated in a simple diagrammatic way as follows:

$$\rightarrow ca^+ \text{ substance} \rightarrow v^+ \text{ substance} \rightarrow cn^+ \text{ substance}$$

In such a scheme, we assume that:

1. The mutant gene ca in some way produces a change such that the chain of reactions is interrupted at some point prior to the formation of ca^+ substance; hence a ca fly lacks ca^+, v^+, and cn^+ substances.

2. Any one of the mutant genes v, cm, p^p, or rb results in a change such that the reaction or reactions leading from ca^+ substance to v^+ substance do not go on; hence the mutants v, cm, p^p and rb lack both v^+ and cn^+ substances but have ca^+ substance. The mutant genes car and g^2 slow down this step in the chain of reactions, hence car and g^2 flies are characterized by a reduced amount of v^+ and cn^+ substances. The mutant gene B interrupts this same step in the chain in the eye, but not in other parts of the body. The mutant gene se results in a change such that the ca^+ substance changes to v^+ substance at a reduced rate in the eye, but at a normal rate in other parts of the body.

3. The mutant gene cn stops a reaction essential for the change of v^+ substance to cn^+ substance; hence a cn fly lacks cn^+ substance but has the ca^+ and v^+ substances.

On the basis of the above scheme, the results of implanting v eye discs in cn hosts can be interpreted as follows: The implant produces no v^+ substance, and, because v^+ substance is an essential step in the formation of cn^+ substance, it likewise produces no cn^+ substance. The host can supply v^+ substance to the implant but cannot supply cn^+ substance. With v^+ substance supplied to the implant by the cn host, there is no block to the formation of cn^+ substance in the implant itself. The implant therefore develops wild type pigmentation in spite of the fact that normally neither the donor nor the host could have produced the cn^+ substance presumably necessary for the production of wild type pigment.

In a somewhat similar way, the results of transplanting B eye discs to v and to cn hosts can be interpreted. The B eye can form no v^+ substance. When transplanted to a v host, v^+ substance cannot move to it from the host, and the pigment developed is therefore v. Because of the absence of the prerequisite v^+ substance, the B eye normally does not itself produce cn^+ substance. But when a B eye disc is implanted in a cn host, the B implant is supplied with v^+ substance from the host and the reaction or reactions from v^+ to cn^+ substances can then go on in the implant itself and wild type pigment is produced.

The results of implanting se eye discs in v and cn hosts can be interpreted in an essentially similar way.

Eye Color Mutant Groups

The eye color mutants in *Drosophila* can be grouped according to their phenotypic characteristics, since mutants differentiated by non-allelomorphic genes can look alike (Morgan, Bridges, and Sturtevant, 1925).

Recently Schultz (1935) has extended this grouping by studying the time of appearance and the rate of formation of pigment, the distribution of pigment in the eye, and the interaction behavior of the different mutants. It is obvious that we can, on the basis of the results given above, classify the mutants with respect to the presence or absence of the three postulated substances. We may then ask if there is any relation between groups such as made by Schultz and the classification according to these substances. If there is such a relation, it is not evident from the data at hand. As an example, the four mutants, v, cn, st, and cd, form one of Schultz's groups, but as we have seen, v lacks two substances, cn one, while st and cd have all three.

The above discussion, we hope, has served to indicate some of the possibilities in the application of the method of transplantation to the study of development in *Drosophila*. The extension of the studies of certain cases to other stages of development is indicated as a logical next step by which we can hope to get at such questions as concern the time of determination of characters and the time of action of genes associated with these characters.

ACKNOWLEDGEMENTS

We are indebted to Professor R. Goldschmidt and to Doctors M. Demerec and N. W. Timoféef-Ressovsky for their kindness in supplying various of the stocks used in the work reported in this paper. To Professor C. Perez and Doctor G. Teissier we wish to express our thanks for facilities for work at the Biological Station at Roscoff. Members of the staff of the Biological Laboratories of the California Institute of Technology, particularly Professor T. H. Morgan, have made many helpful suggestions during the preparation of the manuscript. We are grateful to Professor A. H. Sturtevant for permission to cite unpublished data essential to certain of our arguments.

SUMMARY

Larval optic discs can be successfully transplanted from one larva to another. Such transplanted discs give rise to supplementary eyes, usually lying in the abdominal cavity of the adult fly, which differentiate normally except that they are inverted. The pigmentation of such eyes develops normally.

When optic discs of the mutants cn or v are implanted in wild type hosts, they give eyes with wild type pigmentation, i.e., under these conditions, the cn and v characters are not autonomous in their development. Under the same conditions, bw, ca, car, cd, cl, cm, g^2, Hn^r, lt, ma, p^p, pd, pn, pr, ras, rb, se, sed, sf^2, st and w eye discs implanted in wild type hosts show autonomous development of eye pigment.

In the reciprocals of the above transplants, wild type eye discs implanted in hosts of the mutants mentioned, wild type pigmentation of the implant results in all except one case, a wild type disc implanted in a *ca* host. In this one exception, a genetically wild type eye disc gives an eye with *ca* pigmentation, i.e., *ca*+ does not show autonomous pigment development under these conditions.

If *v* eye discs are implanted in eye color mutant hosts, eyes with wild type pigmentation develop in *bo, bw, cd, cl, cn, Hn^r, lt, ma, pd, pn, pr, ras, se, sed, sf^2, st,* and *w* hosts, i.e., the *v* character is not autonomous in its development when a *v* eye is transplanted to any one of these hosts. But a *v* eye disc implanted in a *ca, cm, p^p,* or *rb* host gives an eye with *v* pigmentation, i.e., the *v* character is autonomous in these cases. It can be concluded that the autonomous or non-autonomous development of the *v* character is determined by the genetic constitution with regard to genes other than *v*, of the tissue environment in which the *v* eye develops.

Implanted in eye color mutant hosts other than *v* or *cn*, a *cn* eye disc behaves in the same way as does a *v* eye disc, showing autonomous pigment development in the same mutant hosts as does *v*, and non-autonomous pigment development in the same hosts as does *v*.

Reciprocal transplants involving *cn* and *v* do not give the same result; a *v* eye disc implanted in a *cn* host gives an eye with wild type pigmentation while a *cn* eye disc implanted in a *v* host gives an eye with *cn* pigmentation.

A *B* eye disc implanted to a *v* host gives a *B* eye with *v* pigmentation. This shows that the *B* gene has an effect on the eye somehow related to the effect of the *v* gene but not of such a nature as to modify the pigmentation of the eye in its normal position. This case shows that the autonomous or non-autonomous develpment of *v*+ pigmentation in an implanted *v*+ eye may be influenced by the genetic constitution, with respect to genes other than *v*, of the implant itself.

A genetically wild type eye disc from a young larva implanted in an older *v* host shows pigmentation intermediate between *v* and wild type. A *se* eye implanted in a *v* host likewise gives pigmentation of an intermediate nature with respect to the *v* character; here the eye is intermediate between *v se* and *se*. The possible relation of these cases to the *B* in *v* results is considered.

A *cn* eye implanted in a *w^av* host gives a *cn* eye, but the eyes of the host are modified from the *w^av* to a *w^a* phenotype.

Ovaries from wild type donors have been implanted in both male and female *v* hosts without any detectable change in the pigmentation of the host eyes.

From the cases of non-autonomous development of the pigmentation of implanted eyes considered in this paper, three substances are postulated, the *v*+, *cn*+, and *ca*+ substances. Their interrelations and the conditions under which they are produced are discussed. A hypothetical scheme accounting for the production and relation of these three substances is suggested, and, in connection with this, questions concerning where and how certain genes might act are considered.

LITERATURE CITED

Beadle, G. W., and Ephrussi, B., 1935a Différenciation de la couleur de l'oeil *cinnabar* chez la Drosophile (*Drosophila melanogaster*). C. R. Acad. Sci. Paris. *201*: 620–622.

———— 1935b Transplantation in Drosophila. Proc. Nat. Acad. Sci. *21*: 642–646.

Caspari, E., 1933 Über die Wirkung eines pleiotropen Gens bei der Mehlmotte *Ephestia kühniella* Zeller. Arch. Entw. Mech. *130*: 353–381.

Dobzhansky, T., 1931 Interaction between female and male parts in gynandromorphs of *Drosophila simulans*. Arch. Entw. Mechan. *123*: 719–746.

Ephrussi, B. and Beadle, G. W., 1935a La transplantation des disques imaginaux chez la Drosophile. C. R. Acad. Sci. Paris. *201*: 98–99.

———— 1935b La transplantation des ovaires chez la Drosophile. Bull. Biol. *69*: 492–502.

———— 1935c Sur les conditions de l'autodifférenciation des caractères mendeliens. C. R. Acad. Sci. Paris. *201*: 1148–1150.

———— 1936 A technique of transplantation for Drosophila. Amer. Nat. In press.

Kühn, A., Caspari, E., and Plagge, E., 1935 Über hormonale Genwirkungen bei *Ephestia kühniella* Z. Nachr. Ges. Wiss. Göttingen. *2*: 1–29.

Morgan, T. H., Bridges, C. B., and Sturtevant, A. H., 1925 The genetics of Drosophila. Bibliogr. Genet. *2*: 1–262.

Schultz, J., 1935 Aspects of the relation between genes and development in Drosophila. Amer. Nat. *69*: 30–54.

Sturtevant, A. H., 1932 The use of mosaics in the study of the developmental effect of genes. Proc. VI Inter. Cong. Genet. *1*: 304–307.

E. L. TATUM and G. W. BEADLE

Crystalline *Drosophila* eye-color hormone

Edward Lawrie Tatum was born in Boulder, Colorado, in 1909. He received his Ph.D. in biochemistry from the University of Wisconsin in 1935, while serving as Assistant in Agricultural Chemistry and Bacteriology there from 1931 to 1936. The following year he spent in Utrecht as Fellow in Bacterial Chemistry, and then returned to the United States as a Research Associate of the School of Biology at Stanford University. He remained at Stanford until 1945, becoming an Assistant Professor in 1941, and then moved to Yale for three years, first as Associate Professor of Botany, then as Professor of Microbiology. 1948 saw him back at Stanford as Professor, and in 1956 Chairman, of the Biology Department. Since 1957 he has been a Professor at Rockefeller University. He is a member of the National Academy of Science, and received the Nobel Prize in Medicine and Physiology in 1958.

His research interests are in nutrition, the biochemistry and genetics of microorganisms, and biochemical genetics.

The development of eye color in *Drosophila* is known to be controlled by specific diffusible substance designated as v^+ and cn^+ hormones. Khouvine, Ephrussi and Chevais[1] and Tatum and Beadle[2] have shown that these substances are amino acid-like in nature. The former authors in testing various amino acids for v^+ hormone activity obtained results which indicated that tryptophane, when added to the larval food, was concerned with hormone production. This "tryptophane effect" was found to be due to the production by certain bacteria of a substance with v^+ hormone activity.[3]

[Previously published in *Science*, 91 (May 10, 1940): 458. Reproduced by permission of author and publisher.]

This bacterially produced v^+ hormone has now been obtained in a pure crystalline state. The bacteria were grown on an agar medium containing dead yeast, sugar and l-tryptophane. The agar and yeast were precipitated in 80 per cent. alcohol. The hormone was then taken up in a mixture of butyl alcohol, ethyl alcohol and water, and was finally precipitated from absolute butyl alcohol. It was then crystallized from 90 per cent. ethyl alcohol. The crystals are very light yellow, elongated plates, usually forming in rosettes. The elementary analysis (made under the direction of Dr. A. J. Haagen-Smit, of the California Institute of Technology) supports the empirical formula $C_{21}H_{34}N_2O_{14}$.

The crystalline hormone has an activity of approximately 20,000,000 v^+ units per gram[4] when a solution is injected into vermilion brown test

TABLE 1

Biological activity of crystalline v^+ hormone[4] (0.28γ injected per larva)

Times hormone recrystallized	Maximum eye-color value	v^+ units per fly	v^+ units per gram hormone
1	3.1	6	21,400,000
2	3.1	6	21,400,000
3	3.3	7	25,000,000
4	2.9	5	17,900,000

larvae. Table 1 shows that within the limits of accuracy of the biological test, repeated recrystallization does not change the activity.

REFERENCES

[1] Y. Khouvine, B. Ephrussi and S. Chevais, *Biol. Bull.*, 75:425, 1938.

[2] E. L. Tatum and G. W. Beadle, *Jour. Gen. Physiol.*, 22:239, 1938.

[3] E. L. Tatum, *Proc. Nat. Acad. Sciences*, 25:486, 1939.

[4] See reference cited in footnote 2 for significance of eye-color values and units.

E. L. TATUM and A. J. HAAGEN-SMIT

Identification of *Drosophila* v+ hormone of bacterial origin

Arie Jan Haagen-Smit was born in Utrecht, Holland, in 1900. He studied at the University of Utrecht, receiving his Ph.D. in organic chemistry in 1928, and served there as Head Assistant and later Lecturer in Organic Chemistry until 1936. The following year he worked in biological chemistry at Harvard University, and then went to the California Institute of Technology as Associate Professor of Biochemistry. In 1940 he became a Professor, and in 1965 Director of the Plant Environment Laboratory, at the same Institute. He is a member of the Royal Netherlands Academy of Science.

His research interests lie in the areas of the chemistry of natural products, and air pollution.

The production of the brown pigment component of *Drosophila* and certain other insect eyes is controlled by diffusible substances, termed eye color hormones. These are sequentially related in *Drosophila* as follows:

$$\text{Precursor} \rightarrow v^+ \text{ hormone} \rightarrow cn^+ \text{ hormone} \rightarrow \text{brown pigment}$$

The properties of these eye color hormones and methods of testing them in *Drosophila* and other insects have been described by several workers (1—4). All the available evidence agrees in indicating their amino acid-like nature. It has been found (5) that certain bacteria can synthesize a substance which is active in *Drosophila* in replacing the first hormone in the

This work was supported in part by funds granted by the Rockefeller Foundation.
[Previously published in *Journal of Biological Chemistry*, 140 (1941): 575–80. Reproduced by permission of publisher and authors.]

series, the v^+ hormone. This substance is formed from tryptophane and has been isolated in pure crystalline form (6). During the time our investigation of the structure of this active substance was in progress, a note by Butenandt, Weidel, and Becker (7) appeared. These authors, following the lead offered by the bacterial synthesis from tryptophane, had systematically tested all known intermediates in tryptophane metabolism and found that *l*-kynurenine had v^+ hormone activity in *Drosophila* and in *Ephestia*. We have confirmed activity of *l*-kynurenine[1] in *Drosophila*. Kynurenine had previously been isolated and characterized by Kotake (8) who showed that it was a product of tryptophane metabolism by *Bacillus subtilis* and by mammals under certain conditions.

Our investigation of the structure of the bacterially produced substance has established that a sucrose derivative of *l*-kynurenine is formed, apparently an ester. The relation of the naturally occurring *Drosophila* v^+ hormone to kynurenine has not as yet been demonstrated, but the evidence indicates that these substances are at least very closely related. The activity of *l*-kynurenine and its production only from *l*-tryptophane make it probable that *l*-tryptophane is likewise the precursor of the *Drosophila* v^+ hormone.

Isolation of Crystalline Material

The preparation and isolation of the pure hormone of bacterial origin have been previously described (6). They involve the production of the substance by the *Bacillus* sp. grown on an agar medium containing *l*-tryptophane, sucrose, and dead yeast. The active substance was extracted from the medium with water-alcohol mixtures, and finally crystallized from hot 90 per cent ethyl alcohol. The yield is about 25 per cent of the theoretical from the *l*-tryptophane added.

Properties of Material

The bacterially produced hormone crystallizes in fine needles from alcohol, often arranged in rosettes. It has no definite melting point, but softens and decomposes, beginning at around 140°. It is optically active. The specific rotation of a 0.74 per cent solution in water is $+13.5°$. The substance is easily soluble in water, and in hot 90 per cent ethyl alcohol, and can be extracted from water by normal butyl alcohol, but is insoluble in absolute alcohols and in other organic solvents. Its activity is not lost on treatment with acid but is easily destroyed with alkali. A water solution gives a strong ninhydrin reaction. These properties agree with those reported for the naturally occurring fly hormones (4) indicating the close relationship.

---

[1] The authors wish to express their thanks to Dr. Clarence P. Berk, State University of Iowa, Iowa City, for his kindness in supplying the samples of *l*-kynurenine, *d*-kynurenine, *d*-tryptophane, and kynurenic acid used in this investigation.

Elementary Composition

The elementary analyses had been provisionally interpreted (6) as indicating an empirical formula of $C_{21}H_{34}N_2O_{14}$. However, the isolation of *l*-kynurenine and sucrose after hydrolysis of the material indicates that the alternative empirical formula $C_{23}H_{32}N_2O_{14}\cdot 2H_2O$ is correct. The material was dried in a high vacuum at 56° and analyzed.

$C_{23}H_{32}N_2O_{14}\cdot 2H_2O$.   Calculated: C 46.31, H 6.08, N 4.70
                        Found: C 46.77, H 6.40, N 5.28 (Dumas)
                                      C 46.49, H 6.39, N 5.11
                                                     N 4.78 (ter Meulen)[2]

That this formula and not a multiple thereof is correct was shown by determining the rate of diffusion through agar blocks, as previously described (4), the concentration in the different blocks being measured by the biological test method.

Hydrolysis with Alkali

Kynurenine is decomposed by hydrolysis with weak alkali with the production of NH_3. The bacterial hormone was inactivated on treatment with hot alkali. The theoretical yield of NH_4OH was obtained on hydrolysis of the material with 0.01 N NaOH.

   4.81 mg gave 0.625 cc 0.0136 N NH_4OH
   4.81 mg gave 0.622 cc 0.0136 N NH_4OH
   $C_{23}H_{32}N_2O_{14}\cdot 2H_2O$.   Calculated: N 2.35; found: N 2.48, N 2.47

Hydrolysis of kynurenine with stronger alkali causes a more complete decomposition in which *o*-aminoacetophenone is produced. This is also true of the bacterial hormone on treatment with hot 1 N NaOH. The *o*-aminoacetophenone, which is easily distinguished by its jasmine-like odor, was extracted from the hydrolyzed product with ether, dried in a vacuum, and the acetyl derivative made by treatment of the residue with acetic anhydride. The derivative was crystallized from alcohol. The acetyl derivative melted at 73° (uncorrected). The reported melting point is 75°.

Acid Hydrolysis

Kynurenine is stable towards acid hydrolysis, and forms an easily crystallizable sulfate. The bacterial product retains its activity on acid hydrolysis, but the sugar residue is removed. The kynurenine may be easily isolated as follows: A hot saturated solution of the bacterial compound in 90 per cent alcohol is made acid with 1 N N_2SO_4 and the solution kept hot for a few minutes. On cooling, kynurenine sulfate crystallizes out. This material

[2] The authors are indebted to Dr. C. B. van Niel for carrying out this determination as well as for many helpful suggestions and criticisms.

darkened at 165° and blackened completely at 180° without melting. The recrystallized material was dried at 80° for 12 hours and analyzed.

$C_{11}H_{10}N_2O_3 \cdot H_2SO_4 \cdot 2H_2O$.   Calculated: C 37.39, H 4.56, N 7.93
                                    Found: C 37.78, H 5.25, N 8.02
                                                       C 37.80, H 5.17

The bromine addition product was made by adding dilute bromine water to a water solution of the sulfate. The product was recrystallized from 50 per cent alcohol. It melted at 206–207° (decomposition). The melting point of the bromine compound made from authentic *l*-kynurenine was the same, as was that of a mixture of the two preparations. The recrystallized bromine derivative was dried at 100° for 24 hours and analyzed.

$C_{11}H_{10}N_2O_3Br_2 \cdot 2H_2O$.   Calculated: C 31.90, H 3.41, N 6.77
                                 Found: C 31.69, H 2.97, N 7.51, 7.68

Identification of Sucrose

A solution of the bacterial hormone reduces Fehling's solution only after acid hydrolysis. Estimation of the sugar as sucrose by determining the reducing power after hydrolysis gave the correct theoretical amount.

$C_{23}H_{32}N_2O_{14} \cdot 2H_2O$.   Calculated: Sucrose 57.3,
                               Found: Sucrose 58.7, 58.4

On hydrolysis with 0.01 N NaOH the sucrose is split from the molecule without further hydrolysis. The kynurenine is decomposed by the alkali and its decomposition products were removed from acid solution with butyl alcohol. The sugar concentration in the remaining solution was estimated to be 0.278 per cent by determining the reducing power on an aliquot after acid hydrolysis. The specific rotation of the sugar solution before, +67.2°, and after inversion, −21.5°, proved that it contained sucrose. The values for pure sucrose are +66.5° and −19.84°, respectively.

It was then found that a short treatment with 0.1 N acid in 90 per cent alcohol solution caused a splitting of the molecule into sucrose and kynurenine without leading to further hydrolysis of the sucrose. After the alcoholic solution was cooled and the crystallized kynurenine sulfate removed, the addition of a little absolute alcohol and ether cause the crystallization of sucrose from the solution. It was dried and analyzed.

$C_{12}H_{22}O_{11}$.   Calculated: C 42.1, H 6.5; found: C 42.0, H 6.6

Constitution of Intact Molecule

After the isolation and identification of both hydrolytic products of the bacterial hormone, *l*-kynurenine and sucrose, there is left only the question of how the two components are combined. No definitive information is available regarding the point of attachment on the sucrose molecule.

Neither carboxyl group can be titrated in water solution. This eliminates a possible linkage of the sugar through an amino group. Only 1 equivalent of aqueous alkali is required for titration in 95 per cent alcohol solution with phenolphthalein. This shows that only one carboxyl group is in equilibrium with a charged basic group, and indicates that the second carboxyl group is not free. It therefore seems probable that the sucrose is esterified with one of the carboxyl groups of kynurenine.

Biological Aspects of Kynurenine Production and Specificity

The production of the active substance by the bacteria is strictly limited to its formation from *l*-tryptophane. A number of related substances have been tested for their ability to replace *l*-tryptophane but all these were ineffective. They include indole, skatole, indoleacetic acid, indolepropionic acid, tryptamine, and *d*-tryptophane. The results showed that only *l*-tryptophane can be used for the bacterial synthesis.

As pointed out previously (5) this synthesis takes place from *l*-tryptophane only under aerobic conditions. It has also been found that it takes place only in the presence of an excess of carbohydrate, glucose or, preferably, sucrose. Presumably in the absence of carbohydrate, the kynurenine formed is further oxidized by the bacteria.

The biological activity in *Drosophila* is also quite specific. *d*-Kynurenine is inactive. Kynurenic acid is also inactive as either the v^+ or the cn^+ hormone.

The absolute activity of the various compounds of *l*-kynurenine has been determined by injection of solutions into vermilion-brown larvae.[3] The results were as follows:

Substance tested	Activity* units per mM $\times 10^6$
Known kynurenine	9
Kynurenine-sucrose derivative	12
Kynurenine sulfate from bacterial derivative	13

* See Tatum and Beadle (4).

It should be pointed out that the unavoidable experimental errors in the biological tests make this agreement quite acceptable.

SUMMARY

The substance produced by certain bacteria from *l*-tryptophane and which possesses v^+ hormone activity in *Drosophila* has been found to be a sucrose ester of *l*-kynurenine. The *l*-kynurenine is the essential active portion of the molecule.

[3] For details of testing and for definition of the unit of activity see Tatum and Beadle (4).

l-Kynurenine, *l*-kynurenine sulfate, and the *l*-kynurenine-sucrose derivative have the same molar activity when tested in *Drosophila* larvae. This value approximates 12×10^6 units per mM.

REFERENCES

1. Beadle, G. W., and Ephrussi, B., *J. Genetics*, 22: 76 (1937).
2. Ephrussi, B., *Am. Naturalist*, 72: 5 (1938).
3. Plagge, E., and Becker, E., *Biol. Zentr.*, 58: 231 (1938).
4. Tatum, E. L., and Beadle, G. W., *J. Gen. Physiol.*, 22: 239 (1938).
5. Tatum, E. L., *Proc. Nat. Acad. Sc.*, 25: 486 (1939).
6. Tatum, E. L., and Beadle, G. W., *Science*, 91: 458 (1940).
7. Butenandt, A., Weidel, W., and Becker, E., *Naturwissenschaften*, 28: 63 (1940).
8. Kotake, Y., *Ergebn. Physiol.*, 37: 245 (1935).

D. F. POULSON

Chromosomal control of embryogenesis in *Drosophila*

Donald Frederick Poulson was born in Idaho Falls, Idaho, in 1910. He received his Ph.D. in genetics from the California Institute of Technology in 1936. In 1936–1937 he was Research Assistant in the Department of Embryology at the Carnegie Institution, and then went to Yale as Instructor in Biology until 1940. In 1940 he became Assistant Professor, and later Associate Professor and Professor, at Yale. He was Gosney Fellow at the California Institute of Technology in 1949. In 1951 he served as research collaborator of the Biology Department of the Brookhaven National Laboratory. In 1957–1958 he was Fulbright Senior Research Scholar of the Commonwealth Scientific and Industrial Research Organization, Canberra, and Fellow of the Guggenheim Memorial Foundation.

His research interests are in cytology, the genetics of *Drosophila*, the embryology and developmental physiology of insects, and the mineral metabolism of invertebrates.

Any full analysis of development and differentiation must rest ultimately on the nature of the hereditary materials, the genes, their reproduction and their activities in the physiological economy of the cell. In spite of the work directed toward the elucidation of the former two, we are in possession of very scanty direct knowledge of the genes themselves. Like other entities of science they are better known by what they do. This and other earlier symposia attest to that. Happily, the day is past when the view that genes have something to do with cellular physiology and development had

[Previously published in *The American Naturalist*, 79 (1945): 340–63. Reprinted by permission of the author and publisher.]

130

to be fought for, and genus versus the cytoplasm raised the heat both of argument and of temper. The preceding papers in this series give rather full accounts of the integral place of genes in the synthetic activities of cells and the interaction between genes and primers which place us in a very advantageous position in considering the problems of development and differentiation. It is the object of this paper to present evidence obtained by approaching these problems in a different way which, together with the above, leads to the closer merging of the disciplines of genetics, embryology and biochemistry.

In the years of research on *Drosophila melanogaster*, especially since the introduction by Muller (1927) of the x-ray technique for the production of mutation, a splendid set of materials has been accumulated for the genetical analysis of developmental processes, but it is only recently that the potentialities of certain types of these materials have begun to be appreciated. The classical method has been to infer the normal activities of a gene by study of differences in effects between alleles. This suffers from the limitations of providing only partial information, and gives often a superficial or even erroneous picture of what a gene is really doing. Ideally, the best approach would be to inactivate completely, or to remove, one gene at a time and investigate the biochemical and developmental consequences. This has undoubtedly been accomplished in some, or perhaps in many, of the cases reported by Horovitz, Bonner, Mitchell, Tatum, and Beadle. However, it is very difficult to distinguish cytologically any changes in the chromosomes of *Neurospora* which would indicate losses or rearrangements of genes. In *Drosophila*, on the other hand, the giant chromosomes of the salivary glands do enable us to distinguish cytological changes on a relatively fine scale. In this respect *Drosophila* has an advantage over *Neurospora*, in establishing the functions of parts of the chromosomes in relation to the standard genetic maps built up by Morgan, Bridges, Sturtevant, and others.

The analysis of mutant types in *Drosophila* has proved that these are not always the result of gene mutation in the ordinary sense, but may represent deficiencies or duplications of greater or lesser portions of chromosomes. In some cases the mutant type is associated with more complex rearrangements in the chromosomes. Rearrangements without gross phenotypic manifestations are also known. But, as clearly foreshadowed by the classical research of Theodor Boveri (1902), most chromosomal deficiencies are lethal when homozygous. Conversely a large proportion of what have been called lethal genes have proved to be deficiencies. Lethal genes have always commanded the interest of the embryologist and have illumined many developmental problems. Witness the work of Bonnevie, Chase, Chesley, Danforth, Dunn, Glücksohn-Shoenheimer, Grüneberb, Mohr, and Wright on mammalian lethals. When a lethal is known to be a

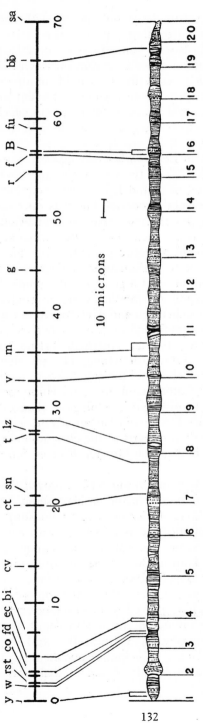

Figure 1. Linkage and salivary gland chromosome maps of the X-chromosome of *D. melanogaster* to show the relative positions of a number of loci. Symbols of the mutants referred to in the text are: y: yellow; w: white; rst: roughest; fa: facet; sn: singled; lz: lozenge; r: rudimentary; fu: fused; sa: spindle attachment region. The numbers below the linkage map give the distances in terms of crossover units from the tip of the X. The numbers beneath the salivary gland chromosome designate the regions according to the system of Bridges. (Adapted and redrawn after Bridges.)

deficiency the simplest explanation of the lethal effects is that the loss involves a gene or genes concerned with some essential processes.

The large number of X-chromosome deficiencies and translocations in *Drosophila melanogaster* and the relative ease with which they may be handled led to the choice of the X-chromosome (Fig. 1), as the starting point for the investigation of the chromosomal control of developmental processes. By appropriate crosses it is possible to obtain zygotes which lack greater or lesser parts of a given chromosome Fig. 2). The missing part may range in size from an entire element to less than a single band of a giant chromosome. Since these deficiencies are almost always lethal to the organism, a means of evaluating the functions of a gene in normal development is made possible by the analysis of the upsets leading to the death of the zygote carrying them. The types of embryological upsets are differ-

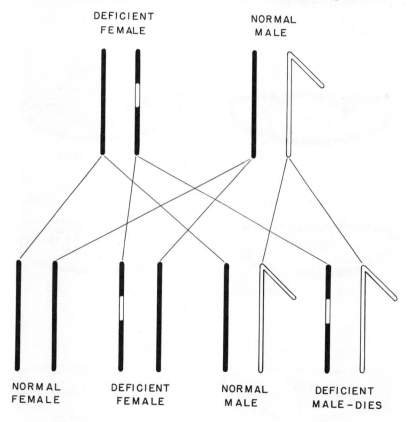

Figure 2. The inheritance of X-chromosome deficiencies through heterozygous females. Of the four classes of zygotes only the deficient male dies at some point in development depending on the deficiency. The embryology of the others is normal.

ent in the several cases studied and make it evident that a large number of chromosomal regions are concerned in embryogenesis. In all the cases considered here the lethal effects appear in the egg stage and have been determined by examining living and fixed eggs from deficiency stocks at successive times after fertilization. This is readily done, as the larva of *Drosophila* normally hatches from the egg within twenty-four hours after fertilization.

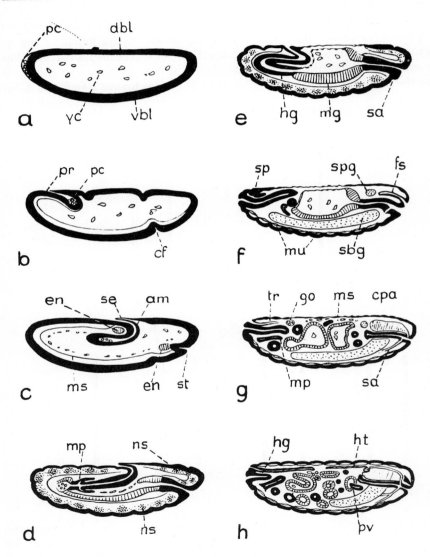

Normal Development

The sequence of embryonic development in Drosophila (Fig. 3), and the higher Diptera is briefly as follows.[1] Fusion of the pronuclei takes place in the anterior portion of the egg followed by seven or eight mitoses after which the number of pre-blastoderm, or cleavage nuclei, reaches about 256. The nuclei first become distributed more or less uniformly through the egg and are connected by cytoplasmic strands and bridges among the yolk spheres and granules. The nuclei then begin a migration into the cortical cytoplasm of the egg. Those which reach the posterior polar plasm are differentiated almost at once to become pole cells, the future germ cells.

The nuclei which reach the cortical layer elsewhere become the blastoderm nuclei (Fig. 4a). Those which remain in the central portion of the egg become the so-called yolk or vitellophag nuclei. After several more mitoses of the blastoderm nuclei cleavage of cytoplasm between the nuclei begins and in a short time a cellular blastoderm is established surrounding the central yolk (Fig. 4d). In the third hour of development foldings in the blastoderm lead to the inturning of mid-ventral cells which constitutes gastrulation, separating outer and inner layers (Fig. 3b). Anterior and posterior portions of the latter give rise to the mid-gut and are therefore referred to as endoderm. Most of the inner layer gives rise to the mesodermal derivatives. At the posterior end of the gastrular furrow the proctodaeum is invaginated; slightly later at the anterior end, the stomodaeum. The dorsal portion of the blastoderm becomes mostly embryonic membrane. The germ band thus laid down increases in length and extends around posteriorly to the dorsal side of the egg, folding up the membranes until the proctodaeum lies just back of the head (Fig. 3c). When this ex-

Figure 3. Outline of morphogenesis and organogenesis in Drosophila from the blastoderm stage to the larva ready to hatch. Blastoderm and ectodermal derivates shown in black, nervous system dotted; the midgut is cross-lined; the mesoderm unlined: (a) blastoderm (2nd hr); (b) gastrulation (3rd hr); (c) extended germ band (4th–6th hr); (d) later germ band showing nervous system (8th hr); contraction of the germ band (11th hr); (f) embryo following contraction (12th hr); (g) differentiation in embryo (16th hr); (h) larva before hatching (22nd hr). Abbreviations: am: amnion; cf: cephalic furrow; cpa: cephalopharyngeal apparatus; dbl: dorsal blastoderm; en: endoderm rudiments of midgut; fs: frontal sac; go: gonad; hg: hind-gut; ht: heart or dorsal vessel; mg: midgut; mp: malpighian tubule; ms: mesoderm; mu: muscle; ns: nervous system; pc: pole cells or germ cells; pr: protodaeum; pv: proventriculus; sa: salivary gland and duct; sbg: suboesophageal ganglion; se: serosa; sp: spiracle; spg: supra-oesophageal ganglion or commissure; st: stomodaeum; tr: trachea; vbl: ventral blastoderm; yc: yolk cells. Only sagittal sections are shown.

[1] This account is based on the work of Huettner (1923, 1924), Parks (1936), Poulson (1937, 1940a, and in press), Rabinowitz (1941), and Sonneblick (1941, and in press).

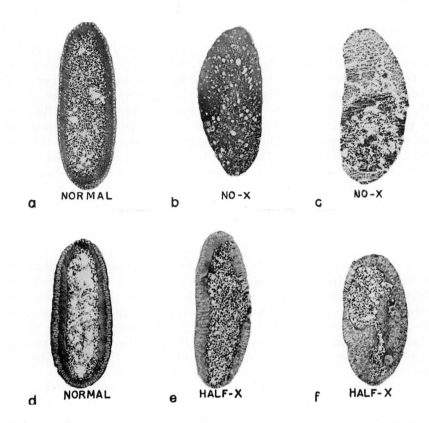

Figure 4. Early development of normal and deficient zygotes: (a) normal embryo just before the establishment of the blastoderm; (b) nullo-X egg at the end of migration showing nuclei at periphery only in anterior half of unincorporated cytoplasm and yolk in posterior part of egg; (d) normal embryo at the time of completion of the blastoderm with cell boundaries fully established; (e) one type of half-X deficient zygote showing incomplete and abnormal blastoderm; (f) the other type of half-X deficiency which becomes abnormal at the time of gastrulation. Photographs of longitudinal sections or iron-hematoxylin preparations. (Enlarged 112 times.)

tension is completed certain cells all along the ventral midline of the embryo become enlarged to form neuroblasts and move beneath the other ventral cells which will become hypoderm or other ectodermal structures (Fig. 3d). The division of neuroblasts involves unequal cytoplasmic division, the smaller products becoming ganglion cells. While this process of neurogenesis is going on groups of ectodermal cells invaginate segmentally to give the tracheal pits from which the tracheal system will arise. These provide the first external evidences of body segmentation, except for the boundary between head and trunk which is present from gastrulation on. Anteriorly lateral groups of ectoderm cells slowly invaginate to form the salivary glands and become pulled in through the stomodaeum.

The mesoderm spreads out between the ectoderm and the developing gut and later separates into somatic and visceral portions. The two mid-gut rudiments approach each other and eventually enclose the yolk which is surrounded by the yolk cells (Fig. 3c and d). The embryo then undergoes a shortening during which the body segmentation becomes clearly apparent and the posterior end of the embryo retreats from behind the head to its more natural position (Fig. 3e and f). The lateral tissues grow out to complete the dorsal portions of the embryonic trunk.

By this time, 11 to 12 hours after fertilization, the principal processes of morphogenesis and organogenesis are completed and subsequent development consists largely of differentiation. There are no further mitoses in any purely larval tissue after this time. All subsequent growth and differentiation of larval tissues proceeds without cell division. In this period the pharyngeal apparatus, the body and visceral musculature, the dorsal vessel and fat bodies are formed, and the chitinization of skin and tracheae takes place (Fig. 3g). During this period the imaginal discs make their appearance, those of the head being distinguishable first. The fully formed larva (Fig. 3h) hatches from the egg between 20 and 24 hours after fertilization depending on the temperature.

Effects of Large Deficiencies

The removal of an entire chromosome has long been known to be lethal, but this was clearly established for the first and fourth chromosomes of *Drosophila* by Li (1927) in his studies on the effects of chromosome rearrangements. Li did not make any developmental analysis beyond determining that mortality was in the egg stage. If zygotes lacking an entire X-chromosome are studied embryologically (these constitute one fourth of the eggs of attached X-females in *Drosophila*) developmental derangements are first evident in the cleavage stages of the egg (Poulson, 1940a). These lead to an abnormal distribution of the nuclei, which remain principally in the anterior half of the egg (Fig. 4b). Although there is cleavage of cytoplasm to form cells, no blastoderm is produced. The result, after several hours, is an anterior cell mass showing no morphogenetic advances and no differentiation. There is usually a clear stratification of the egg into cellular parts, unincorporated cytoplasm, and yolk (Fig. 4c). Yolk nuclei are frequent, but pole cells are rarely produced. The cells of the anterior mass continue division for some hours, becoming progressively smaller and evidently engaging in little or no synthetic activity. Concomitant physiological changes in nullo-X eggs are discussed below and illustrated in Fig. 8. Such drastic upsets as these, in which the whole pattern for further development is deranged, might well be expected when approximately one fifth of the egg's normal complement of genes is removed from the field of action. What will happen in cases of other deficiencies can scarcely be predicted except that, if these are large, the effects will be early and extensive. This is doubtless true for the large autosomes 2 and 3.

Among eggs produced when the X-chromosome is broken in two by a translocation near its center, T (1:4) A1, also known as the CRB translocation, are some deficient for the region between lozenge and the spindle attachment (Fig. 1) and some deficient for the remainder of the chromosome between lozenge and the left end. In each of these cases the morphological upset is drastic and early, but the two portions of this chromosome have clearly different effects. In one (the X_R deficiency ?) these are somewhat similar to the nullo-X (Fig. 4e) in that the distribution of nuclei is disturbed. This leads to the production of an incomplete blastoderm, the cells of which meet a fate much like that of those in the nullo-X eggs. In the other type of egg (X_L deficient ?) a blastoderm is formed, but separation of the germ layers fails (Fig. 4f). Morphogenetic movements are abortive and the embryo ends up as a sac of undifferentiated cells. In both instances cell division continues for some hours, although cytological abnormalities are common.

These large deficiencies clearly show that the X-chromosome has a great deal to do with very early embryonic processes, but it is necessary to turn to smaller deficiencies to separate the effects of the individual regions and individual genes.

The Notch and White Deficiencies

Equally significant and no less spectacular effects have been found in instances of very much smaller deficiencies such as can be demonstrated only with the aid of the giant chromosomes of the salivary glands. Of the many deficiencies obtained in experiments by Dr. M. Demerec, of the Carnegie Institution of Washington, the most extensive series are those involving the loci of white and facet near the left end of the X-chromosome (Figs. 1 and 7). Stocks of these provided by Dr. Demerec, whose kindness is gratefully acknowledged, have made it possible to study in detail a region of the X-chromosome which controls certain very fundamental morphogenetic processes (Poulson, 1940a, b; in press). These deficiencies range in size from one removing 45 bands to those in which no visible loss is apparent. Three principal categories of deficiencies are shown in Fig. 7, those which lack both the white and facet loci, and those which lack white only or facet only.

Embryological studies clearly show that the disturbances in each of the three white deficiencies are essentially the same type. Irrespective of the size of the deficiency, organs of ectodermal origin appear to be more or less normal, but those of endodermal and mesodermal nature show clear ab-

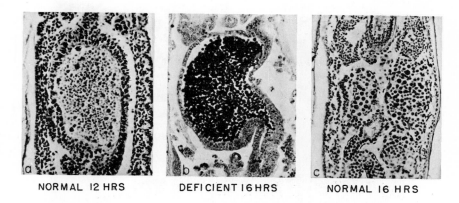

NORMAL 12 HRS   DEFICIENT 16HRS   NORMAL 16 HRS

Figure 5. The abnormal gut and mesoderm of a white-deficient embryo compared with normals: (a) frontal section of a normal embryo at 12 h showing the
midgut as a large sac and the beginning of the differentiation of the body musculature to the right; (b) frontal section of a deficient embryo at 16 hours,
showing only slight morphological advance in the gut, the absence of gut musculature and degeneration of body muscles; (c) frontal section of a normal
embryo at 16 hours showing convolutions of midgut and presence of gut musculature. Photographs *a* and *c* from Bodian preparations, *b* from iron-hematoxylin preparation. (Enlarged 272 times.)

normalities. These become evident between the 12th and 16th hours of
development. Instead of transforming into a long convoluted tube the mid-
gut remains of large undifferentiated sac without any musculature, in striking contrast to the normal condition, as in Fig. 5. This failure of differentiation of the gut is correlated with a failure of the body musculature,
which begins to be laid down and then degenerates. (The same is true for
aorta, fat bodies, etc.) Such embryos, while still alive at the hatching time
of normal larvae, never emerge from the egg, and the yolk remains largely
unutilized in the mid-gut. This is evidence that a gene or genes in the region of 3C1–3C2.3, which is that common to all three deficiencies, is
concerned in the development and differentiation of mesoderm and endoderm.

The facet, or Notch, deficiencies, Fig. 7, all lead to an earlier and
more drastic series of disturbances in which each of the germ layers is involved. The most conspicuous of these abnormalities is that far too many
neuroblast cells are formed from the ventral and cephalic ectoderm so
that there is little or nothing left which can give rise to skin and other ectodermal derivatives. The embryo develops a nervous system which has a
total volume of cells at least three times that of normal, Fig. 6. This hypertrophied nervous system shows considerable differentiation, but the patterns
of the ganglia and fiber tracts are markedly deranged (Poulson, 1943).

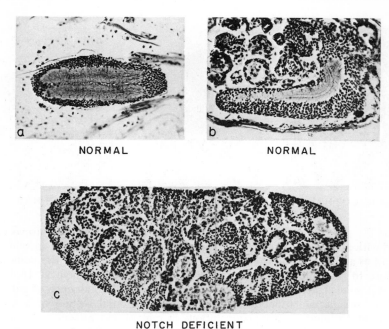

NORMAL   NORMAL

NOTCH DEFICIENT

Figure 6. Notch-deficient embryo and its nervous system compared with the nervous system of normal embryos: (a) frontal section of the highly condensed ventral nervous system of a normal embryo just before hatching; (b) sagittal section of ventral nervous system in a normal embryo of the same age as *a;* (e) sagittal section of a Notch-deficient embryo showing the hypertrophied nervous system, absence of ventral hypoderm, incomplete midgut, and abnormal mesoderm. Photographs from Bodian preparations. (Enlarged 310 times.)

There is no condensation such as typifies the later embryonic period in normal embryos. The nervous system remains naked and uncovered by any outer layer. Only the more lateral and dorsal parts of the hypoderm develop. Tracheal trunks are usually present dorsolaterally and are characteristically chitinized.

The rudiments of the mid-gut fail to unite to form a proper alimentary tract, Fig. 6, and the yolk remains unenclosed by any gut. The yolk mass may occupy any of a number of positions. In Fig. 6c it is seen to lie mid-ventrally, the nervous system being bent around it. The fore-gut is rudimentary and associated structures, such as salivary glands and frontal sac, are lacking. Curiously enough the proventriculus, at the point of union of the fore- and mid-guts, is well developed. The hind-gut is more nearly normal and considerably convoluted. Malpighian tubules are usually present.

The mesoderm remains more or less undeveloped, and muscles, heart, fat-body, etc., are not produced. Partially differentiated spindle-shaped

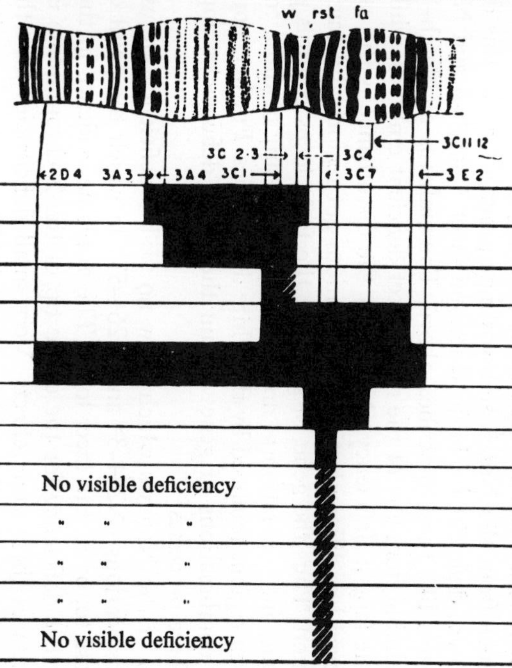

DEFICIENCY	CYTOLOGICAL EXTENT	EMBRIOLOGICAL EFFECT		
		TISSUES AND ORGANS FROM		
		Endoderm	Mesoderm	Ectoderm
W 258 - 11		Abnormal gut	Incomplete musc.	Normal
W 258 - 14		"	"	"
W 258 - 45		"	"	"
NOTCH - 8		Incomplete gut	Undifferentiated	Giant nervous syst. Skin reduced
N 264 - 38		"	"	"
NOTCH - B	No visible deficiency	"	"	"
N 264 - 19		"	"	"
N 264 - 8	" " "	"	"	"
N 264 - 40	" " "	"	"	"
N 264 - 47	" " "	"	"	"
N 264 - 34 (T1, 3L)		"	"	"
N 264 - 53 (T1, 2L)	No visible deficiency	"	"	"

Figure 7. Summary of the cytological extent and morphological effects of the deficiencies referred to in the text. Data on cytological extent from work of Demerec, Slizynska, Sutton, and the author, summarized in Bridges and Brehme (1944). Black indicates visible deficiency; cross-lines no visible detectable deficiency, but definite genetical deficiency.

cells lying irregularly beneath the dorsal and lateral hypoderm are the nearest approach to muscles. Connective tissue is present.

All in all, a kind of hopeless monster is produced which can not develop beyond the embryonic stage, although its constituent cells and parts remain alive for some hours after normal hatching time. Since the results are the same both in the larger deficiencies and those which show nothing visibly missing, it is concluded that in all probability a single gene, which may be the normal allele of facet, is the controlling agent of the processes here deranged. The simplest hypothesis to account for the manifold effects of this gene is to assume that it is normally involved at the time of germ-layer separation and has its effects on the cells of the ventral blastoderm, or possibly only on those along the mid-line, the future mesoderm and endoderm cells. In the latter case, these, when turned under, fail to develop normally and so may influence the overlying ectoderm cells. If this is true it may mean that mesoderm normally plays a role in the induction of the insect nervous system, perhaps comparable in importance to that which it has in vertebrates. Little is known of the factors concerned in the development and differentiation of the arthropodan nervous system and the evidence from the Notch embryos may prove a step in this direction.

Embryos deficient for both white and facet (Notch–8 and N264–38) are monsters like those described above. The embryos of Notch–8 are indistinguishable from any of the other facet deficient embryos, while in the case of the largest deficiency (N264–38) the disturbance is the same, but there is even less differentiation in the various gut regions and tracheae are rarely found. Thus the gene, or genes, at the facet locus controls processes which come into operation at an earlier time than any of those controlled by genes in regions removed by the white deficiencies. Further, none of the genes or combinations of genes within the larger deficiencies appreciably modify these processes.

Two of the Notches which show no visible deficiency are associated with translocations (N264–34 and N264–53) in which the point of breakage is close to, or at, the facet locus. The available evidence in these cases suggests that deficiency for the entire tip of the X-chromosome including facet produces these same effects. Very small deficiencies near the tip of the X-chromosome investigated by Kaliss (1939) and by the writer (Poulson, 1940a) produce their effects very late in the embryo. Other deficiencies in this region reported by Demerec and Hoover (1936), Muller (1935), Sturtevant and Beadle (1936) and Sutton (1940) are the exceptional instances in which both the homozygote and the hemizygote are viable and fertile. Thus it would appear that of all loci at this end of the chromosome facet influences embryogenesis earliest and most extensively, then white and later the other loci. Other genes between bands 3E2 and 8B1 when removed with facet, 3C7, do produce an even greater dislocation of development as indicated in the X_L deficiency. The significance of these loci remains to be investigated with the aid of Notch deficiencies extending further to the right than any now available and with small deficiencies between facet and the locus of lozenge.

It is thus clearly demonstrated that different genes in the X-chromosome have quite different and often clearly separable embryogenetic effects. The individual and additive properties of most of these genes remain to be investigated step by step and related to the structure and chemistry of the chromosome.

The Physiological Effects of Deficiencies

A first step in relating the developmental effects of chromosomes to cellular physiology, in an organism whose cellular physiology is little known, is to obtain some knowledge of the overall metabolic activities in the developing zygote. Students of the physiology and biochemistry of development have been forced to make studies on large numbers of small eggs in order to have adequate material for the methods available. Provided the materials are uniform no special difficulty presents itself. When, however, there is more than one genetic type among the zygotes it becomes imperative to investigate single eggs. The perfection of the Cartesian diver ultramicrorespirometer (Boell, Needham and Rogers, 1939; Boell and Needham, 1939) provided a means of determining the respiratory metabolism of single eggs of D. melanogaster.

A study of the oxygen uptake of normal fertilized eggs of Drosophila (Boell and Poulson, 1939; in press) shows that the consumption is almost uniform with time, having a slight tendency to increase with age during the first twelve hours of development. The rate of oxygen uptake averages 0.026 cu. mm. per egg per hour in the Oregon R wild strain, no sex difference being distinguishable. The rates in normal non-deficient eggs of other strains are of the same magnitude, but significantly different from the Oregon R wild strain. The respiratory rate of unfertilized eggs is lower from the beginning than that of normal eggs, the final value being 0.005 cu. mm. per egg per hour.

Among eggs from attached-X stocks (of which one fourth are nullo-X), the curves for individual oxygen uptake fall into two groups (Fig. 8), that in which the oxygen uptake is as described for fertilized eggs, and one in which it is much lower. Upon microscopic examination eggs with a normal oxygen uptake have always proved to be developing normally, those with a lower rate to be either unfertilized eggs or nullo-X zygotes. In eggs deficient for the X-chromosome respiration is indistinguishable at the outset from that of normal eggs. Several hours after fertilization the oxygen consumption has declined to a value one fifth that of normal eggs. This is maintained for at least 14 hours at a steady rate which is similar to the equilibrium value of unfertilized eggs. The period in which the rate of oxygen consumption is dropping coincides in time with the appearance

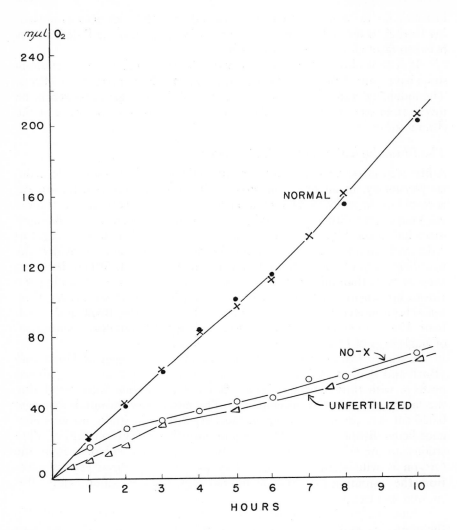

Figure 8. The oxygen uptake of normal, unfertilized, and deficient single eggs of *D. melanogaster* determined with the Cartesian diver ultramicrorespirometer. The time is in hours after the beginning of the experiment, which was seldom less than an hour after eggs had been laid. The oxygen uptake is given in milli-microliters at 25° C.

of the developmental abnormalities which characterize the nullo-X zygotes. The experimental data indicate that while developmental upset is accompanied by failure in respiration, the mechanism for oxygen uptake in deficient eggs is fully functional for a time immediately following fertilization. Furthermore, the cytological studies on nullo-X referred to above

(Poulson, 1940a) show that cell division continues for some hours after the oxygen uptake has dropped to the final value. This raises a number of questions about the role of oxygen uptake in cell division which cannot be discussed fully here (see Needham, 1942). What is clear is that cell division, though not increase in cell size or restoration of nuclear size (which means syntheses), can go on when the oxygen consumption is only one fifth that of normal eggs and of the same magnitude as in unfertilized eggs showing no signs of developmental activity. This suggests that an entire enzyme system has become inactive or has ceased to exist in the nullo-X zygotes. A comparison with the situation in other forms such as the echinoderms where Runnstrom (1930) showed that the respiration of unfertilized éggs is not sensitive to cyanide and is non-ferrous while that of fertilized eggs, proceeding at a much higher rate, is so, inevitably arises. There is also a parallel in the difference between normally developing and diapause eggs of the grasshopper elucidated by Bodine and Boell (1934). Until experiments with respiratory inhibitors have been carried out on the several types of *Drosophila* eggs we can say nothing more than that it is very probable that the difference between fertilized and unfertilized eggs which has been found is due to the inactivity or absence of the cytochrome, or Keilin-Warburg system, in the latter. The difference between normal and nullo-X zygotes is probably the same except that the system appears to be present and functional immediately following fertilization and goes out of action simultaneously with the appearance of the embryological disturbances in the deficient eggs.

Metabolic studies on the smaller deficiencies of the white-facet series have progressed only far enough to say that there are no gross respiratory differences such as just described. It seems unlikely that in these embryos in which morphogenesis and differentiation are proceeding, albeit abnormally, any large or overall effect on the respiratory metabolism would be discernible. The biochemical basis of these abnormalities will have to be approached by other methods.

Interrelations of Chromosomes and Cellular Physiology in Development

From the embryological and physiological observations which have been presented it is clear that the chromosomes are as much concerned in the processes of development and in cellular physiology as they are in hereditary transmission. This is precisely the picture derived from the *Neurospora* studies, and both emphasize the intimate relations between the chromosomes and the enzyme systems of the cell. In *Neurospora* the correspondence between individual genes and enzymes controlling unit processes in synthesis is very close. In *Drosophila* somewhat similar, but less direct, relations between genes and enzymes are indicated, especially by the investigations on the physiology of eye pigmentation (*cf.* review by

Ephrussi, 1942). In all instances the steps between the processes of cellular physiology and the visible ones of development and differentiation require elucidation.

How do genetically identical cells become differently differentiated? Relative positions and gradients (Child, 1941), by themselves, account for some differences and may result in changes in the physiology of a cell, but are not an adequate explanation for so many cases and types of highly specific differentiation. The relations between the chromosomes and units, or elements, in the cytoplasm are most certainly concerned in these cellular specializations. Wright (1941, 1945) has considered theoretically the ways in which genes and cytoplasmic units may be interrelated, and Rhoades (1943) and Sonneborn (1943) have provided specific instances in Zea and Paramecium. There are in Drosophila cases not unlike that which Sonneborn has presented. One is the sex-linked mutant fused (Fig. 1) studied by Lynch (1919). Homozygous fused females produce somewhat fewer eggs than heterozygotes and normals. When fertilized by the sperm of fused males (which are of normal fertility) the eggs of fused females, although they show some signs of embryogenesis, do not produce viable larvae. If fertilized by sperm from normal (not-fused) males they give rise to heterozygous females and normal (not-fused) males, but the fused males die as embryos. The nature of these developmental disturbances remains to be investigated with embryological methods. Another sex-linked mutant, rudimentary, differs from fused only in degree in this respect. Clancy and Beadle (1937) showed that the ovarian eggs of fused females and those of the mutants singed and female-sterile[2] are uninfluenced by the host when transplanted into normal females in larval stages. Thus no diffusible substance is involved within the stages investigated. The simplest hypothesis is that of non-diffusible plasmo genes, or primers, controlled or synthesized by the chromogenes, or nuclear genes, and transmitted through the cytoplasm of the egg. These are exhausted before egg production in singed and female-sterile, but persist in the fused female. Introduction of the normal nuclear gene through a normal sperm into the eggs of fused females starts the synthesis again. Thus the case of fused, as well as other instances of female sterility in which eggs are produced, deserves a thorough biochemical-embryological investigation. Whether any of these mutants may be due to cytological deficiency remains to be established, but it seems unlikely in certain of the cases, such as singed, in view of the numbers of alleles some of which are normal or approach normal in fertility.

Direct evidence of a control of the cytoplasm by the chromosomes is found in the nullo-X eggs (Fig. 4), where there is a breakdown of the cor-

---

[2] Eggs of singed females are abnormal in shape and size and do not develop; those of female-sterile homozygotes never become mature. The latter case may be different in nature from the others cited.

tical layer at the posterior end of the egg at and following the time of migration of the nuclei (Poulson, 1940a). Thus the functional integrity of the cytoplasm depends on the presence of the nucleus in these early stages.

Since there is clear evidence in insect eggs of cytoplasmic segregation during development—widely known in the cases of the pole cells and the neuroblasts—Rhoades' and Sonneborn's suggestions concerning the role of cytoplasmic elements in differentiation apply particularly well to Drosophila. It is not difficult to visualize how the development of a tissue such as the mesoderm, in the white-deficient zygotes (Fig. 5), might proceed normally up to the point at which the primer normally comes into play and then cease differentiating or even de-differentiate. The hypertrophied nervous system of the facet-deficient embryos might arise through a disturbance of cytoplasmic segregation at the time of determination of neuroblasts in the ventral ectoderm, just as well as by the overzealous organizer activity suggested previously. A precise application of this point of view in the analysis of the white and facet deficiencies should prove most illuminating, but will not be attempted here because of limitations of time and space.

Advances in our knowledge of the chemical nature of the chromosomes (Mirsky, 1943; Mirsky and Pollister, 1942, 1943; Gulick, 1944) and of certain cytoplasmic components (Claude, 1941, 1943) demonstrate that the former consist primarily of desoxyribosenucleohistones while the latter are in large part ribosenucleoproteins. The absence of the desoxyribosenucleic acids (Mirsky and Pollister, 1943) from the cytoplasm and the presence of the ribosenucleic acid in both nucleus and cytoplasm suggests that the synthesis of the latter takes place in the nucleus under the influence of the chromosome (Caspersson and Schultz, 1940). The discovery that a desoxyribosenucleic acid is the active substance in the transformations of pneumococcal types by Avery, MacLeod and McCarty (1944) indicates that such substances possess a high degree of specificity and structural complexity. The nucleotide or nucleoprotein nature of many enzymes or coenzymes and the intimate association of some of them with cytoplasmic structures fits very well into the general picture of a system of syntheses. How other types of enzymes such as those of the cytochrome system may be related to this is an important problem.

Ordinarily we do not determine the presence or absence of an enzyme directly, but only by whether or not a reaction or a step in a reaction which it catalyzes is completed. In both Neurospora and Drosophila the enzymes in gene controlled reactions are far from being identified. The biochemical mutants of Neurospora are maintained by supplying the missing products of synthesis. Whether the deficient zygotes in Drosophila can be made to develop if supplied with missing organic molecules or enzymes remains for the future. Even if this be accomplished there will remain unsolved the basic problem of how to pass from a knowledge of the nature of the secondary products of the chromosomes to the intimate structure of the chromosomes themselves, of integrating the isolated systems into the whole dynamic structure. It is a firm conviction of the writer that the patterns of development and differentiation of the organism are implicit in the functional architecture of the cell which in turn has its foundations in the ultimate structure of self-reproducing nucleoprotein systems, chief of which are the chromosomes. Only by filling in the patterns step by step and from level to level, while keeping clearly in mind that there are no boundaries in biological or other science—that genetics, embryology and biochemistry are all approaches to the same thing—can this difficult gap be bridged.

LITERATURE CITED

Avery, O. T., C. M. MacLeod, and M. McCarty 1944. *Jour. Exp. Med.*, 79: 137–158.

Bodine, J. H. and E. J. Boell 1934. *Jour. Cell. Comp. Physiol.*, 5: 97–113.

Boell, E. J. and J. Needham 1939. *Proc. Roy. Soc.*, B 127: 363–373.

Boell, E. J., J. Needham, and V. Rogers 1939. *Proc. Roy. Soc.*, B 127: 322–356.

Boell, E. J. and D. F. Poulson 1939. *Anat. Rec.*, 75 (suppl.): 65–66.

———— In press.

Boveri, T. 1902. V. P. M. G., 35: 67–90.

Bridges, C. B. and K. S. Brehme (Ed.) 1944. "The Mutants of *Drosophila melanogaster.*" Washington: Carnegie Inst. Wash. Publ. 552.

Caspersson, T. and Jack Schultz 1940. *Proc. Nat. Acad. Sciences*, 26: 507–515.

Child, C. M. 1941. "Patterns and Problems of Development." Chicago: Univ. of Chicago Press.

Clancey, C. W. and G. W. Beadle 1937. *Biol. Bull.*, 72: 47–56.

Calude, Albert 1941. *Cold Spring Harbor Symposium on Quant. Biol.*, 9: 263–270.

———— 1943. *Biol. Symposia*, Vol. X: 111–129. Lancaster: The Jaques Cattell Press.

Demerec, M. 1941. *Proc. 7th Int. Genet. Cong.*, 99–103. Cambridge: University Press.

Demerec, M. and M. E. Hoover 1936. *Jour. Hered.*, 27: 207–212.

Ephrussi, B. 1942. *Cold Spring Harbor Symposium on Quant. Biol.*, 10: 40–48.

Gulick, A. 1944. *Adv. in Enzymol.*, 4: 1–39.

Horovitz, N. H., D. Bonner, H. K. Mitchell, E. L. Tatum and G. W. Beadle 1945. *Am. Nat.*, 79: 304.

Huettner, A. F. 1923. *Jour. Morph.*, 37: 385–423.

———— 1924. *Jour. Morph. and Physiol.*, 39: 249–259.

Kaliss, N. 1939. *Genetics*, 24: 244–270.

Li, J. C. 1927. *Genetics*, 12: 1–58.

Lynch, C. J. 1919. *Genetics*, 4: 501–533.

Mirsky, A. E. 1943. *Adv. in Enzymology*, 3: 1–34.

Mirsky, A. E. and A. W. Pollister 1942. *Proc. Nat. Acad. Sciences*, 28: 344–352.

———— 1943. *Biol. Symposia*, Vol. X: 247–260. Lancaster: The Jaques Cattell Press.

Muller, H. J. 1927. *Science*, 66: 84–87.

———— 1935. *Jour. Hered.*, 26: 469–478.

Needham, J. 1942. "Biochemistry and Morphogenesis." Cambridge: University Press.

Parks, H. B. 1936. *Ann. Entom. Soc. Amer.*, 29: 350–392.

Poulson, D. F. 1937. "The Embryonic Development of *Drosophila melanogaster.*" Act. Sci. et Ind., 498, Paris: Hermann et Cie. 51 pp.

———— 1940a. *Jour. Exp. Zool.*, 83: 271–325.

———— 1940b. *Collecting Net*, 15: 172 (Abst.).

———— 1943. *Genetics,* 28: 86 (Abst.).

———— In press. *Genetics.*

Poulson, D. F. In press. Biology of *Drosophila,* Carnegie Inst. Wash. Publ.

Rabinowitz, M. 1941. *Jour. Morph.,* 69: 1–49.

Rhoades, M. M. 1943. *Proc. Nat. Acad. Sciences,* 29: 327–329.

Runnstrom, J. 1930. *Protoplasma,* 10: 106–173.

Slizynska, H. 1938. *Genetics,* 23: 291–299.

Sonnenblick, B. P. 1941. *Proc. Nat. Acad. Sciences,* 27: 484–489.

———— In press. Biology of *Drosophila,* Carnegie Inst. Wash. Publ.

Sonneborn, T. M. 1943. *Proc. Nat. Acad. Sciences,* 29: 329–338.

———— 1943. *Proc. Nat. Acad. Sciences,* 29:338–343.

———— 1945. *Am. Nat.,* 79: 318.

Sturtevant, A. H., and G. W. Beadle 1936. *Genetics,* 21: 554–604.

Sutton, E. 1940. *Genetics,* 25: 628–635.

Wright, S. 1941. *Physiol. Rev.,* 21: 487–527.

———— 1945. *Am. Nat.,* 79: 289.

III

INSECT ENDOCRINOLOGY

STEFAN KOPEĆ

Studies on the necessity of the brain
for the inception of insect metamorphosis

Stefan Kopeć was born in Warsaw in 1888. He studied at the Jagiellonian University in Cracow, where he received his Ph.D. in 1912. He
held the post of Senior Instructor in the Department of Zoology at the
University of Cracow from 1915 to 1918, and then became Head of
the Department of Animal Genetics, and later of the Department of
Experimental Morphology, at the Institute for Agricultural Manage-
ment in Pulawy, Poland. In 1929 he was made Director of the Institute. In 1932 he became Chairman of the Department of Biology of
the Medical School at the University of Warsaw, a post he held when
World War II began. He became a member of the Polish Underground,
was taken prisoner in February, 1941, and in March, together with his
son, was shot.

His research interests were in the areas of developmental physiology, nutrition, insect endocrinology, and developmental genetics.

Gudernatsch (1912, 1914) was the first to describe the acceleration of
metamorphosis in tadpoles fed on thyroid. These results were confirmed for
different amphibians by Laufberger (1913), Cotronei (1914), Brendgen
(1914), Abderhalden (1915, 1919), Kaufman (1917, 1918), Kahn (1916),
Hirschler (1918–19), etc., and first of all by Romeis (1914–19). Adler
(1916) ascertained that changes of temperature of the environment cause
changes of celerity of metamorphosis in tadpoles, together with simultaneous differences in the structure of the thyroid.

Paper from the Embryologico-Biological Laboratory, Jagiellonian University, Cracow,
Poland, presented in the Acad. of Sc., Cracow. *Cf. Bull. Acad. d. Sc. Cracovie*, 1917.
[Previously published in *Biological Bulletin*, 42 (June, 1922): 323–41. Reprinted by per-
mission of the publisher.]

153

The results of the investigations of Loeb (1896) and Wintrebert (1905–11), who cut the spinal cord or the nerves of larvae, contradict the influence of the brain on metamorphosis of amphibians, or at least the influence by means of nerves. On the other hand, Babák (1905) examined the brain of the toad and came to the conclusion that the hind part of the brain affects metamorphosis, since, when it is removed, the processes are arrested. He lays stress on the fact that the removal of the brain effects the changes described only in case the animal is operated upon before the first pair of limbs have grown. Babák (1913) believes that here we have the influence of hypophysis by means of chemical stimuli. Gudernatsch (1912, 1914) by feeding tadpoles on hypophysis did not bring about—it is true— any changes in the rate of development, but there is no doubt that feeding experiments with a certain organ may be considered as decisive only if their results are positive, a fact which is not well understood by certain investigators. In fact, Adler (1914), Smith (1916), and Allen (1916, 1917) confirm that the processes of metamorphosis in tadpoles are arrested by removal of the hypophysis, which, however, is accompanied by changes in the thyroid. On the other hand, Rogers (1918) and Larson (1919) described changes of the hypophysis brought about by removal of the thyroid in tadpoles, and Allen (1918) confirmed the fact that tadpoles deprived of their thyroid do not undergo metamorphosis. The question arises, therefore, whether the essential and decisive factor which regulates the transformation in those animals is the function of the hypophysis or of the thyroid. Hirschler (1918–1919) ascertained that metamorphosis is accelerated by injecting axolotls with iodoform or iodin. From the recent researches made by Swingle (1919a and b), who succeeded in transforming tadpoles deprived of their thyroid by feeding them on iodin with flour, as well as from his own analogous experiments, Allen (1919) draws the general conclusion that the metamorphosis of amphibians depends on iodin stored by the thyroid, and that its secretory function is regulated by the hypophysis.

The relationship of the ganglia of the head to metamorphosis in insects has been studied by Conte and Vaney (1911). These authors made ligatures between the head and the body of caterpillars of *Lymantria dispar* L. and obtained adult moths. They infer from their experiments that the ganglia of the head are of no importance for these processes. The following pages show, however, that their conclusion is false. We shall see that the brain (ganglion supra-œsophageale) exerts a great influence on metamorphosis of insects, and the cause of the erroneous conclusion will be clearly explained.

If we wish to investigate the relation which probably exists between the nervous system and the processes of metamorphosis of insects, we must first of all decide whether, after the removal of single parts of the nervous system, the rate of metamorphosis is in general the same as in normal animals, whether it undergoes acceleration or retardation, or whether it is completely arrested. The problem was to find out a possibly well-defined center which would have a more or less decisive influence on the time of inception or on the rate of metamorphosis. Further, we must consider the means by which this hypothetical influence could act on the processes of metamorphosis. The mechanism of this influence ought to be studied by means of special experiments, and the time at which the influence begins to act ought to be found out. In order to answer this question, I operated on female caterpillars of *Lymantria dispar* L. after their last moult. Thus I was able to consider only the processes of the pupation of caterpillars and the emergence of the adult moths, without taking into consideration the processes of the larval moult.

It must be distinctly remarked that the whole material, experimental as well as that used as a control, came from eggs of one female only. All the caterpillars were reared in precisely identical conditions. Moulting, pupation, and emergence of moths were controlled every 12 hours; thus the error in determining the length of life of caterpillars and chrysalids (see Tables 1 and 2) could not exceed 24 hours.

As to the methods of removal of single ganglia, cf. operations in my former paper (Kopeć, 1918).

A. *The influence of the Brain on the Inception of the Processes of Metamorphosis*

The behavior of caterpillars of *Lymantria dispar* L. deprived of their brain (ganglion supra-œsophageale) allows us to draw the conclusion that this ganglion has a quite specific quality, very important to the whole organism, and characterizing the brain as an organ which excites histolytical processes in the caterpillar and regulates the time of inception of the general processes of pupation. Let us consider the data given in Table 1, which refer to the pupation or to the death of caterpillars, whether normal, brainless, or those used as a control, viz., specimens which have been injured in the same manner as the caterpillars deprived of their brain, and which, in spite of the presence of the brain, refused food as well as the brainless specimens. All these specimens (exclusively females) were operated upon on the seventh day after their last moult and lived under the same conditions of heat, light, and humidity. We see that out of 25 brainless caterpillars only 5 underwent pupation, and in these the instant of beginning pupation exhibits a certain retardation in comparison with the behavior of the specimens used as a control. It is evident that the majority of the brainless caterpillars did not undergo metamorphosis, remained alive for weeks, and did not die until the whole store of fat in their body had been completely exhausted. Large full-blooded and fat caterpillars of 4–5 cm. in length became small during this period, and were often scarcely 1 cm. long in their final state. At the same time their bodies shrank and almost completely dried up, their movements became fainter and fainter, until at last they

TABLE 1

Behavior of the female caterpillars operated upon on the seventh day after their last moult

p. = pupation; d. = death of caterpillars

Caterpillars Deprived of the Brain			Caterpillars Deprived of the Subœsophageal Ganglion (Brain Intact)			Caterpillars Used as a Control; Injuries of the Head as in Caterpillars Deprived of Brain (Brain Intact)			Normal Caterpillars		
Number Corresponding to Each Specimen	Behavior of the Caterpillar	Number of Days the Pupa Lived till the Emergence of the Moth	Number Corresponding to Each Specimen	Behavior of the Caterpillar	Number of Days the Pupa Lived till the Emergence of the Moth	Number Corresponding to Each Specimen	Behavior of the Caterpillar	Number of Days the Pupa Lived till the Emergence of the Moth	Number Corresponding to Each Specimen	Behavior of the Caterpillar	Number of Days the Pupa Lived till the Emergence of the Moth
1	After $12\frac{1}{2}$ days p.	—	1	After $7\frac{1}{2}$ days p.	—	1	After $6\frac{1}{2}$ days p.	21	1	After $6\frac{1}{2}$ days p.	19
2	" $12\frac{1}{2}$ " p.	19	2	" $8\frac{1}{2}$ " p.	17	2	" $6\frac{1}{2}$ " p.	21	2	" 7 " p.	$20\frac{1}{2}$
3	" 14 " d.		3	" $8\frac{1}{2}$ " p.	17	3	" 7 " d.		3	" $7\frac{1}{2}$ " p.	20
4	" $14\frac{1}{2}$ " p.	17	4	" 9 " p.	$20\frac{1}{2}$	4	" $7\frac{1}{2}$ " p.	21	4	" $8\frac{1}{2}$ " p.	20
5	" $14\frac{1}{2}$ " p.	—	5	" $9\frac{1}{2}$ " p.	$18\frac{1}{2}$	5	" $7\frac{1}{2}$ " p.	—	5	" $8\frac{1}{2}$ " p.	$18\frac{1}{2}$
6	" 15 " d.		6	" $9\frac{1}{2}$ " p.	20	6	" 8 " p.	22	6	" $8\frac{1}{2}$ " p.	22
7	" 15 " d.		7	" 10 " d.		7	" 8 " p.	$20\frac{1}{2}$	7	" $8\frac{1}{2}$ " p.	20
8	" 15 " d.		8	" 10 " p.	$19\frac{1}{2}$	8	" 8 " p.	$18\frac{1}{2}$	8	" $8\frac{1}{2}$ " p.	18
9	" 16 " d.		9	" $12\frac{1}{2}$ " p.	16	9	" $8\frac{1}{2}$ " p.	22	9	" 9 " p.	$20\frac{1}{2}$
10	" 16 " d.		10	" $12\frac{1}{2}$ " p.	$19\frac{1}{2}$	10	" $8\frac{1}{2}$ " p.	—	10	" 9 " p.	17
11	" $16\frac{1}{2}$ " p.	21	11	" $12\frac{1}{2}$ " p.	18	11	" 9 " p.	$21\frac{1}{2}$	11	" 9 " p.	18
12	" 17 " d.		12	" 14 " p.	17	12	" 9 " p.	$22\frac{1}{2}$	12	" $9\frac{1}{2}$ " p.	18
13	" $17\frac{1}{2}$ " d.		13	" 14 " p.	19	13	" $10\frac{1}{2}$ " p.	21	13	" $9\frac{1}{2}$ " p.	17
14	" $17\frac{1}{2}$ " d.					14	" 11 " d.		14	" $9\frac{1}{2}$ " p.	17
15	" $21\frac{1}{2}$ " d.					15	" $11\frac{1}{2}$ " d.		15	" 10 " p.	$20\frac{1}{2}$
16	" $22\frac{1}{2}$ " d.					16	" 12 " p.	17	16	" 10 " p.	19
17	" $22\frac{1}{2}$ " d.								17	" 10 " p.	$21\frac{1}{2}$
18	" 23 " d.								18	" 13 " p.	19
19	" 23 " d.										
20	" 23 " d.										
21	" 25 " d.										
22	" 25 " d.										
23	" 27 " d.										
24	" 31 " d.										
25	" 31 " d.										

TABLE 2

Behavior of the female caterpillars operated upon on the tenth day after their last moult

p. = pupation; d. = death of caterpillars

	Caterpillars Deprived of the Brain			Caterpillars Deprived of the Subœsophageal Ganglion (Brain Intact)			Caterpillars Used as a Control; Injuries of the Head as in Caterpillars Deprived of Brain (Brain Intact)			Normal Caterpillars		
	Number Corresponding to Each Specimen	Behavior of the Caterpillar	Number of Days the Pupa Lived till the Emergence of the Moth	Number Corresponding to Each Specimen	Behavior of the Caterpillar	Number of Days the Pupa Lived till the Emergence of the Moth	Number Corresponding to Each Specimen	Behavior of the Caterpillar	Number of Days the Pupa Lived till the Emergence of the Moth	Number Corresponding to Each Specimen	Behavior of the Caterpillar	Number of Days the Pupa Lived till the Emergence of the Moth
	1	After 3 days p.	—	1	After 3½ days p.	21	1	After 4 days p.	19½	1	After 3 days p.	20
	2	" 3½ " p.	—	2	" 3½ " p.	—	2	" 4 " p.	20½	2	" 4 " p.	21
	3	" 4 " p.	21	3	" 4½ " p.	19½	3	" 5 " p.	19½	3	" 5 " p.	20
	4	" 4 " p.	22	4	" 5 " p.	18½	4	" 5½ " p.	19½	4	" 5 " p.	20½
	5	" 4 " p.	22	5	" 5 " p.	18½	5	" 5½ " p.	17½	5	" 5½ " p.	21
	6	" 4 " p.	21	6	" 5 " p.	17½	6	" 6 " p.	—	6	" 5½ " p.	20½
	7	" 4 " p.	21	7	" 7 " p.		7	" 6½ " p.	18	7	" 6 " p.	20
	8	" 4½ " p.	—	8	" 7 " d.		8	" 8½ " p.	—	8	" 6½ " p.	20½
	9	" 5½ " p.	21				9	" 9 " p.	17	9	" 8 " p.	19
	10	" 7 " d.	—				10	" 10½ " d.		10	" 8½ " p.	18½
	11	" 8 " p.	—									
	12	" 8½ " d.	—									
	13	" 9½ " p.	—									
	14	" 10 " p.	17½									
	15	" 10½ " p.	19									

died. Caterpillars deprived of their brain do not, as a rule, die after the operation as a result of any disease induced by the removal of the brain but, on the contrary, they live relatively very long. Only a few specimens die soon after operation as a consequence of mechanical injuries taking place during the removal of the brain. The essential difference between these insects and those used as a control lies only in the fact that histo-lytical processes subsequently followed by metamorphosis can begin only in animals the brain of which has exerted a proper stimulus at the proper time. It is certain that the few brainless caterpillars which succeeded in becoming pupæ attained the stage only because the brain had already in-fluenced the tissues before its removal. In this function, too, the animals exhibit individual fluctuations; here we evidently see specimens in which the brain had begun to perform its stimulative part very early, or had ex-erted it very quickly. It ought to be admitted that, if we could succeed in feeding brainless specimens, their life could be still longer. These cater-pillars, however, would probably not undergo metamorphosis.

The opinion that the brain is of importance for metamorphosis is supported by the following observations, which prove also that the influ-ence discussed sets in at a somewhat definite period, viz., in females of *Lymantria dispar* L. in my breed between the seventh and tenth day after their last moult. Let us observe the behavior of the caterpillars which were deprived of their brain not on the seventh day after the last moult as in investigations hitherto considered, but three days later. From Table 2 it is evident that here the percentages are quite different: almost all cater-pillars undergo pupation. The specimens which did not succeed in becom-ing pupæ lie no longer than the normal larvæ and their death evidently results from the injuries of the operation. In this case the metamorphosis of the caterpillars operated upon does not undergo any retardation.

The above-mentioned experiments of Conte and Vaney (1911) must have been performed on such older specimens. In my previous paper (Kopeć, 1912), in which, like the authors mentioned, I stated that the nervous system is unimportant up to the time of pupation, I relied only on full-grown specimens; in view of my present data, the former opinion can no longer be upheld. It follows from further operations that none of the other nervous ganglia (in contrast to the brain) has any influence on the time of pupation.

The dependence of the metamorphosis of the insect on its brain, already discussed, and its independence of the other ganglia, may be ob-served in one and the same specimen by means of a special method of cutting the caterpillars. Having made ligatures with strong silk round the body of the caterpillar into places chosen *ad libitum*, and having made a section between the ligatures, we may obtain two separate parts from one caterpillar, both of which are able to live. For instance, in one series of experiments the caterpillars were operated upon 7 days after their last moult, and it was found that the parts composed of the head and a few segments of the larval body attained the stage of pupation in from 7 to 9 days after the time of operation. Larger or smaller parts of the hind segments of the body devoid of the brain did not succumb till 35 days after the operation, but at death they exhibited no traces of histolytical processes. When caterpillars a few days older were operated upon both fragments underwent pupation at the normal time.

B. *The Nature of the Influence Exerted by the Brain on the Course of Metamorphosis*

If the influence exerted by the brain on the course of metamorphosis were by means of nerves, it might be supposed that the removal of the suboesophageal ganglion would have the same effect as the removal of the brain, as in this case the continuity between the brain and the remainder of the central nervous system is disturbed. But the corresponding data of Tables 1 and 2 prove that in this case the insects behave normally. The behavior of insects which have been deprived of two or three successive ganglia of the thorax or of the abdomen was also similar: both parts of the body, the part situated in front of the place of operation and that behind it, attained the stage of pupation simultaneously, although the connection between the central nervous system of the two parts had been quite destroyed. After several trials, I convinced myself that processes of regeneration never occur, such as would be able to produce a new nervous communication between the two parts.

At most it must be admitted that the brain is connected with the part of the nervous system situated behind the place of operation by means of the "intestinal nervous system," which is composed of very small ganglia lying in the tissue surrounding the œsophagus and connected in front with the brain. (The "sympathetic nervous system" of the caterpillar undergoes rupture during the removal of the ganglia of the nervous chain. For corresponding anatomical data see the paper of Cattie, 1880.) Owing to the unusually small size of the intestinal system, it was impossible to study it in greater detail by operating. On the other hand, I do not consider it possible that any nervous conduction between the two parts of the larval body operated upon can take place, since I observed several times that the part of the body behind the segment deprived of its nervous ganglion does not respond to any stimuli exerted on the fore-part of the caterpillar operated upon, and *vice versa*. The fore-segments of the operated body may be sharply pinched, injured, cut, or burned, still the hind part does not perform even the slightest movements referable to the stimuli, although under normal conditions even slight excitations of any part of the body produce violent reflexes. In regard to this, there seems to be no doubt that the fore-part of the body of the operated caterpillars is in no nervous connection with the part situated beyond the place of operation. It is, there-

fore, most probable that the brain does not influence the general processes of metamorphosis through the nerves, but that it has rather the
function of an organ of internal secretion, in that it affects the organism
by means of a substance (or substances) which may be supposed to pass
into the blood of the caterpillar from the brain at a certain stage of the
larval life. Experiments bearing on the transplantation either of the organized brain or of its matter might perhaps decide whether this conclusion
is true. It is most probable that the chemical substance (or substances)
here acting is the ferment called "thyrosinase," the aggregation of which
during the pupation of insects and the disappearance of which at the end
of the pupal life has been previously noticed by Dewitz (1905, 1916) and
more recently by Steche and Waentig (1913). In his numerous papers
Dewitz long ago ascribed an important "role" to "thyrosinase" in meta-
morphotic processes.

The mere observation that the brain has an influence on the inception
of histolytical processes in the body of caterpillars gives no idea as to the
physiological nature of this influence. The method of removal of the brain
from the larval body was not adapted to ascertain whether the proper
stimulus effected by the brain is the only factor which excites histolytical
processes in the body of the caterpillar, or whether certain physiological
changes which appear in the organism coöperate spontaneously and independently of the brain in the same direction. In other words, does the
larval organism undergo metamorphosis exclusively because of the stimulus
derived from the brain, or is the brain able to act only when certain physiological changes occur in the tissues of the caterpillar, changes without
which the influence of the brain must remain powerless? The investigation
in this direction had to be made by transplanting the organs of young
caterpillars in which these hypothetical physiological changes in the tissues
themselves had not yet occurred onto full-grown caterpillars, in which the
influence of the brain on the excitement of metamorphosis might already
be noticed. Should the grafted organs exhibit acceleration in their development as a consequence of their new surroundings, the metamorphosis of
the insects would have to be considered as dependent primarily on the
brain, the latter having caused the transformation of the larval organs independently of their age or physiological development. Should this hypothesis
prove false, the coöperation of stimulus of the brain and of the physiological conditions of larval tissues (without which the influence of the
brain would have no effect) would appear to be indispensable.

For these transplantations I used the sexual glands. The gonads of
moths do not belong to those organs which develop in the chrysalis from
the special imaginal discs; they are formed by the growth and histological
changes of the small larval sexual glands whose existence has been observed
for a long time in caterpillars. All four ovarial tubes of caterpillars hitherto
contained in a connective tisue membrane and forming together with it

one apparently globular body grow during the caterpillar's pupation to such a degree that they break out of the membrane. In the testes, on the other hand, the characteristic high cylindrical epithelium which lines the interior of that part of the developing spermiduct adjacent to the testicles is formed at that period from the uniform mass of imperfectly separated cells situated at the base of the gland. At the same time the testicle shrinks considerably and its contents become much compacter. I mention these facts in somewhat greater detail than usual in order to emphasize that, although they do not develop from imaginal discs, the sexual glands exhibit certain distinct evolutive changes during their development. As a consequent of this the study of the behavior of the organs after the transplantation is quite suitable for our present purpose. The ovaries and testicles of caterpillars after the third or fourth moult were transferred to full-grown caterpillars which were to undergo pupation in a few days. Hence, in these caterpillars, the substance which excites histolytical processes had already passed over from the brain into the body. It was found that the rate of evolution of the testes and the ovaries grafted remained unchanged, notwithstanding the new surroundings in which the processes of metamorphosis were just beginning or had already begun. From this follows the important conclusion that the stimulus of the brain is inadequate for metamorphosis of the separate organs of insects, and that it is only able to act when the organism, having attained a certain stage of development, is prepared physiologically to respond to the stimulus.

C. The Independence of the Further Processes of Metamorphosis

I have already mentioned that the brain exerts an influence on the inception of processes of metamorphosis at a certain definite period of the larval life, in females of Lymantria dispar L. of my breed between the seventh and tenth day after their last moult. The question arises as to whether this influence, which excites the inception of histolytical processes in caterpillars, at the same time makes the further course of metamorphosis possible, leading to the formation of the imago; or whether brainless chrysalids are unable to become moths. When the caterpillar has been influenced by the brain sufficiently to undergo pupation, the further evolutive processes, which take place in chrysalids, have been shown to occur independently of the brain. By comparing the data relative to the length of life of the chrysalids in various specimens (brainless, those used as standard, and normal) we see, moreover, that even the rate of formation of the imago from the chrysalis undergoes neither retardation nor acceleration when the brain is removed (cf. Tables 1 and 2). If a caterpillar deprived of its brain undergoes pupation, the emergence of the moth from the chrysalis takes place at the normal time. The removal of the brain or of other ganglia has merely a local effect in that (as I want to point out in another paper) muscles are completely or almost completely absent in the corresponding segments. The absence of muscles, however, is the result of merely local correlation between the presence of the imaginal muscles and that of the nervous ganglion in a segment of the body, but it has no connection with the influence under discussion—i.e., the influence of the larval brain on the *whole* histolytical and evolutive processes during the metamorphosis of insects in all tissues of the *whole* body.

The following experiments were made to demonstrate the above principle, viz., that the further metamorphosis of insects, having once been excited by the influence of the brain, continues independently in a different manner. Evidence ought to be furnished by the metamorphosis of imaginal discs of single parts of the insectal body, if it should take place independently of the surroundings to which they had been artificially transferred. According to recent researches on the development of the Malpighian tubes in moths, the cells of the tubes of full-grown insects are derived directly from the cells of the larval tubes through certain physiological and morphological metamorphosis. (Cf. paper of Samson, 1908.) By grafting fragments of the larval Malpighian tubes into the head or thorax, I hoped to solve the problem as to whether the metamorphosis of these tubes might occur normally, in anomalous surroundings, even in the absence of a connection between the tubes and the intestine. Smaller or larger parts of the tubes taken from various regions were grafted into the head or the thorax of the same caterpillar after the last moult of the animal: some of the caterpillars operated upon had just accomplished this moult, others had lived already 10 to 11 days after the last moult. In other cases the Malpighian tubes were transplanted from female caterpillars 10 days after their last moult into other caterpillars 2 or 3 days after this moult. After a few days the ends of these implanted parts were healed up, and so the contents could no longer come out. In the adult insect or pupa I several times suc-

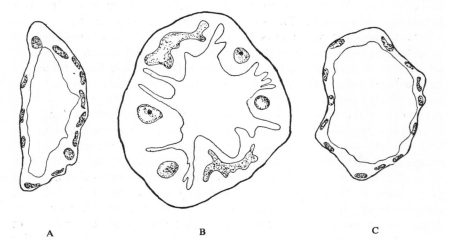

A   B   C

ceeded in detecting microscopically the presence of the implanted tubes, which were here not united with the intestine. The cells of the tube which developed in the head or the thorax (cf. Fig. 1a in text) exhibited different characters from those observed in the caterpillars (Fig. 1b), viz., they corresponded to the normal cells of tubes in the normal adult moth (Fig. 1c). Their height was far lower than in the larval stage of development, sometimes they were twice as low. Their nuclei, having a much more compact chromatine, and a flatter, non-ramified form, were situated nearer the base of the cells. The interior margin of the tubes was not so much notched as in the caterpillar. All these characters prove that the cells of the implanted tubes have undergone normal metamorphosis. This metamorphosis of the Malpighian tubes is consequently independent of the function of this organ, as it is difficult to suppose that the tubes undergoing metamorphosis in heterogeneous surroundings were able to realize their special function in the chrysalis and later in the adult moth, as they were unconnected with the developing intestine, completely grown together and always filled with excrements previously formed during the larval life. If it could be proved without any objection that the Malpighian tubes which have been implanted into the head or thorax had no nervous junction in the new surroundings, the metamorphosis of transplanted fragments of Malpighian tubes would be a further proof for the assertion made in the previous chapter that the brain exerts its influence by means of internal secretion. The probably unchanged rate of metamorphosis of the tubes transferred from caterpillars 10 days after their last moult into those 2 to 3 days after this moult (thus from specimens in which the influence of the brain was already observable into specimens in which there was yet no such influence) points to the conclusion that tissues once stimulated by the brain to transformation undergo further metamorphosis independently.

Should this principle be of general importance, it would be expected that the organs of much older caterpillars (a few days before pupation) grafted on the much younger caterpillars after the fourth moult (and therefore some two to three weeks younger) might also undergo further metamorphosis at the normal rate, in spite of the fact that the organs of the younger specimens do not as yet indicate the slightest trace of the histolytical processes. Transplantations of the germ of wings fully confirmed this hypothesis. I removed the germ of the first left wing from numerous caterpillars shortly before their last moult, and in its place I grafted an analogous germ derived from a full-grown caterpillar, which was to undergo metamorphosis in a few days. In two of the caterpillars somewhat large and black outgrowths—dwarfed and deformed wings—appeared on the place of grafting. In their uniformly dark hue and the thickness and markings of the chitin they formed a striking contrast to the bright-colored tegument of the caterpillar. (Cf. Fig. 2.) The small size and the abnormal forms were doubtless caused by inevitable injuries of the delicate germ during transplantation, as well as by the difficulty of extracting the pupal wing from

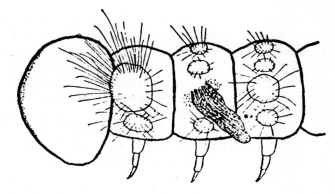

Figure 2

the moulting but not pupating caterpillar. Histologically the development
of the pupal wings was normal. I have also formerly observed (Kopeć,
1911) that the sexual glands of full-grown caterpillars develop at their
normal rate when grafted on the caterpillar after their third or fourth
moult. Such a behavior of the grafted wings and sexual glands strikingly
confirmed the above-stated principle that after the time when the brain
has already exerted its influence on the whole organism—which influence
decides the inception of histolytical processes leading to the chrysalis stage
—the subsequent development and metamorphosis of organs is quite independent of the brain.

The results of my experiments proved that the rate of development
of the grafted organs underwent no change due to the influence of new
surroundings, differing both as to age and physiological state. These results
seem to disagree with analogous researches of Uhlenhuth (1912, 1913) on
amphibians. This author grafted eyes of salamander larvæ on specimens of
a different age and came to the conclusion that the metamorphosis of the
transplanted eyes underwent a distinct retardation when grafted on
younger specimens, and an acceleration in the contrary case—i.e., the transplanted as well as the own eyes of the foster-mother underwent metamorphosis at the same time. But the disagreement of these results with the
behavior of the transplanted insect organs in my investigations is only apparent. The influence of the surroundings on the grafted eye, observed by
Uhlenhuth, was to be remarked only when the age of the specimens on
which the eyes were implanted did not differ much from that of animals
whose eyes were taken for the operation. In the remaining cases—i.e.,
under the conditions which alone corresponded to my investigations on
the transplantation of organs from young caterpillars after their third or
fourth moult to full-grown caterpillars or chrysalids and *vice versa*—the
grafted eyes retained their proper developmental rate without being influenced by the new surroundings, just like the organs of insects transplanted
in my experiments. Nor do my experiments on insects in any way contra-

dict the experiments of Weigl (1913) which were made simultaneously with but independently of those of Uhlenhuth. Weigl studied the same problem in his investigations on the homo- and heteroplastic transplantation of the skin in salamanders and other amphibians. In regard to the course of the metamorphosis of the grafted pieces of skin, he comes to the same general conclusion as Uhlenhuth. In the experiments of Kornfeld (1914) we can also find a parallel to the results I observed on insects. This author, who transplanted the gill of salamanders, agrees in his final conclusion with Uhlenhuth. Uhlenhuth (1913), mentioning my former experiments on the transplantation of gonads in moths, imputes to me results completely different from those which I really obtained (Kopeć, 1911). More recently this error has been corrected by Kornfeld in agreement with Uhlenhuth.

In specimens deprived of the brain or of other nervous ganglia we often may observe certain mechanical difficulties during pupation and emergence of the moth. They are produced by concrescence of the chitin at the place of operation, and cause the appearance of certain deformities of chrysalids or of moths. It must be distinctly noted that all these deformities, caused only by mechanical obstructions during pupation or emergence of the moths, are in no wise dependent on the operation itself, nor consequently on the removal of separate parts of the nervous system. A proof of this is that they also appear—and in the same number of cases— in the specimens with intact nervous system used as a standard and injured similarly as in the operations on the ganglia. Therefore I consider it superfluous to describe these anomalies here.

D. General Conclusions and Summary

From the whole of this paper it follows that my results relative to the influence of the nervous system on metamorphosis in insects show a very great resemblance to the relations observed in amphibians. According to recent investigations (above mentioned), iodin stored by the thyroid glands in amphibians is the direct cause which elicits metamorphosis, but the production of this substance probably depends on the function of the hypophysis. Consequently in both classes of animals metamorphosis would be controlled by the brain, or part of it. In recent years experiments have been performed on the influence of food containing thyroid or hypophysis on the development of the larvæ of insects, but the results of these researches do not as yet furnish an adequate material for any conclusions. Abderhalden (1919) observed that a part of the moths obtained from caterpillars fed on hypophysis was very large; many specimens from caterpillars fed on thyroid, on the contrary, were very small. These data refer, however, to phenomena of growth, and are possibly quiet unrelated to the problem of the rate of transformation here now discussed. Romeis and von Dobkiewicz (1920) studied the rate of development in larvæ of Calliphora fed on thyroid and obtained no distinct changes which might have been attributed exclusively to the specific effect of the thyroid gland. As I mentioned above, negative results of feeding experiments with hypothetical specific influence ought not to be considered as decisive, because it may be inferred from them only that the substance used does not exert any effect on the organism when given *per os*. Hankó (1912), on the other hand, ascertained a very considerable influence of hypophysis on rate of moults in *Asellus aquaticus*. But, as moults in Crustacea are not to be totally identified with moults in insects having complete metamorphosis, these results also have no great importance for our problem. The whole question demands further research in order to elucidate whether and in what degree there exists an analogy between the physiology of transformation of amphibians and that of insects.

The following summary contains the more important results of this paper:

1. The brain (ganglion supra-œsophageale) of the caterpillar of *Lymantria dispar* L. has particular importance in the general processes of metamorphosis. The presence of the brain is indispensable, at least up to a certain period, for the inception of histolytical processes. The influence of the brain in this direction is probably chemical; hence the brain ought to be considered as a gland of internal secretion.

2. At some well-defined time before pupation the quantity of the corresponding substance (or substances) secreted by the brain is already sufficient for the complete pupation of the caterpillar.

3. Tissues of the caterpillar influenced by the brain undergo further metamorphosis independently; the germs of the wings of caterpillars grafted shortly before pupation on younger caterpillars near their last moult are transformed in the larval organism into pupal wings in spite of the absence of histolytical processes in the new surroundings. Analogical results have been obtained by transplantation of Malpighian tubes and gonads.

4. It follows from other experiments on the transplantation of organs that the stimulus coming from the brain is not sufficient by itself for the metamorphosis of caterpillars: this stimulus acts only when the insect organism, having attained a certain stage, is physiologically prepared to answer to this influence. This is shown by the fact that germs of gonads from young caterpillars grafted into full-grown caterpillars do not undergo metamorphosis characteristic of the pupal development of gonads; in other words, the rate of development underwent no acceleration in spite of the histolytical processes occurring in the new surroundings.

5. Other parts of the nervous system have no influence on the general processes of metamorphosis.

6. By making ligatures round the body of the caterpillar and cutting it in different places, we may obtain fragments consisting of front, middle, or hind segments. The front fragments undergo metamorphosis in a normal manner, provided the caterpillar does not die of starvation. On the contrary, the middle and hind fragments undergo pupation only if they have belonged to caterpillars which would have pupated in a few days.

7. The Malpighian tubes are transformed into tubes of the adult insect independently of the intestine and of the performance of their specific functions.

BIBLIOGRAPHY

Papers marked by an asterisk are known to me only from abstracts.

Abderhalden, E. (1915), Studien über die von einzelnen Organen hervorgebrachten Substanzen mit spezifischer Wirkung. 1. Mitteilung. Arch. f. d. ges. Physiol., Vol. 162.

—————— (1919), 2. Mitteilung. Ibidem, Vol. 176.

Adler, L. (1914), Metamorphosestudien an Batrachierlarven. 1. Exstirpation endokriner Drüsen. A. Exstirpation der Hypophyse. Arch. f. Entw. Mech., Vol. 39.

—————— (1916), Untersuchungen über die Entstehung der Amphibienneotenie. Arch. f. d. ges. Physiol., Vol. 164.

Allen, B. M. (1916), Extirpation Experiments in Rana pipiens Larvæ. Science.

—————— (1917), Effects on the Extirpation of the Anterior Lobe of the Hypophysis of Rana pipiens. Biol. Bull., Vol. 32.

—————— (1918), The Results of Thyroid Removal in the Larvæ of Rana pipiens. Journ. of Exper. Zoöl., Vol. 24.

—————— (1919), The Relation of the Pituitary and Thyroid Glands of Bufo and Rana to Iodin and Metamorphosis. Biol. Bull., Vol. 36.

Babák, E. (1905), Ueber die Beziehung des zentralen Nervensystems zu den Gestaltungsvorgängen der Metamorphose des Frosches. Arch. f. d. ges. Physiol., Vol. 109.

—————— (1913), Einige Gedanken über die Beziehung der Metamorphose bei den Amphibien zur inneren Secretion. Zentrbl. f. Physiol., Vol. 27.

*Brendgen, F. (1914), Ueber die künstlich erzielte Metamorphose der Alyteslarven. Anatom. Anzeiger., Vol. 46.

Cattie, J. T. (1880), Beiträge zur Kenntnis der Chorda Supra-spinalis der Lepidopteren und des zentralen, peripherischen und sympatischen Nervensystems der Raupen. Zeitschr. f. wiss. Zoolog., Vol. 35.

Conte, A., and Vaney, C. (1911), Production experimentale des Lépidoptères acephales. Comptes Rend. Acad. Sc. Paris, Vol. 152.

*Cotronei, G. (1914), Première contribution expérimentale à l'étude des rapports des organes dans la croissance et dans la métamorphose des amphibiens anoures. Arch. ital. de Biologie, Vol. 61.

Dewitz, J. (1905), Untersuchungen über die Verwandlung der Insectenlarven. II. Arch. f. Anat. und Physiol., Physiol. Abt., Suppl.

—————— (1916), III. Zusammenfassung früherer Mitteilungen. Zool. Anz., Vol. 47.

Gudernatsch, J. F. (1912), Feeding Experiments on Tadpoles. I. Arch. f. Entw. Mech., Vol. 35.

—————— (1914), Feeding Experiments on Tadpoles. II. Amer. Journ. of Anat., Vol. 15.

Hankó, B. (1912), Ueber den Einfluss einiger Lösungen auf die Häutung, Regeneration und das Wachstum von Asellus aquaticus. Arch. f. Entw. Mech., Vol. 34.

Hirschler, J. (1918–19), Sur la métamorphose provoquée chez l'axolotle à l'aide d'iode et des expérience apparentées. Extrait de Kosmos, Bull. d. l. Soc. Polonaise d. Naturalistes à Leopol.

*Kahn, R. H. (1916), Zur Frage der Wirkung der Schilddrüse und Thymus auf Froschlarven. Arch. f. d. ges. Physiol., Vol. 163.

Kaufman, L. (1918), Researches on the Artificial Metamorphosis of Axolotls. Bull. de l'Acad. d. Sc. de Cracovie. (Prelim. note, ibidem, 1917.)

Kopeć, S. (1911), Untersuchungen über Kastration und Transplantation bei Schmetterlingen. Arch. f. Entw. Mech., Vol. 33.

—— (1912), Ueber die Funktionen des Nervensystems der Schmetterlinge während der sukzessiven Stadien ihrer Metamorphose. *Zool. Anz.*, Vol. 40.

—— (1918), Lokalisationsversuche am zentralen Nervensystem der Raupen und Falter. *Zool. Jahrb., Abt. f. allg. Zool. und Physiol. Bd.* 36.

Kornfeld, W. (1914), Abhängigkeit der metamorphotischen Kiemenrückbildung vom Gesamtorganismus der *Salamandra maculosa. Arch. f. Entw. Mech.*, Vol. 40.

*Larson, M. E. (1919), Effects on the Extirpation of the Thyroid Gland upon the Pituitary Gland in *Bufo. Anat. Record*, Vol. 15.

Laufberger, V. (1913), O vzbuzeni metamorfosy axolotlu krmenim zlazou stitnou. *Lekan. Rozhl.* Prague.

Loeb, J. (1896), Hat das Zentralnervensystem einen Einfluss auf die Vorgänge der Larvenmetamorphose *Arch. f. Entw. Mech.*, Vol. 4.

*Rogers, J. B. (1918), The Effect of Extirpation of the Thyroid upon the Thymus and the Pituitary Glands of *Rana pipiens. Journ. of Exper. Zoöl.*, Vol. 24.

Romeis, B. (1914–15), Experimentelle Untersuchungen über die Wirkung innersekretorischer Organe. II. *Arch. f. Entw. Mech.*, Vols. 40 and 41.

—— (1915), Idem, III. *Zeitschr. f. d. ges. experim. Medizin.*, Vol. 4.

—— (1916), Idem, IV. *Ibid.*, 5.

—— (1918), Idem, V. *Ibid.*, 6.

—— (1919), Idem. VI. *Arch. f. d. ges. Physiol.*, Vol. 173.

Romeis, B., and von Dobkiewicz, L. (1920), Experimentelle Untersuchungen über die Wirkung von Wirbeltierhormonen auf Wirbellose. I. *Arch. f. Entw. Mech.*, Vol. 47.

Samson, K. (1908) Ueber das Verhalten der Vasa Malpighi und die exkretorische Funktion der Fettzellen während der Metamorphose von Heterogenea limacodes Hufn. *Zool. Jahrb., Abt. f. Anat. u. Ontog.*, Vol. 26.

*Smith, P. E. (1916a), Experimental Ablation of the Hypophysis in the Frog Embryo. *Science.*

—— (1916b), The Effect of Hypophysectomy in the Early Embryo upon the Growth and Development of the Frog. *Anat. Record.*

*Steche, O., and Waentig, P. (1913), Untersuchungen über die biologische Bedeutung und Kinetik der Katalase. *Zoologica*, Vol. 26.

*Swingle, W. W. (1919a), Studies on the Relation of Iodin to the Thyroid. I. *Journ. of Exper. Zoöl.*, 27.

—— (1919b), Idem, II. Ibidem.

Uhlenhuth, E. (1912), Die Transplantation des Amphibienauges. *Arch. f. Entw. Mech.*, Vol. 33.

—— (1913), Die synchrone Metamorphose transplantierter Salamanderaugen. *Ibidem*, Vol. 36.

Weigl, R. (1913), Ueber homoplastische und heteroplastische Hauttransplantation bei Amphibien mit besonderer Berücksichtigung der Metamorphose. Ibidem, Vol. 36.

Wintrebert, P. (1905a), Sur la régression de la queu en l'absence des centres medullaires chez Rana viridis. *Comptes rend. Soc. Biol. Paris*, Vol. 58.

—— (1905b), Sur l'indépendence de la métamorphose vis à vis du systeme nerveux chez les Batraciens. *Comptes rend. Acad. Sc. Paris*, Vol. 141.

—— (1906a), Sur l'accomplissement régulier des fonctions de nutrition, de processus d'ontogenèse, de régénération et de métamorphose chez les larves d'Alytes, en l'absence d'une grande étendue de la moëlle. *Comptes rend. Soc. Biol. Paris*, Vol. 60.

—— (1906b), La métamorphose de Salamandra maculosa Laur. en dehors de la moëlle et de ganglions spinaux. Ibidem.

—— (1911), Sur le déterminisme et la métamorphose chez les Amphibiens. Ibidem, Vol. 71.

DIETRICH BODENSTEIN

Leg transplantations in Lepidopterous caterpillars. I. Larval and pupal molting analyzed by means of transplants

Dietrich H. F. A. Bodenstein was born in Corwingen, East Prussia, in 1908. He studied at the Universities of Königsberg and Berlin from 1926 to 1933, and received his Ph.D. in zoology from the University of Freiburg in 1954. From 1928 to 1933 he was Research Assistant in Experimental Morphology at the Kaiser Wilhelm Institute for Biology in Berlin; in 1933 he went to Italy for a year as Research Associate at the Institute of Marine Biology in Rovigno, and from 1934 to 1941 held the same post in the School of Biology at Stanford University. He was Guggenheim Fellow of the Department of Zoology, Columbia University, from 1941 to 1943, and spent the following year as Assistant Entomologist at the Connecticut Experiment Station in New Haven. From 1945 to 1958 he was Insect Physiologist at the Medical Laboratories of the Army Chemical Center in Maryland, and from 1958 to 1960 Embryologist at the Gerontology Branch of the National Heart Institute in Baltimore. Since 1960 he has been Lewis and Clark Professor of Biology and Chairman of the Department of Biology of the University of Virginia. He is a member of the National Academy of Science.

His research interests are in the areas of the experimental morphology and developmental physiology of amphibians and insects, insect endocrinology, and the developmental genetics of *Drosophila*.

INTRODUCTION AND STATEMENT OF PROBLEM

Transplantation has become one of the most useful methods for testing the events and relationships of developmental physiology. Experiments of

[Previously published in Wilhelm Roux' *Archiv fur Entwicklungsmechanik der Organismen*, 3 (April 8, 1933), 565–83. Reprinted by permission of the publisher.]

this sort on the hypodermal organs of lepidopterous larvae have appeared to promise interesting insights into the problem of molting, or metamorphosis. Unfortunately, the stiff chitinous shell and the sensitivity of caterpillars have offered difficulties in this connection. Nevertheless, the legs of caterpillars have now been transplanted successfully, as will be reported in this article.

As is well known, during its growth the lepidopterous larva accomplishes several molts, and at its last molt transforms into a pupa, which then produces the mature insect. The activity of the larval hypodermis in its developmental cycle can be conceived of in any of the following ways:

1. In the course of its development the condition of the hypodermis is changing continuously, and each molt begins whenever a certain level of development has been reached.

2. During development the hypodermis constantly maintains the same larval condition; when the different larval molts will occur and whether a molt is of a larval or a pupal nature are determined by factors located outside the hypodermis, i.e., factors from its environment.

3. Factors in the hypodermis and in its environment work together, so that, on the one hand, the condition of the hypodermis changes, and on the other, definite factors come into being in its environment.

Transplantation of larval legs, which are hypodermal outgrowths, if carried out in manifold combinations should permit a decision as to which of the concepts stated above is the correct one.[1]

MATERIAL AND METHODS

The investigations were carried out on caterpillars of the butterflies *Vanessa urticae* and *V. io*. Larvae in different stages were used for experiment, with the second stage as the lower limit. On hatching, caterpillars were designated first stage, the end of which is succeeded by the first molt. Following the first molt, they are in the second stage, which is succeeded by the second molt, etc. The last fifth larval stage is concluded by the fifth, or pupal, molt.

Bristles, abdominal legs, and thoracic legs were transplanted homoplastically and heteroplastically. As we gained more experience with the technique, the thoracic legs proved to be the most suitable; thereafter they were used almost exclusively. The site of transplantation was usually the back of the caterpillar, at the location of a median dorsal bristle, but on occasion other places were chosen.

[1] Once again I owe sincere thanks to my esteemed chief, Professor Mangold, for his kind assistance in this work.

TABLE 1

Summary of the homoplastic transplantations of bristles, thoracic legs and abdominal legs in *Vanessa urticae* and *Vanessa io*. All cases heterotopic, except for 10 orthotopic cases (5 of them positive) which were done as anaplastic transplantations of 2nd stage thoracic legs onto the 3rd stage.

Donor → Host	Stages the same				Anaplastic					Kataplastic		
	Stage 2 → Stage 2	Stage 3 → Stage 3	Stage 4 → Stage 4	Total	Stage 2 → Stage 3	Stage 3 → Stage 4	Stage 3 → Stage 5	Stage 4 → Stage 5	Total	Stage 4 → Stage 3	Stage 5 → Stage 4	Total
Bristles:												
Total			144	144								
Positive			1	1								
Thoracic legs:												
Total	4	6	22	32	30	69	12	21	132	28	106	134
Positive	1		12	13	7 (+3?)	18 (+2?)	(2?)	3 (+1?)	30	9	9 (+2?)	18
Abdominal legs:												
Total			9	9								
Positive			1	1								
Total				185					132			134
Positive				15					30			18

171

Complications in the operation occurred when large transplants from older caterpillars were implanted into earlier stages. Here the number healing into the host was small; hence, many specimens had to be operated on in order to obtain a few positive cases. Only those cases were considered positive in which the molted shell of the transplant could be shown to be attached to the cast skin of the host. It should be remarked at this point that the failure of larger transplants to heal into small hosts has nothing to do with healing capability as such in transplantation between stages so different; rather, mechanical obstacles thwart healing in these instances.

Tables 1 and 2 summarize the experiments. Altogether 343 operations were carried out; of these 321 were homoplastic and 22 heteroplastic. Of the 321 homoplastic ones, 311 were heterotopic and 10 orthotopic. Altogether, 69 cases—63 homoplastic and 6 heteroplastic—were positive. Distribution of the cases over the different groups of operations is shown in Tables 1 and 2. For the reasons mentioned above, the greatest number of experiments were done with the thoracic legs.

TABLE 2

Summary of heteroplastic transplantations of abdominal legs and thoracic legs between *Vanessa urticae* and *Vanessa io*. All cases heterotopic.

Donor V. *io* ↓ Host V. *urticae*	Stage the same			Anaplastic	
	Stage 2 ↓ Stage 2	Stage 4 ↓ Stage 4	Total	Stage 3 ↓ Stage 4	Total
Thoracic leg:					
Total	3	6	9	8	8
Positive	1	1	2	2	2
Abdominal leg:					
Total		5	5		
Positive		2	2		
Total			14		8
Positive			4		2

Anesthetization was with ether. It was important that the larvae not get onto the cotton pad soaked with the narcotic; this was managed by placing a small bottle of ether in the actual anesthesia vessel. Proper exposure to the anesthetic is highly important, as it controls the degree of bleeding. If the larvae are insufficiently stupefied, the wound bleeds severely in consequence of their violent movements, and this bleeding lifts the transplant off. The proper condition of stupefaction has been reached when the caterpillar shows only very weak quivering movements of bristles or legs. The operation was done under the binocular microscope. Dissection was not sterile, but was as clean as possible, and the instruments were disin-

Figure 1. Pair of thoracic legs of *Vanessa urticae*. E.K.: Terminal claw of the fourth leg segment. *Gl. 1–4:* First to fourth leg segment. (Enlarged 19 times.)

fected in alcohol before each use. For extirpation I used finely pointed Wecker scissors and for transplantation two pairs of carefully whetted watchmaker's forceps. The transplant must fit the wound precisely; with the proper degree of narcosis the blood then clots at the place of union into a protective scab. The operation as such has no effect on the developmental rhythm of specimens that are well maintained. As was shown earlier (1930), specimens with several wounds molted synchronously with the controls. The caterpillars were maintained singly, or in groups of three to five, in small glass dishes with glass covers. Fresh food was never provided. In these containers the specimens were able to remain until emergence of the adult. For histological study Carnoy's solution was used as a fixative; imbedding was via methyl benzoate–celloidin (according to Peterfi); and the sections, 10–15 μ thick, were colored in Delafield eosin.

For further comprehension of the exposition that follows, it should be pointed out that it was hypodermal larval organs (caterpillar legs) which were transplanted, and that the imaginal anlagen of the future adult legs, which lie in the basal segment, have been left out of consideration, since we wished to acquaint ourselves only with the accomplishments and potencies of the larval hypodermis in its developmental cycle. The interesting problems brought up by the transplantation of imaginal leg discs are being worked on and will be reported later.

Butterfly larvae have three pairs of thoracic legs and four pairs of abdominal legs. In the terminal segment there is an additional pair of legs, sometimes called "pushers." The thoracic leg of *Vanessa urticae* consists of four joints or articles, usually called segments (Fig. 1), if the proximal basal segment is reckoned as the first. This part is not set off from the

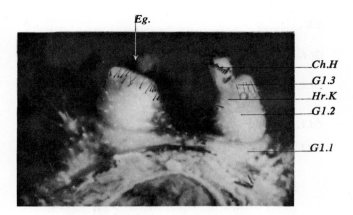

Figure 2. Pair of abdominal legs of *Vanessa urticae*. *Gl. 1–3:* First to third leg segment. *Ch.H.:* Wreath of chitinous hooks on the third segment. *Hr.K.:* Distal wreath of hairs on the second segment. *Eg.:* Retracted third segment. (Enlarged 19 times.)

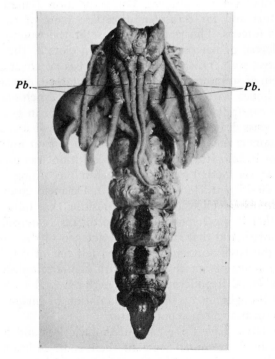

Figure 3. Pupa of *Vanessa urticae*, immediately after it had stripped off the larval skin. *Pb.:* The pupal legs, formed from the imaginal leg anlagen. (Enlarged 4½ times.)

thorax by any joint; it is more an evagination of the hypodermis. The color of the leg is a glistening black; the light-colored segmental boundaries stand out clearly. The cross section is slightly oval. The abdominal leg of *Vanessa urticae* (Fig. 2) consists of three segments. The first, the basal segment, is partly fused with the body, so that only the lateral face stands out in relief. The second segment is the largest; the proportion of its basal diameter to the length (in the fifth larval stage) is about 2:1. The distal margin of the second segment bears a wreath of coarse hairs, which in some places encircle the leg completely in two rows. The third segment is shiny and hairless; it can be protracted and retracted. It is about half as long as the second segment; its distal end bears a U-shaped wreath of chitinous hooks, which is open laterally. The pupal legs, which supply the later imaginal legs, are formed from imaginal anlagen at the base of the larval legs. During the process of pupation the imaginal discs of the legs become strongly extended and press their way into the caterpillar leg. The epidermis of the larval leg apparently forms pupal hypodermis over the anlage of the pupal leg, without developing the typical shape of the leg (the

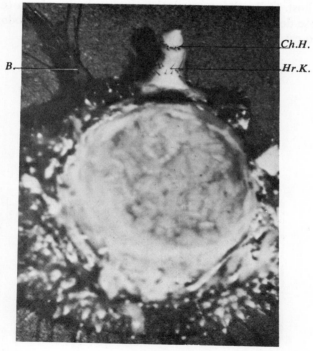

Figure 4. Heterotopically homoplastically transplanted abdominal leg of *Vanessa urticae. Ch.H.:* Chitinous hooks of the third leg segment. *Hr.K.:* Distal wreath of hairs on the second leg segment. *B.:* Dorsal bristle. (Enlarged 19 times.)

process is not yet fully clarified). At pupation the empty chitinous shell of the caterpillar leg is cast off, and in its place the pupal leg appears (Fig. 3).

EXPERIMENTAL DATA

A. *Heterotopic Homoplastic Transplantation*

Leg I, urt. x urt. (Fig. 4) May 27, 1931. The abdominal leg of a donor larva in the fourth stage was implanted into the fifth segment of a caterpillar of the same age, in place of a dorsal median bristle. The implant comprised the two distal segments. The donor died during anesthesis. The host molted 3 days later and the implant synchronously. The segments of the implanted leg are normal in form and coloration (Fig. 4). At the boundary of the distal and proximal segments, as is normal, there is evident a wreath of coarse hairs (*Hr.K.*). At the end of the distal segment there stands the typical U-shaped wreath (*Ch.H.*) of chitinous hooks. Inspection of the sections showed that the implant had healed fully into place (Fig. 5). Its hypodermis is continuous, without any scar, with that of the host. Cell size is normal; there are no broken-down cells.

This case depicts the heterotopic transplantation of an abdominal leg between two caterpillars of the same age and species.

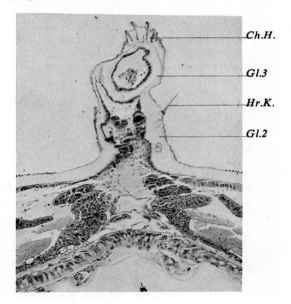

Figure 5. Leg 1. Section through the heterotopic homoplastic abdominal leg transplant. *Ch.H.*: Chitinous hooks of the third leg segment. *Hr.K.*: A hair from the distal wreath of hairs on the second leg segment. *Gl. 2–3*: Second and third leg segments. (Enlarged 58 times.)

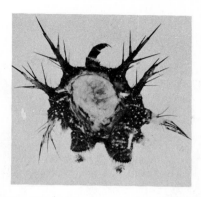

Figure 6. Leg 77_1. Heterotopically homoplastically transplanted thoracic leg of *Vanessa urticae*. (Enlarged 10 times.)

Leg 77_1, urt. x urt. (Fig. 6). May 29, 1932. The host was a caterpillar of the fourth stage; the thoracic leg of a donor of like age was transplanted into it in place of a dorsal median bristle. On June 1 the donor died. The host molted on June 2, the implant synchronously with it (Fig. 6). The implant is situated in the seventh segment and consists of three well-formed completely normal segments; the intersegmental membranes are light in color. The distal segment is slightly inclined laterally, to the left, and bears the typical terminal claw of a thoracic leg. This leg transplant should be compared with the normal *urticae* thoracic leg shown in Fig. 1.

This case depicts the heterotopic transplantation of a thoracic leg between two caterpillars of the same age and species.

B. *Heterotopic Homoplastic-Kataplastic Transplantation*

a. *Donor fifth stage, recipient fourth stage*

Leg 22_2, urt. x urt. (Fig. 7). Aug. 8, 1931. A larva in the fourth stage served as host, one in the fifth stage as donor. The second through the fourth segments of a thoracic leg constituted the transplant. The site of implantation was the place of the dorsal median bristle in the fifth segment. The donor died during anesthesia. Two days later the host caterpillar was very lively; the leg seemed to have grown in very well and had its flexor side directed cephalad. It appeared to move autonomously. Suddenly, without any visible stimulus, the two distal segments would bend and after a few seconds snap back just as suddenly into the resting position. The caterpillar molted on Aug. 14, 1931, six days after the operation, the transplant in synchrony with it (Fig. 7). The segments of the implant have the character of a normal thoracic leg; thus no pupal molt has taken

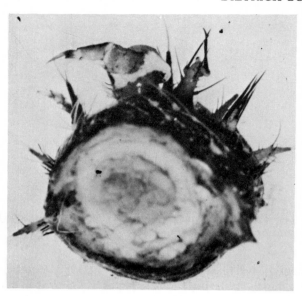

Figure 7.   Leg 22_2. Heterotopically homoplastically-kataplastically transplanted thoracic leg of *Vanessa urticae*. (Enlarged 19 times.)

place. Segment 2 is markedly swollen and the intersegmental membrane considerably stretched. The color of the leg is clearly weaker than that of a normal caterpillar leg (see Fig. 1). The specimen was fixed in this condition. Histological examination shows that here too the unification of donor and host hypodermis is complete. The muscles in the implant have not grown together with those of the host. The size of the cells of the implant corresponds approximately to that of the host cells.

This case depicts the transplantation of a fifth-stage leg into a caterpillar of the fourth stage. The transplanted leg molts synchronously with the host. It retains its larval character, hence has undergone five instead of four larval molts. Its intensity of pigmentation is weakened somewhat.

Leg 48, urt. x. urt.   May 24, 1932. The thoracic leg of a fifth (last) stage larva was transplanted into the site of the dorsal median bristle in the seventh segment of a fourth stage larva. On May 28 the host molted, in synchrony with the transplant. The transplant retained its larval character. It had grown in well but was slightly deformed, yet the boundaries of hairs on the segments were still clearly recognizable. The donor was lively and still feeding; it did not pupate until May 30.

Here, too, as in case 22_2, the transplanted leg undergoes a supernumerary larval molt and molts synchronously with the host. Further, there is clearly an acceleration of molting of the transplant versus that of the donor.

b. Donor fourth stage, host third stage.

Leg 81$_1$, urt. x urt.   (Figs. 8 and 8a). May 30, 1932. The thoracic leg of a fourth stage larva was implanted in place of a dorsal median bristle of a third stage larva—June 3. The donor is still lively and feeding; the host has molted. The implant, which molted synchronously, is on the tenth segment, consists of three leg segments, and has a normal shape. It stands quite upright, with the tip pointing to the right and cephalad.—June 4. The donor has spun in preparation for molting. The host is lively and feeding.—June 5. The donor has molted. The host is still feeding.—June 6. The host has spun in preparation for the final larval molt. The donor is lively and feeding.—June 7. The host has molted; the implant, molting in synchrony with it, has clearly grown larger (Fig. 8). Otherwise as in the

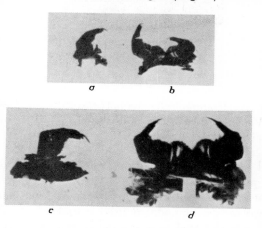

Figure 8a–d. Leg 81$_1$. Heterotopically homoplastically-kataplastically transplanted thoracic leg of Vanessa urticae. (a) Cast skin of the transplant after the second molt following the operation; (b) the associated integumental leg shell of the host; (c) cast skin of the transplant after the third (last) postoperative molt; (d) the associated integumental leg shell of the host. (Enlarged 10 times.)

preceding stage. The donor is still feeding.—June 12. The donor has pupated. The host is still active and feeding.—June 13. The host has spun in preparation for molting.—June 14. The host has pupated. The transplant on the cast skin is hollow. On the pupal abdomen the transplant has been transformed into a pupal leg (Fig. 8a).

However, the transformation of the transplant into a pupal leg does not prove that the hypodermis of the implant has also changed to pupal hypoderm. Rather, the phenomenon shows only that the simultaneously transplanted imaginal leg anlage was able to realized its tendency to pupate. Yet the hollowness of the transplant, shown in the examination of

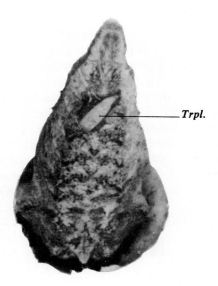

Trpl.

Figure 8a.   Leg 81₁. Heterotopically homoplastically-kataplastically transplanted thoracic leg of *Vanessa urticae*, transformed into a pupal leg, on the abdomen of the host pupa. (Enlarged 6 times.)

the histological sections, permits the conclusion that its hypodermis too has changed to pupal hypodermis.

Once again the divergent molting rhythms of donor and host are very clear. The transplant accommodated itself completely to the host; apparently it shifted over to pupal substance in correspondence with the influences from the host.

Fig. 9 shows yet another last-stage *urticae* caterpillar, with a heteroplastic homoplastic-kataplastic transplanted thoracic leg in the ninth segment (stages at operation: donor fourth stage, host third stage). This transplant was dislodged at pupation.

C. Heterotopic Homoplastic-Anaplastic Transplantation

a. Donor fourth stage, host fifth stage.

Leg 72, urt. x urt.   May 28, 1932. The host was in the fifth stage. In place of one of its median dorsal bristles, a thoracic leg from a fourth stage donor was implanted—June 1. The donor has molted, and thus has entered the fifth stage. The host is lively and feeding. The transplant looks completely healthy, and seems to have grown as well—June 3. The donor is active and feeding. The host, which has been creeping agitatedly about in search of a place to pupate, is fixed in Carnoy. Examination of the sections shows that the transplant has healed on well; its hypodermis displays

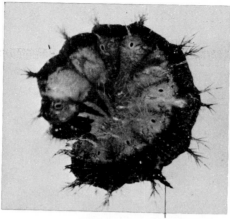

Trpl.

Figure 9. Leg 82. Thoracic leg of a fourth stage larva, transplanted heterotopically and homoplastically into a third stage host. Photo after the second (last) postoperative larval molt. *Trpl.*: Transplant. (Enlarged 2⅓ times.)

the same molting phenomena as the host's hypodermis. Thus the transplant must have responded to the influences toward pupation emanating from the host. But whether the molting phenomena in the transplant are to be regarded as characteristic of larval or pupal molting cannot be decided, because the leg epidermis of the transplant displays essentially no structural qualities.

When transplants from the fourth or third stages are put into fifth stage hosts, they heal in well. They are determined for molting by host influences. However, whether they will perform larval or pupal molts cannot be decided from study of the sections. At the pupal molt the transplants are cast off; and where they were located can be discerned only from a slight scar on the pupa.

b. Donor third stage, host fourth stage.

All positive cases of this combination, save those which were attacked by parasites and had to be fixed on this account, remained alive until pupation. Here too the transplants were cast off at the pupal molt, and on the pupa only a slight scar indicated where the transplant had been.

Leg 89₁, urt. x urt. (Fig. 10). May 31, 1932. The thoracic leg of a third stage larva was implanted in place of a dorsal median bristle of a fourth stage larva—June 3. The host molted, in synchrony with it the transplant. The implant is in the third segment. It consists of three segments and a little basal material (Fig. 10). The implanted leg is shaped

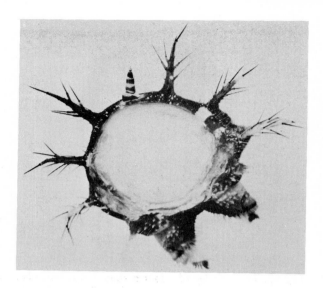

Figure 10.   Leg 89_1. Heterotopically homoplastically-anaplastically transplanted thoracic leg of *Vanessa urticae*. (Enlarged 10 times.)

normally, its intersegments are good and light in color; only the intensity of its pigmentation is a little weaker than normal—June 6. The donor molted and entered the fourth stage. Shortly after the molt a parasite left the donor, which was therefore discarded as unusable—June 11. The host is weak; it had also been stung by a parasite and hence was fixed in Carnoy. In section the transplant showed the same degree of elevation of the old cuticle as the host. However, it is impossible to say whether the molting phenomena would have led to larval or pupal molting.

Leg transplants from the third into the fourth stage heal in well. Here, too, the moment of molting depends on that of the host. When the host pupates, the transplants are shed with the last larval skin. At the pupal molt, influences from the host cause the transplant to exhibit definite molting phenomena. However, study of the sections leaves in question whether these are directed toward larval or pupal molting.

D. *Orthotopic Homoplastic-Anaplastic Transplantation*

In these experiments the thoracic leg of a second stage larva was transplanted in place of the extirpated thoracic leg of a third stage larva.

Donor and host were *urticae* caterpillars. At the site of transplantation the extirpating cut was made in such a way that the whole basal segment was retained and the first segment was left more or less incompletely as a stump. Then the transplant with as much basal material as possible, almost complete, was caused to heal onto this base. After the first molt, the transplants had healed in well, although they did not cover the entire wound surface but were displaced slightly laterad. The rings of the individual segments of the transplant were short. Growth in diameter rather than in length seemed to have occurred. Otherwise the organization of a thoracic leg had retained well. These growth relationships seem to have their cause in the unfavorable positional relationships that had come about at operation, for the small size of the object prevented good orientation of the transplant. But perhaps some weight should be given to influences from the stump, namely, to its regenerative tendencies, and perhaps to the reduction in nourishment. After the second molt following transplantation there was a remarkable phenomenon. The stump regenerated two new legs and pushed the transplant to the side, so that it was now situated on the regenerated distal segment of the local leg (Fig. 11). In all of the few (5) applicable cases, the same thing was observed. Hence the stump had maintained its independence. Its regenerative potencies were not suppressed by the transplant. There had been no coordination to produce a single responding organ system.

Figure 11. Orthotopically homoplastically-anaplastically transplanted thoracic leg of *Vanessa urticae*. (Integumental shell after the last larval skin had been shed). (Enlarged 19 times.)

Studies of sections of the transplants fixed after being shed at the final molt show that in two of the five cases the implant is completely hollow. Hence its cells must have been transformed into pupal hypodermis. In the last two cases there were still present remains of the imaginal disc, which apparently had been transplanted simultaneously. A definite epidermal layer could not be discerned.

Our results with orthotopic leg transplantation in lepidopterous caterpillars, and the characteristic findings made in this connection, seem, so far as can be seen at present, to agree well with the results of orthotopic leg transplantation in Amphibia (see P. Weiss, 1933). In Weiss's experiments the orthotopic leg transplants (in Salamandra) were pushed out by the regenerates that formed from the extirpation stump, so that the transplants finally were situated directly on top of the local regenerate. The conditions making possible the regeneration of the stump are, according to Weiss, to be sought especially in the positional relationship of the transplant. If the orientation was such that the transplant did not cover the entire surface of the stump, then a regenerate was formed from the open portion of the wound. With precise placement—when the transplant fitted exactly the surface cut made during extirpation, and tissues of the same sort came together—there was no regeneration. In our own cases the transplant was too small, and did not cover the entire wound surface of the stump; thus the latter's regenerative tendencies could be activated. The complications in the regenerate, inhibited by the transplant, which occurred in the experiments with Amphibia—such as were manifest in the delay of regeneration from the stump and the defective differentiation of the form of the regenerate—cannot be analyzed thoroughly in our few cases. These interesting questions are under investigation and will be reported on later elsewhere.

E. Heterotopic Heteroplastic Transplantation

Leg 13, io x urt.   On June 16, 1931, the thoracic leg of a fourth-stage io caterpillar was transplanted into an urticae caterpillar of the same next-to-last stage (4). The site of implantation of the two-segmented transplant was the locus of the dorsal median bristle in the fifth segment.

The donor died under anesthesia. Five days later the host molted, and with it synchronously the transplant. In the transplant the two segments are fully normal in development. At its base the transplant is connected with the host hypodermis by a lighter-colored zone. In this condition the specimen was fixed in Carnoy. Study of the sections from this case shows, as in homoplastic transplantation, the complete union of host and implant hypodermis.

Thus heteroplastic transplantation of legs between two different species (of Vanessa) is possible. Molting of the implant occurs in synchrony with that of the host.

F. Heterotopic Heteroplastic-Anaplastic Transplantation

Leg 95₂, io x urt. (Fig. 12)   June 16, 1932. The thoracic leg of a third stage larva of Vanessa io was transplanted into the dorsal midline of the eighth segment of a fourth stage Vanessa urticae caterpillar, in place of a bristle.—June 20. The host molted, as did the transplant synchronously. The transplant consists of three segments; it is inclined slightly cephalad and its apical claw points caudad (Fig. 12).—On June 25 or even as early as June 24, the donor molted; the host was still lively and feeding —June 27. The host is fixed in Carnoy; it is ripe for pupation. The donor is still in the fourth stage, lively and feeding.

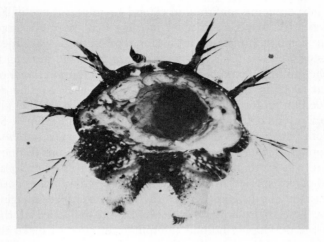

Figure 12. Leg 95_2. Thoracic leg of *Vanessa io*, transplanted heterotopically and heteroplastically-anaplastically onto *Vanessa urticae*. (Enlarged 10 times.)

Thus heteroplastic-anaplastic transplantation between two different species of *Vanessa* is possible. The transplant accommodates itself to the molting rhythm of its host.

DISCUSSION OF RESULTS

A. *What Determines When Molting Occurs?*

Information on the question whether the time of molting is already established in the hypodermis or whether environmental factors determine it is given by all our experiments. It was invariably observed that the transplants molted synchronously with the host. Of special significance here are the cases where continued rearing of donor and host was successful. This was so in several instances, of which Leg 48 (p. 178) was described. Here the earlier molting (two days) of the transplant in contrast with that of the donor is shown clearly. Those experiments in which the donor could not be maintained point in the same direction, for it was impossible always to match two larvae of exactly the same age as regards their molting condition. Of course, some uncertainty is caused by the circumstance that the molting rhythm of different individuals is very variable. It might be objected that the operation as such influences the molting rhythm of donor and host. But this possibility could not explain the synchrony of molting, which is possible only with a definite correlation of host and transplant.

Thus we must conclude that the time of molting is not determined by autonomous changes in the hypodermis, but rather that factors situated in the host outside the transplant determine the time of molting.

These experiments confirm and extend the observations of Koller and von Buddenbrock, who succeeded in showing that the molts were accelerated when hemolymph from just-molting caterpillars was injected into caterpillars of the same stage that were distant from the molting time. Apparently the molting phenomena and their realization are based on certain factors that occur in the caterpillars at definite intervals. The dependent nature of certain localized developmental processes are attested also by the unpublished results of Bytinski-Salz (personal communication). Salz transplanted from pupae of the species hybrids *Cel. galli* x *Cel. euphorbiae* and *Cel. euphorbiae* x *Perg. elpenor*—which for genetic reasons did not develop —anlagen of wings and ovaries into developing caterpillars and pupae from the normal parent species. In these cases he achieved a further development of the transplanted organ anlagen, all the way to complete imaginal formation. Thus these transplanted organs, under the influence of the stimuli present in the developing normal caterpillar, are able to make the proper local response. In this connection the experiments of Umeja (1930) must also be mentioned. He transplanted larval ovaries between univoltine and bivoltine races of *Bombyx mori* and found that the voltinism always followed that of the host. However, it was possible by change of temperature to alter the voltinism, so that the determination of the latter must be regarded as quite labile.

B. What Determines the Number of Molts?

The question now is: Is the number of molts fixed in the hypodermis? Normally *Vanessa urticae* caterpillars undergo four molts. Of course there are exceptions, but these may be ignored here. In our experiments by transplantation from the fifth to the fourth and from the fourth to the third stage, the transplanted leg underwent five instead of four molts. In a few most fortunate cases it was also possible by rearing the donor to establish that the transplant came from a donor with a normal number of molts (see Legs 48, p. 178 and 81$_1$, p. 179). This result strengthens our conclusion that molting is released not by factors inherent in the hypodermis but rather by extrahypodermal factors. It shows further that the hypodermis is able to carry out more molts than it normally does. Of course, whether it can carry out an unlimited number is questionable. Probably definite limits are set for it, for, according to other discoveries in research on developmental physiology (Mangold, 1926, p. 1174; 1929, p. 687; Schulze, 1924, pp. 341–42) the assumption is that it cannot remain indefinitely in a condition where the skin is larval.

C. The Quality of the Extrahypodermal Larval Molting Factors

The extrahypodermal factors effective during larval molting may differ from one another within the different stages. In this connection the following observations are of interest. A fourth stage leg implanted into a fourth stage host responds exactly as if it had been implanted into a third stage host. In fact, even a third stage leg transplanted heteroplastically into a fourth stage host behaves as though the host were the same species of the same stage. From this we can conclude that the extrahypodermal factors probably are alike in the different stages.

D. *Special Stimuli Causing Larval and Pupal Molting*

The processes of larval and pupal molting, as may without further ado be deduced from their results, are obviously different. This is shown also by the experiments of Frew (1928), who cultured *in vitro* imaginal discs of flies in larval and pupal hemolymph. Metalikow (1907) also was able to demonstrate a difference in the effectiveness of pupation blood and molting blood: blood taken from caterpillars shortly before pupation had a toxic action when injected into younger stages, while blood from younger caterpillars was not poisonous. However, how much significance should be attached to these findings is questionable, since Kopec (1911) in similar experiments found that even the blood of younger caterpillars evokes paralytic symptoms. At a larval molt the hypodermis of a larval leg once again forms the covering of a larval leg, but at the pupal molt, where the larval leg is lost, it apparently contracts (the process is not precisely described) and makes the customary pupal hypodermis without any special form construction over the imaginal anlage of the extremity. Since in the homoplastic-kataplastic experiment we were able to release in the hypodermis a larval instead of a pupal molt, it must be concluded that the extrahypodermal factors do not determine merely "molting," but rather "larval molting" or "pupal molting"; thus they also influence the nature of the process. With some limitations this is indicated also in the transplantations of younger legs (Stage 3) onto older hosts (Stage 4). These transplants first completed smoothly the forthcoming larval molt of the host and later the subsequent pupal molt. But strikingly, pupal molting succeeded smoothly in only certain cases (2 out of 5) of the orthotopic transplantations; that is to say, the empty chitinous shell was cast off, while the hypodermis apparently remained on the host. In the other cases, thus in all of the heterotopic ones and in three of the five orthotopic ones, the chitinous shell was pinched off together with the epidermis. In these the epidermis of the transplant had clearly been lifted away from the chitinous shell, and thus likewise displayed molting phenomena. But whether these should be regarded as pupal or larval molts cannot be decided. Hence there are apparently at least two kinds of extrahypodermal molting factors to be distinguished, namely, "factors for larval molting" and "factors for pupal molting."

The accomplishment in our experiment of a supernumerary larval molt in place of the pupal molt is to an extent in contradiction with the results of Kopeć (1922a, b). Kopeć transplanted the wing anlagen, eyes, and Malphighian tubules from caterpillars close to pupation into earlier stages, and found that these structures developed in accordance with their origin and thus were not subject to any influences from the host. The contradiction in the two results is easily explained from the different ages of the operated animals. In Kopeć's experiments, the donor had obviously begun metamorphosis, and the various organs had already experienced an impulse toward metamorphosis. In our experiment, on the other hand, the donor was far distant from pupation. Evidently relationships here are similar to those in amphibian metamorphosis, as was shown by means of kata- and anaplastic experiments by Uhlenhut, Sidonya Vertelowna, and Stone et al. for the eye (see Mangold, 1931, pp. 303, 304). Uhlenhut, using larvae of *Salamandra maculosa*, transplanted the eye bulb heterotopically behind the jaw region and found that in general it carried out the darkening of the iris, which appears at metamorphosis, synchronously with the metamorphosis of the host (synchronic metamorphosis). But when one of the two partners, differing in age, had already initiated metamorphosis, the implanted eye metamorphosed too early—with older donors—or too late —with older hosts—(heterochronic metamorphosis).

E. *The Performance of the Hypodermis*

The smooth execution of the supernumerary larval molts in transplantations from the fifth to the fourth and from the fourth to the third stage shows that the potencies necessary are at the disposal of the hypodermis, no doubt for a longer than normal time. Now the question is: For how long and in what stages does the hypodermis possess the capacity of carrying out a pupal molt? Here our experiments permit no certain conclusions, for surprisingly almost all transplants were shed completely (i.e., integument and epidermis) at the pupal molt, no matter whether of the same stage as, younger than, or older than the host, and also whether they had been transplanted heterotopically or orthotopically. There were only three exceptions, two (out of five) orthotopic-anaplastic and one heterotopic-kataplastic (Leg 81₁, p. 00). In these, as in a normal pupal molt, the chitinous shell of the transplant was cast off without epidermis; here apparently the epidermis had been incorporated into the pupal hypodermis. But these instances are not sufficient proof of the presence in earlier stages of a capacity for pupation.

Why the transplants were cast off at the pupal molt is unclear. Several causes are to be considered and might have worked singly or together, for instance, (1) the capacity or lack of capacity, discussed above, of the younger material to respond to the pupation stimulus; (2) mechanical or chemical alterations in the host hypodermis at pupation, which have an adverse influence on the transplant; and finally (3) the possibility that the implant is not reached at all by the pupation stimulus. The first possibility comes into question only for the anaplastic transplantations, not for those of the same stage and for the kataplastic ones. Against this likelihood there is a certain amount of evidence from the two cases with positive pupal molts, mentioned above. The second possibility has much in its favor, since pupation is accompanied by appreciable contractions in the neighborhood of the transplant, by which superfluous material is naturally easily cast off. The third possibility is on the whole quite improbable, since the stimulus for a larval molt has evidently reached the implant. Yet there might be here a significant difference between larval molting and pupal molting, which will not be discussed further, since it leads too far into the realm of speculation.

In respect to the capacity of the hypodermis for molting, we find that the old hypodermis, ready for the pupal molt, can still perform larval molts and that thus the number of larval molts is not precisely fixed. Whether young hypodermis can also carry out a pupal molt at all times is still uncertain, however.

Our results naturally do not exclude the possibility that parallel with the internal processes in the animal there occur changes in the hypodermis that enable the hypodermis to carry out its acts independently, changes that are suppressed in the transplantation experiment by the effective extrahypodermal factors. If this were the case, the molts would be doubly assured. Experience in experimental research on amphibia indicates that this is not improbable. Such changes in the hypodermis are not demonstrable for the caterpillar hypodermis in our experiments. Perhaps the observed fact that after molting a few transplants did not have the normal intensity of coloration is a clue of sorts. However, little significance can be attached to this with reference to our question; at best it shows that the caterpillar skin is subject to certain weakening influences which interfere with its capacity for becoming colored. But even if all performances are deemed to go to completion in the total absence of extrahypodermal factors, to the latter must still be ascribed a role as releasers and to the hypodermis the totality of the potencies requisite for execution.

F. The Nature and Localization of the Extrahypodermal Factors

The experiments by Koller and von Buddenbrock already mentioned made it seem rather likely that molting and pupation depend on the action of factors in the blood which should be regarded as hormones. Perhaps the factors called "extrahypodermal" in our experiments should be equated with these molting hormones.

The results of heteroplastic transplantation show that the extrahypodermal factors that determine molting are not species-specific.

SUMMARY

1. Using caterpillars of *Vanessa urticae* and *Vanessa io*, bristles, abdominal legs, and thoracic legs were transplanted homoplastically and heteroplastically,

heterotopically and orthotopically, between specimens of like and unlike ages. In the heterotopic combination the site of transplantation was mostly the locus of a dorsal median bristle on the caterpillar's back; occasionally other places were selected. The transplants healed in well and made autonomous movements.

2. The implants invariably molted synchronously with the host; factors in the host determined the time of molting (cf. synchronous metamorphosis in Amphibia).

3. The implants are able to go through one more larval molt than they normally do. Hence the number of larval molts is not defined in the hypodermis.

4. At the pupal molt, surprisingly, the transplants were regularly cast off, no matter whether they were younger, the same age, or older than the host. The question whether early transplants can be brought prematurely to the pupal molt must therefore remain open.

5. Probably at least two extrahypodermal molting factors, larval and pupal, are to be distinguished.

6. The factors for the several larval molts are evidently alike.

7. They are also not species-specific and perhaps correspond to the molting hormones discovered by Koller and von Buddenbrock.

8. In orthotopic-homoplastic-anaplastic transplantation, the stump of the excised host extremity regenerated, without regard to the transplant, an extremity that was situated on top of and lateral to the transplant.

REFERENCES

Bodenstein, D.: Experimentelle Untersuchungen über die Regeneration der Borsten bei *Vanessa urticae* L. *Z. Insektenbiol. 25* (1930).

Buddenbrock, W. von: Beitrag zur Histologie und Physiologie der Raupenhäutung, mit besonderer Berücksichtigung der Versonschen Drüsen. *Z. Morph. u. Okal. Tiere 18*, H. 4 (1930 a). Untersuchungen über die Häutungshormone der Schmetterlingsraupen. *Z. Physiol. 14*, H. 2 (1930 b).

Frew, J. G. H.: A Technique for the Cultivation of Insect Tissues. *Brit. J. Exper. Biol.* 6 (1928).

Koller, F.: Die innere Sekretion der wirbellosen Tiere. *Naturwiss. Mh. biol.-chem., geogr. u. geolog. Unterr. 27*, H. 4 (1930). Leipzig: B. G. Taubner.

Kopeć, S.: Untersuchungen über Kastration und Transplantation bei Schmetterlingen. *Arch. Entw. mechan. 33* (1911).

――― Mutual Relationship in the Development of the Brain and Eyes of Lepidoptera. *J. of Exper. Zool. 36* (1922 a).

――― Physiological Self-Differentiation of the Wing-Germs grafted on Caterpillars of the Opposite Sex. *J. of Exper. Zool. 36* (1922 b).

――― Studies on the Necessity of the Brain for the Inception of Insect Metamorphosis. *Biol. Bull. 42* (1922 c).

Korschelt, E.: *Regeneration und Transplantation.* Vol. 2, T. I. *Transplantation.* Berlin: Gebr. Bornträger 1931.

Loewe, S.: Hormonale Sexualität bei den Schmetterlingen. *Naturwiss. 1931*, H. 37.

Mangold, O.: Ueber formative Reize in der Entwicklung der Amphibien. *Naturwiss. 14*, H. 50/51 (1926).

――― Experimente zur Analyse der Determination und Induktion der Medullarplatte. *Roux' Arch. 117*, Spemann-Festschr. T. 2 (1929).

——— Das Determinationsproblem III. Das Wirbeltierauge in der Entwicklung und Regeneration. *Erg. Biol.* 7. Berlin: Julius Springer 1931.

Metalnikow, S.: Zur Verwandlung der Insekten. *Biol. Zbl.* 27 (1907).

Plotnikow, W.: Ueber die Häutung und einige Elemente der Haut bei den Insekten. *Z. Zool.* 76 (1904).

Przibram, H.: *Experimental-Zoologie, 2. Regeneration.* Leipzig-Wien: F. Deuticke 1909.

Schröder, C.: *Handbuch der Entomologie.* Jena: G. Fischer.

Schulze, W.: Weitere Untersuchungen über die Wirkung nekretorischer Drüsensubstanzen auf die Morphogenie. III. Ueber die Sprengung der Harmonie der Entwicklung. *Arch. mikrosk. Anat. u. Entw.mechan. 101,* H. 1/3 (1924).

Umeja, J.: Studies on the Vigor of Silkworms, *Bombyx mori. Genetics 15* (1930). *mikrosk. Anat. u. Entw.mechan.* 99, H. 1 (1923).

Weiss, P.: Transplantation von entwickelten Extremitäten bei Amphibien. II. *Arch.*

V. B. WIGGLESWORTH

The physiology of ecdysis in *Rhodnius prolixus* (Hemiptera). II. Factors controlling moulting and metamorphosis

Vincent Brian Wigglesworth was born in Kirkham, Lancashire, in 1899. He studied at Repton and at Caius College, and was graduated in physiology and biochemistry from the University of Cambridge. He received his M.D. from St. Thomas' Hospital in London. From 1926 to 1935 he was Lecturer in Entomology at the London School of Medical Hygiene and Tropical Medicine, and then held the post of Reader in Entomology at the University of London. From 1945 to 1952 he was also Director of an A.R.C. unit. Since 1952 he has held the post of Quick Professor of Biology at the University of Cambridge. He is a Fellow of the Royal Society, and was knighted in 1964.

His research interests are in physiology, and in the metamorphosis, comparative physiology, and endocrinology of insects.

In the blood-sucking bug *Rhodnius prolixus* there are five nymphal stages, throughout which the morphological characters remain comparatively constant. At the fifth moult, when the insect becomes adult, there are striking changes in all parts of the body. It is convenient to refer to the appearance of these adult characters as 'metamorphosis'—though without suggesting that this change is exactly homologous with metamorphosis in endopterygote insects. Thus in the growth of *Rhodnius* there are two distinct phenomena to be considered: simple moulting, and moulting coupled with metamorphosis. In a previous paper (Wigglesworth, 1933) the histo-

[Previously published in *Quarterly Journal of Microscopial Sciences*, 77 (1934): 121–222. Reprinted by permission of the publisher and author.]

logical changes in the epidermis during moulting and metamorphosis have been described; in the present paper an attempt will be made to analyse some of the factors which regulate these processes.

According to current opinion moulting in insects is induced by a hormone secreted into the blood (Bodenstein, 1933*b*). Koller (1929) accelerated the onset of moulting in normal Sphingid larvae by injecting the blood from other larvae in which moulting had begun. v. Buddenbrock (1930) repeated these experiments on a larger scale. He failed to obtain a definite acceleration of moulting; but moulting was not delayed; whereas, if the blood of normal larvae was injected, moulting was delayed—from which he inferred that the blood of the moulting larvae had actually caused an acceleration. More convincing evidence was obtained by Bodenstein (1933*a*), who showed that limbs transplanted from one caterpillar to another, moulted at the same time as their new host.

As regards the pupation of caterpillars, Kopeć (1922) showed that in the last stage larvae of *Lymantria* the removal of the brain before a certain crictial stage of growth arrested development. Section of the nerve-cord had not this effect, from which he concluded that pupation was induced by a hormone secreted by the brain. The presence of such a hormone was demonstrated also by tying a silk thread round the larvae. If this was done before the critical stage, only the anterior fragment pupated; if done after the critical stage, both fragments pupated.[1] These experiments provide the starting-point of the present inquiry.

THE CAUSATION OF MOULTING

The Effect of Decapitation on Moulting

Moulting in *Rhodnius* occurs at a definite interval after feeding, only one meal being necessary in each stage. The fifth nymph, at 24° C., requires on an average about 28 days between feeding and moulting; the fourth nymph requires about 15 days; the earlier nymphs rather less. Insects at all stages have been decapitated at different times after feeding, and the effect on development observed. The head was removed by drawing a thread tightly round the neck in the larger insects; it was cut off with scissors in the smaller insects, the wound in each case being sealed with paraffin wax melting at 52° C.

The results are given in Fig. 1, where it can be seen that in each stage (as Kopeć (1922) found in the pupation of *Lymantria*) there is a critical period before which the head is necessary for moulting to occur. After this period moulting is no longer prevented by decapitation. In the fifth nymph

---

[1] Similar results, with fly larvae, have been reported in a preliminary note by Fraenkel (1934).

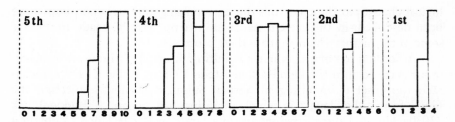

Figure 1. Charts showing the proportion of insects which moulted out of batches (numbering from 6 to 30) decapitated at different times after feeding. Figures on base line represent days after feeding. The uppermost level represents 100 percent moulting.

the critical period occurs between the sixth and eighth days after feeding; in the earlier nymphs, from the third to the fifth day.

These headless insects digest their meal and excrete normally. Where they fail to moult they survive for long periods—several fifth nymphs survived more than 200 days, and one survived more than a year (Fig. 4, Pl. I)—far longer, indeed, than normal insects fed at the same time and kept under the same conditions. Where they moult, the process goes forward as already described (Wigglesworth, 1933). The insect usually dies when part way out of its old skin; in many cases the only sign that moulting is complete is the appearance of a film of air beneath the old cuticle—due to the absorption of the moulting fluid; but in one instance, that of a fourth nymph decapitated 4 days after feeding, the insect freed itself completely from the old skin.

The Effect of Decapitation on the Histological Changes in the Epidermis

In order to throw some light on the nature of the influence the head exerts, a series of fourth nymphs was fed on the same day, half being decapitated 24 hours later and half serving as controls. On each succeeding day for a week after feeding, the tergites of the abdomen were removed from a decapitated insect and a control insect, stained, and mounted as already described (Wigglesworth, 1933), and the appearances in the epidermis compared.

There are visible differences in the epidermal cells within 24 hours after decapitation. In the normal insects the cytoplasm gradually becomes denser and more deeply staining. By the fourth day after feeding the nuclei are swollen, the chromatin being often clumped at the centre, and occasional mitoses can be seen. By the fifth and sixth days mitoses are very numerous. In the decapitated insects, on the other hand, these signs of growth are entirely wanting: the cytoplasm remains pale and somewhat vacuolated, and no cell divisions occur. The dermal glands behave alike in both: the saccular dilatations of their ducts show up as clear areas, but the glands themselves show no sign of secretory activity in either group of insects. During the first week the oenocytes become progressively swollen and lobulated in the decapitated as in the normal insects. In the normal insects (Wigglesworth, 1933) they become reduced again as the new cuticle is formed; in a decapitated insect mounted 21 days after feeding, they were still enormously enlarged.

Thus the histological criterion of the 'critical period' (3 to 6 days after feeding, in the fourth nymph) is the onset of mitosis in the epidermal cells; but in the normal insect there are signs of growth in these cells even before this period. In the decapitated insect these growth changes are absent.

Comparable results were obtained by taking twelve fifth nymphs, all from the same batch, decapitating six of them 7 days after feeding, and mounting the abdominal tergites of the other six on the same day. Only one of the decapitated insects failed to moult. The six insects mounted 7 days after feeding could be arranged in a series according to the stage of growth of the epidermis; and in only one of this series had mitosis not begun.

The results, coupled with the experimental effects of decapitation, suggest that the head is necessary for the production of a growth or moulting hormone; and that this hormone increases in amount until it reaches a critical concentration. At this stage (the critical period) mitoses in the epidermal cells begin, and thereafter the head is no longer needed.

Demonstration of a Moulting Hormone in the Blood

If this idea is correct, the blood from an insect that has just passed the critical period should induce moulting in an insect decapitated before that period. This has been tested by cutting through the prothorax of the two insects, one shortly after the critical period, the other 24 hours after feeding, and fastening them together with paraffin wax so that the blood can flow freely from one to the other. In the early experiments the mixing of the blood was ensured by gently squeezing the two insects alternately; but this proved unnecessary.

In the first experiment, six fifth nymphs decapitated 8 days after feeding were joined to six fifth nymphs decapitated 1 day after feeding (Fig. 1, Pl. I). Two of the former moulted, and both induced moulting in their partners. This experiment has been repeated many times with nymphs at different stages, and in every case where the insect decapitated soon after the critical period has moulted, it has induced moulting in its partner decapitated 24 hours after feeding.

It is interesting to note that cross-circulation in this way seems to reduce the proportion of insects moulting after decapitation on a given day; as though in some cases mixture and dilution with the blood of the second insect reduced the concentration of the moulting hormone below the criti-

1   2   3

4   5   6

7   8   9

cal level. Thus in the above experiment only two out of the six insects moulted; whereas after the simple decapitation at 8 days (Fig. 1) five out of six fifth nymphs moulted. And of fourth nymphs simply decapitated at 5 days, six out of six moulted (Fig. 1); whereas after decapitation combined with transfusion six out of eleven moulted. But a great many experiments would be required to establish this point with certainty.

It is interesting to note also that in the first experiment, although there was an interval of 7 days between the feeding of the two members of each pair, both members became ripe for moulting (that is, air appeared beneath the old cuticle) simultaneously: in one pair 29 and 36 days, respectively, after feeding; in the other pair 33 and 40 days. This simultaneous moulting has occurred with such constancy that it cannot be due merely to coincidence. Altogether forty-seven pairs of these cross-circulated insects have moulted—insects in many cases belonging to different nymphal stages —and in forty-two pairs moulting occurred in both members during the same day. In several cases it was definitely seen to take place within the same hour. In the remaining five pairs it took place at an interval of 1 or 2 days.[2]

Now if the living nymphs are examined with a dissecting microscope while the epidermal cells are becoming separated and the new cuticle is being laid down, the body surface can be seen to go through a definite sequence of changes; and by observing these changes the stage of development can be approximately gauged. If daily observations are made on two insects that have been joined together, the onset of moulting is seen to be accelerated in the second insect (so that it may reach in 6 days a stage normally reached in 9 or 10 days), while the progress of moulting in the first insect appears to be delayed. This delay seems to last until the second insect has caught up the first; thereafter they develop together.

[2] These figures do not include experiments where transfusion has been performed in the later stages of moulting (see p. 198).

PLATE I

Figure 1.   Two fifth nymphs joined together after decapitation.
Figure 2.   Decapitated fifth nymph joined to a decapitated fourth nymph.
Figure 3.   Two decapitated fourth nymphs joined together.
Figure 4.   Living fifth nymph photographed 10 months after decapitation.
Figure 5.   Decapitated fifth nymph joined to a fourth nymph with the tip of the head removed.
Figure 6.   Decapitated first nymph attached to tip of head of fifth nymph.
Figure 7.   Unexpanded wing of normal adult.
Figure 8.   The same from adult produced from decapitated fifth nymph by joining it to fourth nymph decapitated 7 days after feeding (as in Figure 2).
Figure 9.   The same from insect produced from a decapitated fifth nymph by joining it to a fourth nymph with only the tip of the head removed (as in Figure 5).

Thus it appears that not only is moulting initiated by a hormone, but the entire process is regulated, and parallel development in all parts of the body is ensured, by chemical substances in the blood. It is inconceivable that a single external factor should secure this exact co-ordination. These observations can only mean that the growing tissues themselves are communicating with and controlling one another by chemical means. This is a fundamental idea but it is beyond the scope of the present work, which is concerned only with the external or overriding factors which provide the initial stimuli to growth.

How Long Does the Moulting Hormone Persist in the Blood?

In all the transfusion experiments so far described, the insects providing the moulting hormone were decapitated immediately after the critical period. In order to see how long the hormone persists in the blood, the experiments were repeated with fourth nymphs decapitated 7, 8, 9, 10, and 12 days after feeding. All those up to 10 days caused their partners to start moulting, showing that the hormone remains active until development is well advanced. But, as can be seen in Table 1, when the nymphs are cross-circulated in the later stages of moulting the development of the first insect is no longer delayed by the presence of the second; so that the first insect

TABLE I

Simultaneous and independent moulting of cross-circulated nymphs

Day after feeding	No. of experiments	No. failing to moult	No. moulting simultaneously	No. moulting independently
(a) Fourth nymphs cross-circulated (at different times after feeding) with fourth nymphs decapitated 24 hours after feeding.				
5	5	2	3	0
6	6	1	5	0
7	6	0	5	1
8	6	0	2	4
9	6	0	0	6
10	6	0	1	5
12	6	0	0	6
(b) Fourth nymphs cross-circulated (at different times after feeding) with fifth nymphs decapitated 24 hours after feeding				
5	6	3	3	0
6	5	1	4	0
7	4	1	3	0
8	4	0	3	1
9	6	0	0	6

moults independently. As soon as it has moulted development in the second insect seems to be arrested and it fails to complete its moult. That may be the reason for the failure of the 12-day insects to induce moulting: the first insect of each pair moulting before visible changes were apparent in the second. But the significance of these results has not yet been explored.

The Source of the Moulting Hormone

From the foregoing results it is clear that the moulting hormone must either be secreted in the head or by some organ innervated from the head. Various suggestions have been put forward in the past. (1) Koller (1929) suggested that the oenocytes might be concerned. But these have no nerve supply, they reach the height of their secretory activity when the new cuticle is being laid down—long after moulting has begun (Wigglesworth, 1933)—and we have seen that they go through the same changes, at least up to the critical period, in both normal and decaditated insects. (2) Buddenbrock (1930) and Hoop (1933) believe the dermal moulting glands to be responsible. But in *Rhodnius* these glands clearly serve to digest the old

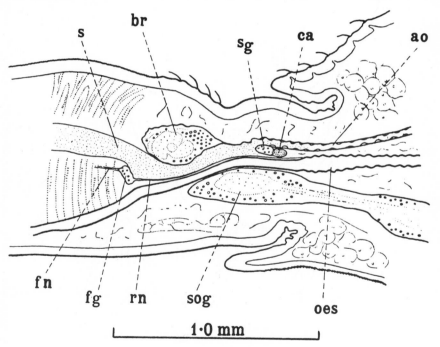

Figure 2. Longitudinal section of the posterior part of the head and the prothorax of *Rhodnius* (composite figure), *ao:* aorta; *br:* brain; *ca:* corpus allatum; *fg:* frontal ganglion; *fn:* frontal nerve; *oes:* oesophagus; *rn:* recurrent nerve; *s:* sinus receiving blood from aorta; *sg:* sympathetic ganglion; *sog:* suboesophageal ganglion.

cuticle in the later stages of moulting; moulting has definitely begun before
the new glands become active (Wigglesworth, 1933); and there is no difference in the changes in the old glands in normal and decapitated insects.
(3) Kopeć (1922) supposed that the brain itself secreted the hormone.

By analogy with vertebrates it is more likely that the hormone should
be produced by some discrete glandular organ. Such an organ is the corpus
allatum, which is usually regarded as a gland of internal secretion of unknown function (Nabert, 1913). Like the endocrine organs of vertebrates it
is budded off from the epidermis at an early stage of development, and it is
well supplied with nerves. Fig. 2 represents a longitudinal section of the
head and prothorax showing the position and relations of the corpus allatum. In *Rhodnius* it is a single median structure, more or less spherical,
situated at the posterior part of the head, where this is invaginated into the

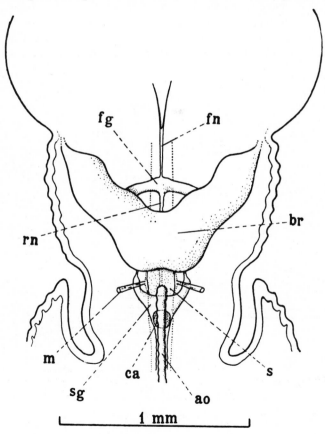

Figure 3.   Approximate reconstruction of the brain and associated structures
viewed from above. *ao:* aorta; *br:* brain; *ca:* corpus allatum; *fg:* frontal ganglion;
fn: frontal nerve; *m:* muscle attached to gut; *rn:* recurrent nerve; *s:* sinus receiving blood from aorta; *sg:* sympathetic ganglion.

prothorax. Fig. 3 is a rough drawing of the brain and associated organs seen from above, based partly on dissections, partly on reconstruction from horizontal sections. A detailed description of these structures is not necessary for our present purpose. Fig. 4 shows the corpus allatum and its immediate relations on a larger scale. It is made up of a great number of closely packed cells staining rather deeply. Immediately in front is the posterior sympathetic ganglion from which it receives a nerve entering at a hilus. It is invested by some large pale-staining cells which injections of ammonia carmine have proved to be pericardial cells. Directly above it lies the aorta, which ends immediately beyond the sympathetic ganglion by discharging downwards into a large sinus with membranous walls. This sinus runs forwards through the brain, but it also discharges backwards around the corpus allatum, which thus enjoys a very rich blood supply.

Serial sections of the head and thorax of *Rhodnius* fifth nymphs, double embedded in celloidin and paraffin, have been prepared at all stages of the moulting process: that is, in the fasting insect, at intervals of 1 day up to 10 days after feeding, and thereafter at intervals of 2 days up to the time of moulting at 28 days. One series was prepared at each day; except around the critical period, when two were made at 6 days after feeding, four at 7 days, and two at 8 days. The sections were stained with Ehrlich's haematoxylin and eosin, and compared by having two microscopes side by side.

The only organ in the head which was found to show a definite cycle of changes coinciding with the critical period was the corpus allatum. During the sixth, seventh, and eighth days, particularly the seventh day after feeding, the cells of the corpus allatum are swollen; the cytoplasm is homo-

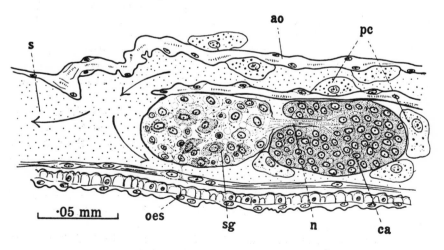

Figure 4. Longitudinal section of corpus allatum and related structures. *ao:* aorta; *ca:* corpus allatum; *n:* nerve entering corpus allatum; *oes:* oesophagus; *pc:* pericardial cells; *s:* blood sinus, *sg:* sympathetic ganglion. The arrows indicate direction of blood flow.

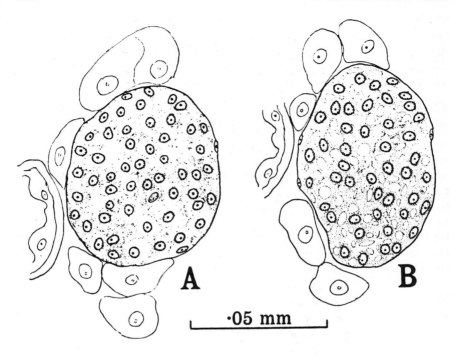

Figure 5. Transverse sections of corpus allatum of fifth nymph. A: 7 days after feeding; B: 12 days after feeding.

geneous and somewhat eosinophil, and the cell boundaries are distinct (Fig. 5A). Before and after this period the cells tend to shrink away from one another, leaving indefinite vacuolated spaces between, the cell boundaries being difficult to make out (Fig. 5B). During the moulting of the fifth nymph there appears to be no multiplication of cells in the corpus allatum; the gland as a whole does not increase in size, and no mitoses have been seen.

A similar series of preparations was made from the moulting fourth nymphs. Here there is a great increase in the number of cells in the corpus allatum, mitoses being very numerous during the third, fourth, and fifth days after feeding. At no period do these young growing cells show the swollen eosinophil appearance described above. But there is a group of cells, mostly in the central part of the corpus allatum, which, during the critical period (the third, fourth, and fifth days after feeding), do show precisely this change.

The histological evidence therefore favours the idea that the corpus allatum is responsible for secreting the moulting hormone. But we have seen that moulting is co-ordinated by hormones which must be derived from the growing cells themselves (p. 198), and this raises the question whether the general epidermal cells may not be responsible for the initial moulting hormone. This possibility cannot be entirely excluded; but the epidermal cells are not innervated (p. 206), and it is therefore probable that any hormones they secrete appear only when their own growth has been stimulated by the hormone from the head.

The Stimulus to Moulting

The next question is the nature of the stimulus which brings about secretion of the moulting hormone. In the earlier paper (Wigglesworth, 1933) it was shown that the time required for moulting is substantially the same whether the insect is fed a week after the previous moult or 9 weeks. The moulting cycle is clearly initiated by the new meal. Now if a succession of small meals is given at intervals, so that the stomach always contains a small amount of blood, moulting does not occur. (This was observed also by Kemper (1931) in the bed-bug, *Cimex.*) It cannot therefore be the state of nutrition alone which determines moulting. It appears rather to be the abdominal distension.

This notion was tested experimentally as follows. After a meal of blood *Rhodnius* rapidly eliminates a large amount of fluid, quickly reducing the abdominal distension (Wigglesworth, 1931). By occluding the anus with paraffin immediately after feeding, the distension for a given size of meal can be artificially exaggerated; and it is thus possible to study the effect of distension apart from that of nutrition. Fig. 6 summarizes the results obtained. Normal fifth nymphs, which weigh from 30 to 50 mg. according to the time since they moulted, usually take a feed of between

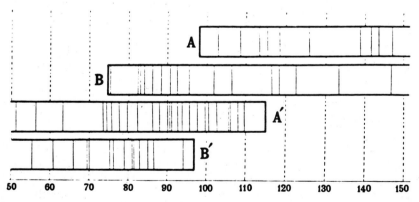

Figure 6. Chart showing the effect of occluding the anus immediately after feeding on the size of meal necessary to cause moulting in fifth stage nymphs. The figures represent milligrams. The vertical lines indicate weights of blood taken by individual insects. A: normal insects which subsequently moulted; A': normal insects which failed to moult; B: insects with anus occluded, which moulted; B': ditto which failed to moult.

200 and 300 mg. of rabbit blood. A meal as large as 420 mg. was noted in one instance. As shown in Fig. 6A, the smallest meal after which any normal nymph moulted was 98.6 mg.; the largest meal which failed to cause moulting was 115 mg. (Fig. 6A′). When the anus was occluded immediately after feeding, the smallest meal to cause moulting was 74.8 mg. (Fig. 6B); and the largest which failed to cause moulting was 96.7 mg. (Fig. 6B′).

Thus stretching of the abdomen, combined of course with adequate nutrition,[3] is probably the requisite stimulus to moulting. We have seen that the presence of the head is necessary for moulting to occur. This suggests that stretching exerts its effect by way of the nervous system. (Excessive stretching, produced by occluding the anus immediately after a large meal, caused great delay in moulting and in some cases has inhibited it altogether. Kemper (1931) observed that excessive feeding of *Cimex* delayed moulting. Perhaps that was the same phenomenon.)

Effect of Cutting the Nerve-Cord

The part played by the nervous system has been tested by cutting through the nerve-cord immediately behind the neck 24 hours after a full meal. The prothorax in front of the first pair of legs was cut through with a fine lancet up to the level at which the sections showed the nerve-cord to lie (Fig. 7,

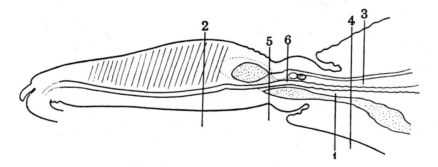

Figure 7. Longitudinal section of head and thorax of *Rhodnius* showing the positions at which experimental cuts were made.

cut 1), the wound being sealed with paraffin. Some of the earlier insects upset the experiment by swallowing enormous quantities of air and so causing their death. Later this was prevented by waxing over the proboscis. Of thirty-two fifth nymphs treated in this way, only six moulted. Serial longitudinal sections of these were cut; and in all of them it was found that the nerve-cord had been incompletely severed, though in three of these the part that remained could not have been more than 1 per cent of the

[3] Insects becoming distended with lymph alone, as occasionally happens with first-stage nymphs, do not moult. This has been observed also in *Cimex* by Kemper (1931).

total nerve-cord. In these three, moulting was enormously delayed. They were fixed 44, 49, and 56 days after feeding, and yet the new cuticle was not nearly fully formed. Serial longitudinal sections were cut from five of the nymphs which failed to moult. In these the break in the cord was found to be complete; but the contents of the head, including the corpus allatum, were perfectly normal in appearance.

Thus it appears that nervous impulses to the brain, due to stretching of the abdomen, provoke the secretion of the moulting hormone. But it is remarkable how slender a nerve connexion will suffice for this purpose.

The Innervation of the Abdomen

The central nervous system of *Rhodnius* is concentrated in the head and thorax; but a great number of slender nerves run backwards to the abdo-

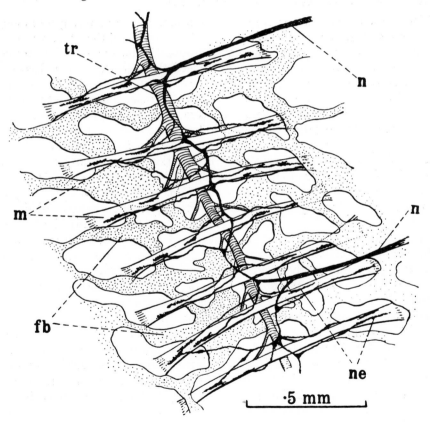

Figure 8.   Small group of intersegmental muscles on sterna of fifth nymph. Head of insect lies to the right. (Dogiel's method.) *fb*: fat body; *m*: intersegmental muscles; *n*: nerves from thoracic ganglia entering nerve plexus; *ne*: nerve endings; *tr*: trachea.

men. In the hope of demonstrating the receptors of the stretching stimulus, the distribution of these nerves has been studied by Dogiel's method (the injection of 0.05 percent methylene blue in Ringer's solution into the living insect and the fixation of the tissues several hours later with saturated ammonium picrate). There is no innervation of the general epidermal cells. Fibres can be traced to the sensory cells below the cuticular bristles. But the vast majority of the nerves end in rich plexuses, which lie transversally along the intersegmental membranes, and supply an abundance of branches to the numerous intersegmental muscles—particularly on the sterna (Fig. 8). Many of these nerves must convey afferent impulses due to muscle tension. It is highly probable that it is they which are stimulated by the stretching of the abdominal wall.

Section of the Nerves to the Corpus Allatum

Now if the corpus allatum is indeed the source of the moulting hormone, as the histological evidence suggests (p. 202), removal of this gland without injury to the brain should prevent moulting. Unfortunately, the corpus allatum of *Rhodnius* is so awkwardly placed that this experiment has not yet been successfully performed.

Moulting should also be prevented by cutting the nerve connexion between the brain and the corpus allatum. But the nerve-fibres from the brain enter the sympathetic ganglion so low down that it is necessary to cut more than half-way through the head from the dorsal aspect to sever them. Cuts of varying depth were made in this position in twelve insects (Fig. 7, cut 6). Shallow cuts scarcely delayed moulting. Deep cuts delayed it greatly—moulting being still incomplete 77 days after feeding; and in two insects, moulting was completely inhibited (there was no sign of moulting even beginning 90 days after feeding). Serial longitudinal sections of these various insects were cut, but the tissues had been so much disorganized by the operation that it was impossible to be certain that the nerve connexions were completely severed in the insects which failed to moult; incompletely severed in the others. These results are therefore inconclusive; but their general resemblance to the effects of incomplete and complete section of the ventral nerve-cord is very suggestive.

Certain other experiments, the results of which are compatible with this hypothesis, may be referred to very briefly. (1) Removal of the head in front of the eyes (Fig. 7, cut 2) (performed in six insects) delayed moulting up to 50 days but did not prevent it. (2) Section through the dorsal half of the prothorax, dividing the aorta (Fig. 7, cut 3) (performed in six insects) merely delayed moulting up to 52 days). (3) Section of the aorta at the anterior end of the abdomen, without injury to the other abdominal contents (performed in four insects) delayed moulting up to 65 days but did not prevent it. (4) Section through the prothorax, with replacement of the head (Fig. 7, cut 4) (performed in ten insects) entirely prevented moulting; although the tissues, at least in the posterior part of the head, survived for a considerable time. (5) Section immediately behind the brain but in front of the corpus allatum (Fig. 7, cut 5) with removal of the anterior fragment (performed in eight insects) entirely prevented moulting. (6) Transplantation of the posterior half of the head of the insect into its own abdomen 24 hours after feeding (performed in twenty insects) did not result in moulting; although, when sections were cut 6 weeks later, the cellular contents of the transplanted head still appeared healthy, though considerably disorganized.

THE CAUSATION OF "METAMORPHOSIS"

The adult *Rhodnius* presents many structural characters which distinguish it from the nymphal stages. It has well-developed membranous wings, whereas the nymphs have only small leathery lobes, rather more conspicuous in the fifth nymph. The adult has sexual appendages which are totally unlike in male and female. In the earlier nymphs the sexes cannot be distinguished; though in the fifth nymph, as Gillett (1934) has recently shown, there are slight but definite sexual differences. The adult has a climbing organ on the anterior and middle tibiae which is wanting in the nymphs (Gillett and Wigglesworth, 1932). There are numerous differences in the integument of the abdomen: the epicuticle shows a deep stellate folding in the nymphs, a slight transverse folding in the adult; the adult has a deep pleat along the side of the abdomen; the bristles are totally different in form; the dermal glands differ in form and in distribution, and so on (Wigglesworth, 1933). In this paper the development of these adult characters will be referred to as metamorphosis.

Control of Metamorphosis by the Blood

There are two possibilities in the causation of metamorphosis. There may be an inherent change in the body-cells of the fifth nymph, so that these give rise to adult structures although the moulting hormone remains the same; or the change in the type of differentiation at metamorphosis may be due to a change in the chemical factors in the blood.

This question is readily settled by transfusing blood (by the technique already described) from a fifth nymph decapitated after the critical period, into a fourth nymph decapitated 24 hours after feeding (Fig. 2, Pl. I). When this is done both insects moult simultaneously, and the fourth nymphs are found to have suffered a premature metamorphosis and to have developed all the adult characters mentioned above. As a single illustration Fig. 9 shows the female genitalia of a normal adult and an "adult" derived from a fourth nymph, together with the corresponding parts in a normal female fifth nymph.

It is worth noting that transfusion in this way has no influence on the sexual characters of the insects: the pair may be of the same or opposite

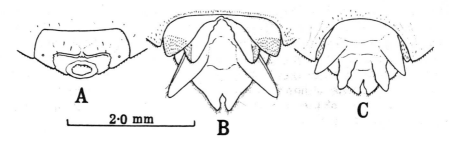

Figure 9.   A: terminal segments of normal female fifth nymph viewed from below; *B:* the same in normal adult female, with valves extruded; *C:* the same in
"adult" derived from fourth nymph cross-circulated with a moulting fifth nymph.

sexes. This bears out the conclusion of other authors that sexual characters
in insects are not influenced by chemical substances in the blood (Koller,
1929).

   This same experiment has been repeated with first nymphs. These
were decapitated 24 hours after feeding, and fixed with paraffin wax on to
the tip of the head of fifth nymphs fed 8 days previously (Fig. 6, Pl. I).
Out of six experiments, four of the first nymphs moulted successfully and
all gave rise to diminutive adults. One of these is shown in Fig. 10, where
its general appearance and its genitalia are contrasted with the corresponding parts of a normal second nymph.

Inhibition of Metamorphosis in the Early Nymphal Stages

These experiments clearly prove that metamorphosis is due to chemical
differences in the blood. But two kinds of chemical difference are con-
ceivable: either (*a*) the moulting hormone of the fifth nymph differs from
the moulting hormone of the earlier nymphs; or (*b*) the hormone is always the same, but the earlier nymphs produce in addition an inhibitory
hormone which restrains metamorphosis.

   This question was tested by joining six fourth nymphs decapitated 5
days after feeding to six fifth nymphs decapitated 24 hours after feeding.
Three of the fourth nymphs moulted, and each of them induced moulting
in the fifth nymph to which it was joined.

   This clearly proves that the moulting hormone is the same at metamorphosis as at earlier moults. Absence of metamorphosis in the younger
insects must therefore be due to an inhibitory factor. And if that is so we
should expect to find, in the above experiment, where the fifth nymphs
contain blood from moulting fourth nymphs, that the adults produced
from these fifth nymphs would show the effects of this inhibitory factor.
This has proved to be the case; though the effects were very slight, consisting only of small imperfections in the male and female genitalia.

   But it must be remembered that the body volume of the fifth nymph
is between two and three times that of the fourth nymph; and, therefore,

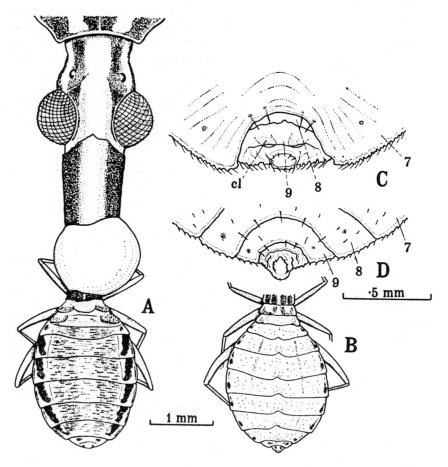

Figure 10. A: precocious "adult" produced from first nymph by joining it to head of a moulting fifth nymph; B: normal second nymph for comparison; C: terminal segments of the precocious "adult" (male); D: the same in normal second nymph. Figures indicate homologous sterna; *cl:* claspers (Cf. Figure 11.)

when the blood of the two insects is mixed the hypothetical inhibitory factor will be greatly diluted. If this dilution of the inhibitory factor from the fourth nymphs is really the cause of its feeble action upon the fifth nymphs, we should expect to find the fourth nymphs themselves in these experiments showing at least partial metamorphosis.

That also proved to be the case. Indeed, the three fourth nymphs showed almost complete metamorphosis. Furthermore, those fourth nymphs which produced the best-formed genitalia were found to be united to those fifth nymphs which developed genitalia with the least impairment —suggesting that in these the inhibitory factor was in very low concentration.

These experiments were repeated with fourth nymphs decapitated 6 days, 7 days, and 8 days after feeding, in the hopes that the inhibitory factor might be present in greater quantities. The results justified this expectation: adults of both sexes with genitalia incompletely formed and with wings intermediate between the fifth nymph and the normal adult were produced (Fig. 11 B, and Fig. 8, Pl. I).[4] But the effect was still relatively slight; and in all these experiments the fourth nymphs again developed adult characters (although, as a rule, these were not so well formed as in those decapitated and cross-circulated at 5 days)—showing that the inhibitory factor was still very limited in amount.

In might, of course, be argued that the metamorphosis of the fourth nymphs in these experiments was due, not to the dilution of an inhibitory factor as we have supposed, but to factors produced by the metamorphosing organs of the fifth nymphs. This possibility was tested by joining fourth nymphs decapitated at 5 days after feeding with fourth nymphs decapitated 24 hours after feeding (Fig. 3, Pl. I). Three of these pairs moulted, and both members of each pair were found to have undergone metamorphosis. When the experiments were repeated, using nymphs decapitated 6 days and 7 days after feeding, the results were the same. In every case both members of each pair showed adult characters, although, at least in the case of the 7-day insects, these were not so perfectly developed.

Thus at no stage does the inhibitory factor seem to reach a sufficient

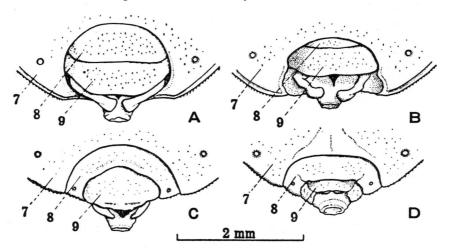

Figure 11.   A: terminal segments of normal adult male seen below; B: the same in adult male produced from decapitated fifth nymph by joining it to fourth nymph decapitated 7 days after feeding; C: the same in an insect produced from a decapitated fifth nymph by joining it to fourth nymph with only the tip of the head removed; D: normal male fifth nymph. Figures indicate homologous sterna.

[4] I am indebted to Dr. H. B. Newham for the photomicrographs of these wings.

concentration in the blood to prevent metamorphosis in a second insect. But acting on the assumption that the inhibitory factor is secreted in the head, and in the hope that an increased demand for this factor might lead to its production in increased amounts, a number of fourth nymphs in which only the tip of the head had been removed (6 days after feeding) were cross-circulated with fourth nymphs decapitated 24 hours after feeding. The results were as anticipated: five pairs of insects moulted, and both members of each pair gave rise to normal fifth nymphs. Metamorphosis had been completely inhibited.

An attempt was therefore made to inhibit metamorphosis in fifth nymphs in the same way: by decapitating them 24 hours after feeding, and joining them to fourth nymphs in which the tip of the head had been removed 6 days after feeding (Fig. 5, Pl. I). Three such fifth nymphs moulted. In the characters of the wings (Fig. 9, Pl. I), and the cuticle and pigmentation of the abdomen, and in the absence of a lateral pleat in the abdomen, they were almost exactly like giant nymphs. The genitalia showed partial development towards the adult form (Fig. 11 c). Two of them moulted 17 days after feeding; whereas the moult from fifth nymph to adult requires 28 days.

Effect of Simple Decapitation on Metamorphosis

It is evident from the foregoing experiments that the head is necessary for the secretion of the inhibitory hormone as well as the moulting hormone. It is probably legitimate to conclude, also, that the quantity of the in-

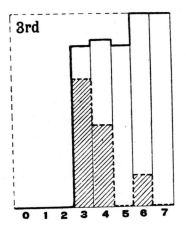 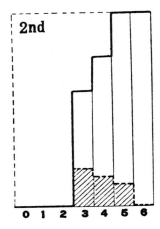

Figure 12. Charts showing proportion of insects developing adult characters when decapitated at different times after feeding. Figures on base line are days after feeding. The continuous line shows proportion of insects moulting; the broken line (above shaded area) shows proportion of insects developing adult characters.

hibitory hormone normally produced is very small, and that it is secreted
after the moulting hormone has become active.[5] If that is so, it should be
possible to decapitate early nymphs at a time when the moulting hormone
is already active, but the inhibitory hormone is absent, and so to bring
about premature metamorphosis.

This has proved to be the case. For if the head is removed from a
large number of fourth, third, second, even first nymphs around the critical
period, certain of them suffer a precocious metamorphosis, and develop
into diminutive adults. The results in the case of second and third nymphs
are summarized in Fig. 12. As was to be expected, the proportion of insects
moult increases. In other words, premature metamorphosis occurs only in
insects decapitated immediately after their critical period.

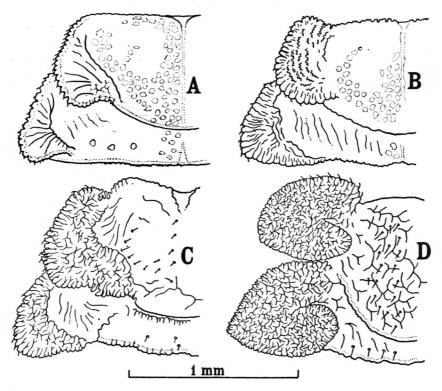

1 mm

Figure 13.   Dorsal view of left side of thorax in four insects produced by decapitating third stage nymphs on the third and fourth days after feeding. A:
normal fourth nymph; *B* and *C*: intermediate forms; *D*: extreme "adult" form.

[5] It has been pointed out to me by Dr. C. H. Waddington that the results described in
this paper could all be explained by supposing that a single hormone only is present,
which causes the appearance of adult characters at low concentrations, and of nymphal
characters at higher concentrations. Further work will be needed to test this possibility.

showing adult characters diminishes as the proportion of insects which

Now if this interpretation is correct, it should be possible to remove the head when varying amounts of the inhibitory factor are present, and so to obtain nymphs with adult characters developed in varying degree. And, in fact, if a number of these early nymphs decapitated around the critical period are closely examined when they are ripe for moulting, it is possible to arrange them in an unbroken series, with normal nymphs at one end, extreme adult forms at the other end, and all grades of intermediates between. These results are illustrated in Figs. 13–15, which represent four insects produced by decapitating third nymphs at the third and fourth days after feeding. In each case, A represents a normal fourth nymph, D the most extreme adult form obtained, B and C intermediates.

Fig. 13 shows the second and third thoracic segments and the wings. The progressive development of the adult type of wing is obvious. The changes would be more striking, of course, if the wings were expanded; those of D would then be seen to come very near the adult proportions. Fig. 14 shows a bristle from the dorsum and the margin of the abdomen from the same four insects, Fig. 14 E being corresponding bristles from a normal adult This series illustrates also the changes in the type of folding in the epicuticle. Fig. 15 shows the external genitalia. These four insects were all males. A corresponding series of females was also obtained.

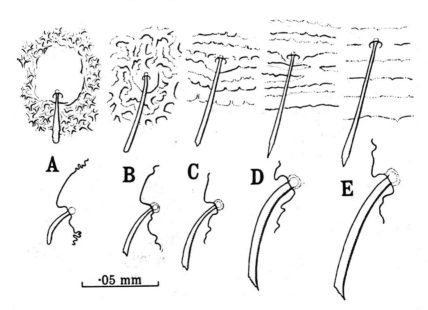

Figure 14. Bristles from dorsal surface of abdomen (upper row) and from margin of abdomen (lower row). A–D: from the insects represented in Figure 13; E: from a normal adult.

It is important to note that the abnormal change, even in insects showing the least degree of abnormality, is towards the adult form. Even in B (Fig. 15) rudimentary claspers are present in the male genitalia; whereas, even in the fifth nymphs of *Rhodnius* there are no definite claspers in the male (Gillett, 1934). The same applies to all their characters. Clearly, therefore, all these insects are intermediate adults, and not merely nymphs which have jumped a stage or two.

The tergites of these precocious adults have been stained and mounted. The epidermal cells are about the same size as in normal adults, and there are about the same number of cells to a unit area. Thus the outward form is that of the adult; but it may be built up by less than one hundredth part of the normal number of cells.

The Source of the Inhibitory Hormone

Definite evidence as to the source of the inhibitory factor is wanting. But it is almost certainly secreted in the head; and it is natural to turn again to the corpus allatum. We have seen (p. 202) that there is a difference between the changes in the corpus allatum during moulting in the fifth nymph and the earlier nymphs. In the former, all the cells become swollen and eosinophil during the critical period; in the latter, only a part of the cells shows this change. It is therefore an attractive hypothesis to suppose

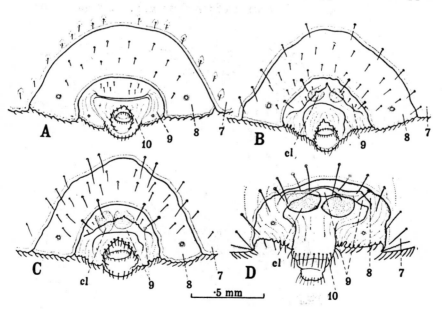

Figure 15. Genital segments from the four insects represented in Fig. 13. B, C, and D are males. Figures indicate homologous sterna; *cl:* claspers. (Cf. Fig. 11.)

that while the eosinophil cells secrete the moulting hormone, the remaining cells secrete the hormone which inhibits metamorphosis; which hormone is absent, of course, in the fifth nymphs.

DISCUSSION

Moulting and Metamorphosis in Other Insects

The number of moults in *Rhodnius* is absolutely fixed. No departures from the normal five nymphal stages have been observed among hundreds of these insects reared in the laboratory. This constancy is associated with the fact that moulting is definitely initiated by a large meal—a meal large enough to provide for the requisite degree of growth. That is not the case with all insects. Many species show wide variations in the number of ecdyses: in the clothes moth *Tineola*, these may range from four to forty (Titschack, 1926); and certain insects (*Tineola, Tenebrio*, etc.) may continue to moult though starved. In such insects the secretion of the moulting hormone must be brought about by other factors, and not solely by stretching of the body-wall as in *Rhodnius*. Exactly what controls this secretion will doubtless be different in different insects.

As regards the metamorphosis or pupation of holometabolic insects, it has long been realized that some influence is at work during larval life which restrains the development of the imaginal germs. We need not recapitulate here the many mechanisms of this restraint that have been suggested. Kopeć (1924) advanced the view that the restraining influence is a hormone secreted by the brain. His only evidence for this hypothesis was that starvation of *Lymantria* larvae, while prolonging larval life, shortened pupal development; and in a later paper (Kopeć, 1927), having obtained opposite results, Kopeć himself cast doubt upon this evidence. The observations of Bodenstein (1933a) that limbs transplanted from one caterpillar to another of different age are cast off when their new host pupates, led him to suggest that the hormones associated with pupation differ from those which cause larval moulting; and that the larval epidermis is capable of metamorphosis at a comparatively early stage. These conclusions have been substantiated in *Rhodnius*.

Diapause

The life-cycle of many insects is interrupted from time to time by periods of arrested development during which digestion and metabolism continue (usually at a reduced rate) but growth and development cease. These periods of "diapause" may be brought to an end or "broken" by various stimuli: freezing, pricking, the oviposition or development of parasites, and so forth (Readio, 1931; Varley and Butler, 1933). Now we have seen that *Rhodnius* nymphs which have repeated small meals of blood fail to grow because they lack the necessary stimulus of abdominal distension; and insects decapitated soon after feeding fail to grow, even though they have received a full-sized meal, because they lack the moulting hormone. Such insects are in a state of diapause. Growth or moulting can take place in them only if the requisite hormone is introduced into the blood. And this naturally suggests that diapause in other insects (when it is not brought about by the direct effect of the environment (Cousin, 1932) may result from the temporary failure of growth-promoting hormones, due sometimes perhaps to an inborn rhythm, sometimes perhaps to the indirect effect of environmental factors.

Prothetely and Metathetely

It is not an uncommon thing in artificial cultures of certain beetles and Lepitoptera for a few of the larvae to develop visible wing pads or other pupal structures. These monstrous individuals are sometimes regarded as larvae showing a premature formation of pupal characters (prothetely), sometimes as pupae whose metamorphosis has been imperfect (metathetely or neoteny) (Singh Pruthi, 1924; Chapman, 1926). The phenomenon is most simply explained as due to a disturbance in the hormones which regulate metamorphosis (v. Lengerken, 1924). Thus Goldschmidt (1923) regards such abnormalities as resulting from an upset in the proper timing of developmental velocities ("zeitlich abgestimmte Reaktionsgeschwindigkeiten"). The results recorded in the present paper fit in well with this hypothesis. For we have seen that the secretion of the moulting hormone precedes secretion of the hormone inhibiting metamorphosis; and if the early nymphal stages are decapitated before the latter hormone is fully formed, they develop adult characters in greater or lesser degree; that is, they show prothetely (p. 211). Whereas if the fifth or final nymphs receive the blood of earlier nymphs containing the inhibitory hormone (p. 211), they develop into adults showing imperfect metamorphosis (metathetely).

SUMMARY

The five nymphal stages of *Rhodnius prolixus* are more or less alike. The adult differs markedly from the nymphs. There are thus two phenomena to be considered: simple moulting and moulting coupled with metamorphosis.

1. Causation of Moulting

Moulting occurs at a definite interval after feeding, only one meal being necessary in each stage. There is a "critical period" in the moulting cycle (about 7 days after feeding in the fifth nymph, about 4 days in the earlier nymphs) and removal of the head of the insect before this period prevents moulting. The critical period corresponds with the time when mitotic divisions in the epidermis begin.

The blood of insects that have passed the critical period contains a factor or hormone which will induce moulting in insects decapitated soon after feeding.

It is suggested that this moulting hormone may be secreted by the corpus allatum, since the cells of this gland show signs of greatest secretory activity during the critical period.

Stretching of the abdominal wall provides the stimulus which causes secretion of the moulting hormone. This stimulus is conveyed by nerves to the brain: moulting is prevented by section of the nerve-cord in the prothorax.

Section of the nerves between the brain and the corpus allatum appears to prevent moulting; but these experiments were inconclusive.

Insects sharing the same blood moult simultaneously. The whole process of growth must therefore be co-ordinated by chemical means, the factors concerned being produced presumably by the growing cells themselves.

2. *Causation of Metamorphosis*

If fourth or even first nymphs, decapitated soon after feeding, receive the blood from moulting fifth nymphs, they suffer a precocious metamorphosis and develop adult characters. Metamorphosis is therefore brought about by chemical differences in the blood.

If fifth nymphs decapitated soon after feeding receive blood from moulting fourth nymphs, they also moult; showing that the moulting factor is the same at all stages.

The absence of metamorphosis in normal nymphs before the fifth stage must therefore be due to an inhibitory factor or hormone in the blood. This is proved by the fact that if a fifth nymph decapitated soon after feeding receives the blood from a moulting fourth nymph (not deprived of its head) it develops characters much more like those of a nymph than an adult.

The inhibitory hormone is normally produced in such small quantities that simple dilution of the blood of a moulting fourth nymph with that of another fourth nymph (decapitated soon after feeding) causes them both to suffer metamorphosis.

The head is necessary for the secretion of the inhibitory hormone.

This hormone seems to be secreted after the moulting hormone. Thus if series of fourth, third, second, or first nymphs are decapitated around the critical period, some of them show more or less complete metamorphosis. Others show characters intermediate between those of nymphs and adults.

The bearing of these results on the phenomena of diapause and prothetely is discussed.

REFERENCES

Bodenstein, D. (1933 *a*)—"Beintransplantationen an lepidopteren Raupen. I. Transplantationen zur Analyse der Raupen- und Puppenhäutung", 'Arch. Entw. Mech.', cxxviii. 564–83.

———— (1933 *b*)—"Zur Frage der Bedeutung hormoneller Beziehungen bei der Insektenmetamorphose", 'Naturwiss.', xxi. 861–3.

Buddenbrock, W. v. (1931)—"Untersuchungen über die Häutungshormone der Schmetterlingsraupen", 'Zeitschr. f. vergleich. Physiol.', xiv. 415–28.

Chapman, R. N. (1926)—"Inhibiting the process of metamorphosis in the confused flour beetle (Tribolium confusum, Duval)", 'Journ. Exp. Zool.', xlv. 292–9.

Cousin, G. (1932)—"Étude expérimentale de la diapause des insectes", 'Bull. Biol. Fr. et Belg.', Suppl. xv, 341 pp.

Fraenkel, G. (1934)—"Pupation in flies initiated by a hormone", 'Nature', cxxxiii. 834.

Gillett, J. D. (1934).—Unpublished work.

Gillett, J. D., and Wigglesworth, V. B. (1932)—"The climbing organ of an insect, Rhodnius prolixus", 'Proc. Roy. Soc. B.', cxi. 364–76.

Goldschmidt, R. (1923)—"Einige Materialen zur Theorie der abgestimmten Reaktions-geschwindigkeiten", 'Arch. mikr. Anat.', xcviii. 292–313.

Hoop, M. (1933)—"Häutungshistologie einiger Insekten", 'Zool. Jahrb., Abt. Anat.', lvii. 433–64.

Kemper, H. (1931)—"Beiträge zur Biologie der Bettwanze (Cimex lectularius L.). II. Ueber die Häutung", 'Zeitschr. Morph. Oekol. Tiere', xxii. 53–109.

Koller, G. (1929).—"Die innere Sekretion bei wirbellosen Tieren", 'Biol. Rev.', iv. 269–306.

Kopeć, S. (1922).—"Studies on the necessity of the brain for the inception of insect metamorphosis", 'Biol. Bull.', xlii. 322–42.

——— (1924).—"Studies on the influence of inanition on the development and the duration of life in insects", 'Biol. Bull.', xlvi. 1–21.

——— (1927).—"Ueber die Entwicklung der Insekten unter dem Einfluss der Vitamin-zugabe", 'Biologia Generalis', iii. 375–84.

Lengerken, H. v. (1924 a).—"Prothetelie bei Coleopteren-Larven", 'Zool. Anz.', lviii. 179–85.

——— (1924 b).—"Prothetelie bei Coleopterenlarven (Metathelie)", 'Zool. Anz.', lix. 323–30.

Nabert, A. (1913).—"Die Corpora allata der Insekten", 'Zeitschr. wiss. Zool.', civ. 181–358.

Readio, P. A. (1931).—"Dormancy in Reduvius personatus (Linnaeus)", 'Ann. Ent. Soc. Amer.', xxiv. 19–39.

Singh Pruthi, H. (1924).—"Studies on insect metamorphosis. I. Prothetely in mealworms (Tenebrio molitor) and other insects", 'Proc. Camb. Phil. Soc. Biol.', i, 139–47.

Titschack, E. (1926).—"Untersuchungen über das Wachstum, den Nahrungsverbrauch und die Eierzeugung. II. Tineola biselliella", 'Zeitschr. wiss. Zool.', cxxviii. 509–69.

Varley, G. C., and Butler, C. G. (1933).—"The acceleration of development of insects by parasitism", 'Parasitology', xxv. 263–8.

Wigglesworth, V. B. (1931).—"The physiology of excretion in a bloodsucking insect, Rhodnius prolixus", 'Journ. Exp. Biol.', viii. 411–51.

——— (1933).—"The physiology of the cuticle and of ecdysis in Rhodnius prolixus (Triatomidae, Hemiptera); with special reference to the function of the oenocytes and of the dermal glands", 'Quart. Journ. Micr. Sci.', lxxvi. 269–318.

SOICHI FUKUDA

Induction of pupation in silkworm by transplanting the prothoracic gland

Soichi Fukuda was born in Wakayama Prefecture, Japan, in 1907. He studied at the Institute of Zoology, Tokyo Imperial University, and received his Ph.D. in 1944. From 1936 to 1953 he was Research Assistant at the Katakura Sericultural Experiment Station in Matsumoto City, and from 1954 to 1960 was head of the same station. In 1957 he also became Director of the Katakura Industrial Company, a post which he held until 1961. In 1960–1961 he was a member of the Science Council of Japan. In 1962 he became Professor, and in 1965 Chairman, of the Biological Institute of Nagoya University.

His research interests are in the developmental physiology and experimental morphology of insects.

It was found that by removing the head of the silkworm at the moulting stage by means of a ligature the pupation of the remaining part cannot be prevented. But I found, as Muroga (1939) did, that when a ligature is applied behind the prothoracic segment, no pupation takes place in the part posterior to it, although the anterior part including the prothoracic segment is able to pupate, while if the same operation is performed on the older larva after it has spun the greater part of its cocoon, the posterior part without the prothoracic segment pupates. From these results it seems probable that the prothoracic segment represents a center of internal secretion which at a critical period releases into the blood some stimulating substance responsible for the pupation of the silkworm. It remains to be seen what organ in the prothoracic segment produces this active substance.

[Previously published in *Proceedings of the Imperial Academy, Tokyo*, 16 (1940): 414–416. Communicated by N. Yatsu, Oct. 12, 1940.]

The only likely organ responsible here is the prothoracic gland[1] which attaches to the inner side of each of the prothoracic spiracles and extends anteriorly along the tracheae running toward the head region. The function of this gland has so far remained obscure.

In this paper the results of the transplantation experiments of the gland will be presented briefly.

MATERIAL AND METHOD

The silkworms of Chinese bivoltine race on the 2nd day of the last instar were used as the recipients. A prothoracic gland of a larva of European race on the 6th day of the 5th instar was pushed into the postgonadal segment (9th segment) through a small slit made on the right side of the dorsal vessel. The experiments were controlled with the larvae transplanted with some such organs as salivary gland, prothoracic ganglion, fat-body.

The silkworms thus operated passed the remaining larval life normally and moulted at about six days after transplantation. At this stage the silkworms were ligatured either at the level between the mesothoracic and metathoracic segments or at the level between gonadal and postgonadal segments.

RESULTS

As is shown in Table 1, many of the posterior parts of the silkworms with the transplanted prothoracic gland pupated, while none of the controls did (Fig. 1).

It was observed that the onset of pupation in the posterior parts was generally delayed by one or two days in comparison with that in the anterior parts or in the unoperated silkworms of the same batch.

[1] The gland so designated by Ke (Bult. Sci. Fakult. Terkult., Kjusu Imp. Univ. 4, 1930) is identical with the prothoracic glandular band of Tanaka (Santai Kaibōgaku Kōgi, 1928).

TABLE 1

TRANSPLAN-TATS	NO. OF SILKWORMS TRANS-PLANTED	NO. OF POSTERIOR PARTS SURVIVED	NO. OF POSTERIOR PARTS WHICH FAILED TO PUPATE	NO. OF POSTERIOR PARTS PUPATED
Prothoracic gland	70	44	19	25
Salivary gland	43	29	29	0
Prothoracic ganglion	18	14	14	0
Fat-body	41	17	17	0

Figure 1. (a) Control transplanted with salivary gland. (b) Experimental. (c) Control transplanted with fat body. (d) Experimental. Larval skin of pupated part was removed as the ligatured silkworms could not moult by themselves. (Natural size.)

DISCUSSION AND CONCLUSION

From the above-mentioned results it seems highly probable that the prothoracic gland is a pupation-inducing center which releases at a critical period its active principles into the blood.

It may be added that according to my experiment the result of which has not as yet been published, if a prothoracic gland of a 5th instar larva is transplanted into the abdomen of a silkworm whose anterior part including the prothoracic segment has been removed by a ligature at the moulting stage, the rear part does not pupate. I think the failure of the establishment of air supply to the transplanted glands by the tracheal branches of the hosts may be responsible for the negative result. This is borne out by the fact that the anterior parts of the larvae including the prothoracic segments are unable to pupate, if the spiracles are closed by an artificial means. Evidently the prothoracic glands do not function normally when the oxygen supply is impeded. When the transplantation is made on such younger larvae as those used in the present experiment, the tracheal supply of the transplanted glands may be established by the time of the moulting and consequently the posterior parts pupate.

REFERENCE

Muroga, H. (1939), *Nippon Sansigaku Zassi,* 10.

Hormonal control of molting and pupation in the silkworm

In a previous paper (Fukuda, 1940) it has been shown that the prothoracic gland of the silkworm is an organ of internal secretion which releases into the blood its active principles responsible for the onset of pupation. Furthermore, I have recently obtained some evidences showing that the molting in the silkworm larva is also controlled by hormones secreted by the prothoracic gland.

MATERIAL AND METHODS

The 4th instar silkworms of Japanese bivoltine race called "Syō-haku" were used in the experiments.[1] In the 4th instar larvae, the feeding period at 23–25.5° C is on an average 129 hours. The age of the silkworms was calculated from the time they began to take food after previous molting.

Two series of experiments were made: (1) decapitation of the larvae by a ligature at the level between head and prothorax and (2) ligaturing the larvae behind prothoracic segment either (A) at the level between mesothoracic and metathoracic segments or (B) at the level between gonadal and postgonadal segments.

TABLE 1

Decapitation of 4th instar silkworms at different ages

AGE AT OPERATION IN HOURS	NO. OF SILKWORMS DECAPITATED	NO. OF SILKWORMS PUPATED	NO. OF SILKWORMS MOLTED	NO. OF SILKWORMS REMAINED AS LARVAE
50	50	0	0	50
60	50	3	0	47
70	50	6	2	42
80	50	21	3	26
90	50	8	21	21
100	50	0	40	10
110	50	0	48	2

[1] Normally the silkworm pupates at the 5th molting.

RESULTS

1. Pupation and Molting in Decapitated Silkworms

Neither pupation nor molting occurred in the larvae decapitated at 30 or 50 hours of age.

But as is shown in Table 1, some of the silkworms decapitated between 60 and 90 hours underwent a precocious pupation without preceding larval molting, resulting in small headless pupae (Fig. 1, f).

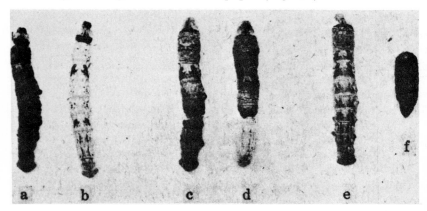

Figure 1. (a, b) Silkworms ligatured at level between mesothoracic and methoracic segments at 90 hours of age. (a) Both parts have molted. (b) Anterior part alone has molted. (c, d) Silkworms ligatured at level between gonadal and post-gonadal segments at 90 hours of age. (c) Both parts have molted. (d) Anterior part alone has molted. (e) Decapitated silkworm molted. Operation at 90 hours of age. (f) Pupa obtained from silkworm decapitated at 80 hours of age. (Natural size.)

However the larval molting (Fig. 1, e) also took place in some silkworms decapitated at the ages older than 70 hours, and the later the larvae were operated the more numerous were the molted ones. The time of onset of molting in the decapitated larvae was almost the same with that in the unoperated controls.

2. Molting in Silkworms Ligatured behind the Prothoracic Segment

In every case neither part of the larvae was able to pupate. However, larval molting took place in some cases. Table 2 gives the combined results obtained from the groups A and B.

The larval molting occurred in the anterior parts of some larvae ligatured at the ages older than 70 hours, while in the posterior parts the molting took place only in the larvae operated at the ages older than 90 hours (Fig. 1, a–d).

TABLE 2

Ligation of 4th instar silkworms behind prothoracic segment at different ages
(Combined results from groups A and B)

AGE AT OPERATION IN HOURS	NO. OF SILKWORMS LIGATURED	ANTERIOR PART ALONE MOLTED	BOTH PARTS MOLTED	NEITHER PART MOLTED
50	100	0	0	100
60	100	0	0	100
70	100	7	0	93
80	100	31	0	69
90	100	53	21	26
100	100	28	57	15
110	100	0	100	0

There was no marked delay in the onset of molting in either part of the larvae as compared with that in the unoperated controls. The larval parts not molted at normal time always remained as such until death.

DISCUSSION AND CONCLUSION

The occurrence of precocious pupation in the larvae decapitated during the 4th instar seems to indicate that something may be present in the head of the silkworms of this age which controls the onset of molting and its removal induces a sudden pupation. The only organs which seem to be of importance in this respect are the corpora allata, since it has already been found that their extirpation at a certain time in the 4th instar silkworm larvae brings about a precocious pupation without preceding larval molting (Bounhiol, 1937; Kin, 1939; Fukuda, unpublished).

It should be mentioned that the molting takes place in the decapitated silkworms and in the anterior parts including the first two thoracic segments of the ligatured silkworms if the operations are performed at the ages older than 70 hours. On the other hand, in the posterior parts excluding the thoracic segments the molting is only possible when the larvae are ligatured at the ages older than 90 hours. This may show that there is an organ in the thoracic segments which plays some role in the onset of molting by pouring its product into the blood between 70 and 90 hours of age. The organs which seem responsible here are the prothoracic glands.

The larval molting in silkworms and probably also in other lepidopterous larvae may be induced by two different hormones discharged in succession into the blood from the corpora allata and the prothoracic glands. On the other hand, for the onset of pupation only the hormone from the prothoracic gland may be necessary. The precocious pupation following the removal of the corpora allata or the decapitation performed prior to a certain age, i.e., about 90 hours, may be due to the exclusion of the hormone of the corpora allata and the operated larvae affected by the hormone of the prothoracic glands alone undergo pupation without preceding larval molting.

It is highly probable that in the last instar larvae the corpora allata have lost their endocrine activity and the prothoracic glands alone seem to become active. It has already been observed that in the last instar silkworms neither extirpation of the corpora allata (Kin, 1939) nor decapitation (Fukuda, unpublished) can bring about noticeable acceleration of the pupation time.

The role played by the corpora allata and the prothoracic gland for the inception of molting and pupation in the silkworm have also been demonstrated in my experiments of the transplantation of the larval skin, which will shortly be published elsewhere. But suffice it to mention here that when a piece of skin taken from a last instar larva at the beginning of its cocoon formation was transplanted into the body cavity of a silkworm at about the middle of the 4th instar, the transplanted skin underwent a pupal molting simultaneously with the larval molting of the host. On the contrary if similar transplantation of the skin was made into a younger 4th instar larva the larval molting took place in the transplanted skin at the molting of the host.

According to Piepho (1940) in *Galleria mellonella* the transplantation of the corpora allata of young larvae into a last instar larva has brought about excessive larval molting. He has attributed this to the pupation-inhibiting effect of the transplanted corpora allata. However, this explanation seems to have missed the point judging from the above-mentioned results of my experiments.

LITERATURE

Bounhiol, J. J. (1937), C. R. de la Soc. Biol., 126.
Fukuda, S. (1940), Proc. Imp. Acad., 16.
Kin, J. (1939), Nippon Sansigaku Zassi, 10.
Piepho, H. (1940), Biol. Zbl., 60.

ADOLF BUTENANDT
and PETER KARLSON

Concerning the isolation in crystalline form of an insect metamorphosis hormone

Adolf Butenandt was born in Bremerhaven, Germany, in 1903. He studied at the Universities of Marburg and Göttingen, and received his Ph.D. in chemistry from the latter in 1924. From 1931 to 1933 he was Head of the Department of Biochemistry at the University of Göttingen, and then Professor of Organic Chemistry at the Technische Hochschule, Danzig, until 1936, when he became Director of the Max Planck Institute for Biochemistry in Berlin. From 1945 to 1956 he was Professor of Physiological Chemistry and Director of the Institute of Physiological Chemistry at the University of Tübingen, and from then until 1960 Professor and Head of the Department of Physiological Chemistry at the University of Munich. Since 1960 he has been President of the Max Planck Institute for the Advancement of Science. He was awarded the Nobel Prize in 1939.

His research interests are in the biochemistry of hormones, vitamins, and carcinogens, and the biochemistry of hormones in insects.

Peter Karlson was born in Berlin in 1918, and received his Ph.D. in chemistry from the University of Tübingen in 1942. From 1942 to 1954 he was Research Assistant at the Max Planck Institute for Biochemistry in Berlin and Tübingen. In 1953 he became Docent of Physiological Chemistry, and in 1954 Research Assistant of the Institute of Physiological Chemistry, at the University of Tübingen. In 1956 he went to Munich, first as Research Associate of the Max Planck Institute for Biochemistry, and then as Research Associate of the Department of

[Previously published in *Zeitschrift für Naturforschung*, 9b (May 8, 1954), 389–91. Reprinted by permission of the publisher.]

226

ry of the University of Munich. From 1960 to
ing Head of the department. Since 1964 he has
id of the Department of Physiological Chemistry
arburg.
rests are in the areas of biochemistry in general,
)chemistry of insect hormones.

stigations of active agents produced by insects
lt, Weidel, and Schlossberger, 1949), in the
nts the object of which was the concentration
morphosis hormones. We have now succeeded
rmones in crystalline form and in characteriz-
ical, physical, and physiological data.

THOD OF TESTING

of evaluation, in concentrating the active ma-
terial, we used Becker and Plagge's test (1939) on *Calliphora* maggots, as
modified by us (Karlson and Hanser, 1952): *Calliphora* larvae shortly before pupation are ligated in the anterior third with a cotton thread. Only
those specimens that have formed "half-pupae" after twenty-four hours—
i.e., only the anterior portion of which pupated—are used for the test. The
pupated anterior part is removed, and precisely 0.01 ml of an aqueous solution of the substance to be tested is injected through the cut into the
isolated abdomen. Puparium formation (browning and hardening of the
cuticle) of the surviving posterior portion within twenty-four to thirty
hours after the injection is considered a positive hormonal response. Cal-
culation of the percentage of pupating abdomens was made in the way
previously described (Karlson and Hanser, 1953); deviating therefrom,
we today define as a *Calliphora* unit (C.E.) the amount of substance that
releases pupation in 50–70 percent of the test animals.[1] In over two thou-
sand experimental series the test has proved to be satisfactorily reproducible
and very dependable.

STARTING MATERIAL

In order to obtain potent extracts, we initially used pupae of the fleshfly
Calliphora erythrocephala Meig. according to the procedure of Becker
(1941). More recently (since 1947) we have used almost exclusively pupae

[1] Detailed description and discussion of the testing method in Karlson (1953).

of the silkmoth, *Bombyx mori* L., since these are more easily procured. From German cultures of the summer of 1953 we had at our disposal for the first time rather large amounts of fresh *Bombyx* pupae, some 500 kg (almost exclusively ♂ ♂).[2]

METHODS OF PREPARATION

The 500 kg of pupae, stored in methanol, was compressed at 50 atm, the press juice (ca. 650:1) concentrated to 30:1 under reduced pressure and extracted several times with butanol. The butanol solution was washed with 1 percent sulfuric acid, 10 percent caustic soda, and 5 percent acetic acid, and concentrated by evaporation.[3] The residue of red-brown oil (79 g) was dissolved in pure butanol and filtered through a ten-fold amount of aluminum oxide (Brockmann activity V: Brockmann and Schodder, 1942); the butanol filtrate was dried, taken up with water, and extracted with ether and ethyl acetate. The aqueous phase was evaporated, leaving 1.15 g of a red-brown oil that contained a *Calliphora* unit in about 0.5 γ.

With carefully performed chromatography on aluminum oxide of Brockmann activity IV, using mixtures of ethyl acetate–butanol (3:1) and ethyl acetate–methanol (3:1), we succeeded in separating from the oil 167 mg of a highly potent fraction (1 C.E. = 0.1 γ), from which an effective crystalline product was obtained by grinding with ethyl acetate and a small amount of methanol. From 500 kg of fresh pupae, 35 mg of this crude crystalline material was obtained; after a single recrystallization from ethyl acetate–methanol, 25 mg remained.

In order to check the identity of the crystallized material with the active substance, a countercurrent distribution was carried out with 10 mg, in the system butanol (4 parts)— cyclohexane (6 parts)/water (10 parts) (Fig. 1), and showed the expected distribution of activity. The distribution coefficient amounts to 1.28 (at 19° C); the material recovered from the distribution, recrystallized from methanol–ethyl acetate and methanol–acetone, contains a *Calliphora* unit in 0.0075 (in the test, 41 percent pupation with 0.005 γ; 69 percent with 0.0075 γ; 80 percent with 0.01γ).

[2] For their support in procurement of the *Bombyx* cocoons we thank Dr. M. Cretschmer, Bundesforschungsanstalt für Kleintierzucht, Celle, and Mr. E. Poerschke, Arbeitsgemeinschaft der Seidenbauer, Celle.

[3] These procedures were carried out in the factory of the Deutschen Hoffmann-LaRoche Gesellschaft, Grenzach, on the basis of our laboratory experience and under our supervision. Thanks are due here too to the Deutschen Hoffmann-LaRoche Gesellschaft, particularly to Dr. Saenger, for their indispensable assistance; to Miss Ingeborg Brachmann for conscientious conduct of the animal experiments and for technical assistance; and to the Deutsche Forschungsgemeinschaft for a generous grant toward procurement of the starting material.

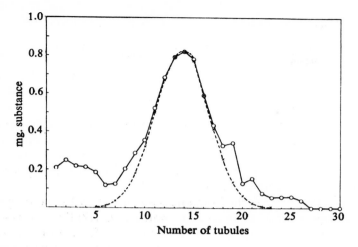

Figure 1. Countercurrent distribution of the hormone (preparation once re-crystallized) in the system cyclohexane (6) butanol (4)/water (10) at 19° C. Volume proportion ⅔, $n = 30$. Fractions 27–30 extracted in a single phase. Calculated according to P. Karlson and E. Hecker, Z. *Naturforsch.* 5b, 237 (1950), taking into account the volume proportion ⅔. o ————— o experimentally determined distribution curve, x — — — — — x theoretical curve for $K = 1.28$.

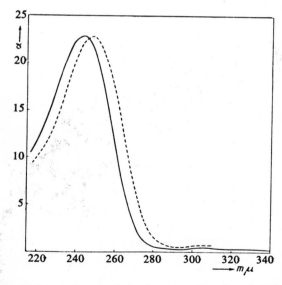

Figure 2. Ultraviolet spectrum of the hormone in ethanol (solid line) and in water (dashed line). On the ordinate is plotted the absorption coefficient

$$a = \frac{1}{c \cdot d} \cdot \log \frac{I_0}{I}$$

CHARACTERIZATION OF THE SUBSTANCE

The pure hormone crystallizes from ethyl acetate or water in silky, matted needles (Fig. 3), which when tested rapidly under the Kofler heating microscope undergo a shift (lost of water of crystallization) at 161–162°, in doing so partly melt and recrystallize, and then finally melt at 235–237°. The substance is optically active [a] $D^{20°} = +58.5° \pm 2°$, [a] $546^{21°} = 82.3° \pm 2°$ (7.00 mg in 2 ml ethanol). The ultraviolet spectrum (see Fig. 2) shows a conspicuous maximum at 244 mμ (in ethanol) or at 249 mμ (in water). In alkaline solution there is a rapid breakdown of the substance, accompanied by a change in the spectrum. The infrared absorption spectrum shows a sharp band at 6.12 μ.

To our astonishment the hormone—in contrast to the accompanying substances isolated earlier (Butenandt, Karlson, and Zillig, 1951)—is free of nitrogen. When dried, the crystals precipitated from water undergo a weight loss of 10.2 percent (probably loss of water of crystallization).

From the elemental analysis of the dried substance (found C 69.58, H 9.62, O 21.17 percent) an atomic proportionality of $C_{4.4}H_{7.3}O_1$ is calculated. Because of the insolubility of the substance in camphor, a molecular weight determination could not be made.

The substance described here is to our knowledge *the first hormone from the insect kingdom to be isolated in pure form.* From biological experiments regarding the hormonal regulation of insect metamorphosis

Figure 3.   Crystals of the hormone (from water). (Enlarged about 418 times.)

(Piepho, 1951; Wigglesworth, 1949, 1952; Williams, 1952a, b), it is known that three hormonal glands contribute to this: the brain with its neurosecretory cells, the prothoracic glands, and the corpora allata. Each molt is initiated by an adenotropic hormone from the brain which affects the prothoracic glands and causes them to secrete a second hormone. The hormone from the prothoracic glands induces molting and guides it in a direction toward the imaginal state unless simultaneously the hormone from the corpora allata takes effect and impresses a larval character on the molt (cf. the scheme in Karlson and Hanser, 1953). Proper allocation in this context of the substance isolated by us was made possible by the cooperation of Professor Carroll M. Williams, who tested it on his experimental material. According to his observations, the hormone described here is capable of inducing imaginal development in diapausing pupae of the saturniids *Samia walkeri* (*Cynthia*) and *Platysamia cecropia*; it is effective both on pupae whose brain has been extirpated and on the isolated pupal abdomen that no longer contains any endocrine glands. According to experiments to date,[4] the dose required in this test amounts to about 12.5 γ per specimen. Since the resumption of development by the isolated abdomen is to be regarded as a specific response to the action of the prothoracic gland, the substance isolated by us must be the *prothoracic gland hormone*.

SUMMARY

By means of methanol extraction and concentration there was obtained from silkworm pupae a crystalline uniform substance with MP 235–237° that was active in the test with the ligated abdomen of *Calliphora* larvae. 0.0075γ is effective in the *Calliphora* test. As shown by experiments on saturniid pupae (C. M. Williams), the substance is the hormone of the prothoracic glands.

REFERENCES

Becker, E. (1941), *Biol. Zbl.*, 61:360.
Becker, E., and Plagge, E. (1939), *Biol. Zbl.*, 59:326.
Brockmann, H., and Schodder, H. (1942), *Ber. dtsch. chem. Ges.*, 74:73.
Butenandt, A. (1949), *Angew. Chem.*, 61:262.
Butenandt, A., Karlson, P., and Hannes, G. (1946), *Biol. Zbl.*, 65:41.
Butenandt, A., Karlson, P., and Zillig, W. (1951), *Hoppe-Seyler's Z. Physiol. Chem.*, 288: 125, 279.
Butenandt, A., Weidel, W., and Schlossberger, R. (1949), *Z. Naturforsch.*, 4b:242.
Karlson, P., "Habilitationsschrift". Tübingen, 1953.
Karlson, P., and Hanser, G. (1952), *Z. Naturforsch.*, 7b:80.
――――― (1953), *Z. Naturforsch.*, 8b, 91.
Piepho, H. (1951), *Verh. dtsch. zool. Ges.*, 1951:62.
Wigglesworth, V. B. (1949), *Bull. Biol. Suppl.*, 33:174.
――――― (1952), *J. Exper. Biol.*, 29:620.
Williams, C. M. (1952a), *Biol. Bull.*, 103:120
――――― (1952b), *Harvey Lectures*, 47:126.

[4] Private communication.